Understanding Law School

An Introduction to the LexisNexis Understanding Series and Tips on How to Succeed in Law School

Various Authors

ISBN#: 0-8205-6193-2

Editorial Offices
744 Broad Street, Newark, NJ 07102 (973) 820-2000
201 Mission St., San Francisco, CA 94105-1831 (415) 908-3200
701 East Water Street, Charlottesville, VA 22902-7587 (804) 972-7600
www.lexis.com

(Pub.1376)

Author and Publication Credits

Chapter 1 excerpted from
Understanding Civil Procedure

Gene R. Shreve

Richard S. Melvin Professor of Law
Indiana University School of Law, Bloomington

Peter Raven-Hansen

Glen Earl Weston Research Professor of Law
George Washington University Law School

Chapter 2 excerpted from
Understanding Contracts

Jeffrey Ferriell

Professor of Law
Capital University Law School

Michael J. Navin

Former Professor of Law
Pennsylvania State University
Dickinson School of Law

Chapter 3 excerpted from
Understanding Property Law

John G. Sprankling

Associate Dean & Distinguished Professor and Scholar
McGeorge School of Law
University of the Pacific

Chapter 4 excerpted from
Understanding Torts

John L. Diamond

Professor of Law
University of California,
Hastings College of the Law

Lawrence C. Levine

Professor of Law
University of the Pacific,
McGeorge School of Law

M. Stuart Madden

Distinguished Professor of Law
Pace Law School

Chapter 5 excerpted from
Understanding Constitutional Law

Norman Redlich

Dean Emeritus and Judge Edward Weinfeld Professor of Law Emeritus
New York University School of Law

John Attanasio

Dean and William Hawley Atwell Professor of Constitutional Law
Southern Methodist University

Joel K. Goldstein

Professor of Law
Saint Louis University School of Law

Chapter 6 excerpted from
Understanding Criminal Law

Joshua Dressler

Frank R. Strong Chair in Law
Ohio State University College of Law

Chapter 7 excerpted from
Understanding Evidence

Paul C. Giannelli

Albert J. Weatherhead, III and Richard W. Weatherhead Professor of Law
Case Western Reserve University School of Law

Chapter 8 excerpted from
Understanding Corporate Law

Arthur R. Pinto

Professor of Law
Co-Director of the Center for the
Study of International Business Law
Brooklyn Law School

Douglas M. Branson

W. Edward Sell Chair in Business Law
University of Pittsburgh
School of Law

Chapter 9 excerpted from
Understanding Criminal Procedure

Joshua Dressler

Frank R. Strong Chair in Law
Ohio State University College of Law

Chapter 10 excerpted from
Understanding Lawyers' Ethics
Monroe H. Freedman

Professor of Law
Hofstra University
School of Law

Abbe Smith

Professor of Law & Co-Director
Criminal Justice Clinic and E. Barrett Prettyman Fellowship Program
Georgetown University Law Center

Appendix A
"How to Succeed in Law School"
Lazar Emanuel

Appendix B excerpted from
American Legal Systems: A Resource and Reference Guide
Toni M. Fine

Lecturer in Law & Director of Graduate and International Programs
Yeshiva University
Benjamin N. Cardozo School of Law

Preface to *Understanding Law School*

LexisNexis is pleased to present **Understanding Law School,** a book specifically designed for first-year law students. This book contains sample chapters from some of our leading *Understanding* treatises. The LexisNexis *Understanding Series*, a collection of accessible treatises on a variety of topics, includes nearly forty individual titles. The concise, yet comprehensive, analysis contained in each *Understanding* title provides a foundation for true understanding of the subject and facilitates more than mere rote learning.

Understanding Law School contains the first chapter of each of the following leading treatises:

Understanding Civil Procedure
Understanding Contracts
Understanding Property Law
Understanding Torts
Understanding Constitutional Law
Understanding Criminal Law
Understanding Evidence
Understanding Corporate Law
Understanding Criminal Procedure
Understanding Lawyers' Ethics

Each Understanding title is designed to provide a solid grounding in the subject covered and to help you succeed in gaining a mastery of the subject. The chapters presented in this **Understanding Law School** volume are intended for your review as part of your preparation for your first class meetings. As the semester progresses and you begin to explore issues of increasing complexity in your various courses, you will likely find that reference to the full text of the *Understanding* titles listed above will better prepare you for class. Copies of most, if not all, Understanding treatises are available for purchase at your school's bookstore.

The appendix in this **Understanding Law School** volume contains some very useful reference material, including a chapter on the *Basic Concepts of American Jurisprudence*. This chapter is reprinted from **American Legal Systems: A Resource and Reference Guide**, a unique book that provides an overview of American legal institutions and sources of law, and presents a guide to the interrelationships between and among those institutions and legal authorities. Please contact your school's bookstore to purchase a copy of the full text of **American Legal Systems**.

The appendix also contains additional helpful material, including guidance on how to brief a case and how to write a good course outline, a segment on cite verification, and information about participation on law review, moot court, law school seminars, and law school clinics.

LexisNexis also publishes a line of student study aids, our *Questions & Answers Series*. Each guide in our *Q & A Series* contains over 150 multiple-choice and short-answer questions, as well as a comprehensive "practice final exam"-to help you prepare for course study and for final exams. Each multiple-choice question is accompanied by a detailed answer that indicates which of four options is the best answer and explains, in detail, why that option is better than the other three. Each short-answer question (designed to be answered in no more than fifteen minutes) is followed by a thoughtful, yet brief, model answer. Our *Q & A* titles are also available for purchase at your school's bookstore.

LexisNexis is a publisher of casebooks, treatises, and study guides designed for legal education, criminal justice, and other academic programs. LexisNexis is also a global leader in comprehensive and authoritative legal, news, and business information and tailored applications. The LexisNexis® Total Research System offers an extensive range of online and print legal and regulatory information products, tools, customized Web applications, and critical filing services that help legal professionals reach confident decisions and comply with the law.

The LexisNexis Law School home page (http://www.lexisnexis.com/lawschool/) provides students with access to a comprehensive search form that offers quick retrieval of a full-text single legal document, Lexis® Search Advisor, *Shepard's*® Citations Service, Lexis® Get & Print, and other key sources as well as the option to perform research using the Lexis-Nexis® Total Research System.

Your LexisNexis Law School Representative may be located by visiting the "My School" portion of the LexisNexis Law School home page. Your Law School Representative is available for group and individualized training and to answer questions about the LexisNexis® Total Research System, your comprehensive resource for case law, statutes, *Shepard's*® Citations, and more.

We trust that you will find this **Understanding Law School** volume useful as an introduction to our *Understanding Series* and we wish you the greatest success in your law school career.

LexisNexis Law School Publishing Staff

TABLE OF CONTENTS

Page

CHAPTER 1
UNDERSTANDING CIVIL
PROCEDURE

By

Gene R. Shreve

Richard S. Melvin Professor of Law
Indiana University School of Law, Bloomington

Peter Raven-Hansen

Glen Earl Weston Research Professor of Law
George Washington University Law School

Chapter 1

INTRODUCTION

§ 1.01 What is Civil Procedure?

[1] Approaching the Subject

Like all law, the law of civil procedure can be seen as a series of expedients to influence, punish, reward and authoritatively explain human behavior. Perhaps the reason that beginning students sometimes find civil procedure especially difficult is that it is preoccupied with *litigation* behavior, and students come to the course with little sense of what litigation is.

Litigation is often described as a game. Litigants are like players and judges like umpires. The litigation game is remorselessly competitive and is often thought to have winners and losers. Its rules, like those of many other games, are difficult to understand in the abstract. They are given life and meaning by the experience of the game itself. Thus, the more we understand the phenomenon of civil litigation, the easier it will be to understand civil procedure.

Litigation differs from most games, however, in at least two important respects.

First, most games exist for the pleasure they give to participants or spectators. So long as they are relatively harmless, they are not difficult to justify. In contrast, the litigation game carries a heavy burden of justification. The game may impose onerous costs upon the parties, the court and the public, and frequently has only one enthusiastic player — the plaintiff.

Civil procedure cases and problems can therefore appropriately be considered from the perspective of cost control or resource allocation. Could the factual dispute between the parties have been resolved by any means that would have eliminated the need for litigation? Should particular tactics employed by litigants be viewed as legitimate procedural means to substantive ends, or unreasonably burdensome means that are disproportionate to the ends? What should the balance be between litigant autonomy and judicial control?

Inquiry about the most appropriate use of judicial resources also requires a developing appreciation of the different roles trial and appellate courts play. The law of civil procedure recognizes that some issues resolved by trial

3

judges should rarely, if ever, be reviewed,[1] because appellate courts have an inferior vantage point or because redecision does not seem to justify expenditure of scarce appellate resources. Where and how the line should be drawn between matters freely reviewable and matters committed to the trial court's discretion (hence, largely unreviewable) is a recurring question in the civil procedure course.

A second difference between litigation and most games is that games are usually not of central importance to (at least amateur) participants or to society. In contrast, the plaintiff may be forced to play the litigation game in order to avert or recover from a crushing setback in life. To deny claimants opportunities to become effective players in the litigation game might make meaningless the rights secured by substantive law (e.g., torts, contracts, civil rights).

Readers of Dickens' *Bleak House* will recall how the redundant and prolonged Chancery procedure consumed the merits of the case. And, as Kafka's *The Trial* suggests, too little procedure can be just as bad. At its worst, procedure displaces or blocks substance. This can happen either when the expense and delay of too much procedure makes it impossible for a player to stay in the game long enough to reach the merits, or when potential players are shut out of the game because there is too little procedure. We must also be sensitive to possible differences between rules in theory and in application. As Anatole France observed, "the law in its majestic equality forbids the rich as well as the poor to sleep under bridges, to beg in the streets and to steal bread."

Ultimately, then, the game analogy must be used cautiously because it risks trivializing both the costs and stakes of litigation. Unlike a game, civil litigation does not exist for its own sake. Civil Procedure works best when it validates substantive law (the merits) in the most expeditious, accessible and unobtrusive way possible.[2]

[2] Substance and Procedure

The study of the formation and content of substantive rules of decision — the standards by which society controls and affects "primary decisions respecting human conduct"[3] — is the subject of the traditional first year law courses of contracts, torts, property, and substantive criminal law. Civil procedure concerns itself with enforcing substantive rules by civil lawsuits.

---

[1] When the losing party can appeal a trial judge's procedural order and does so, the appellate court must decide whether the order under review should be upheld. Whatever it decides, the appellate court acts by issuing an order of its own, *e.g.,* to affirm, to reverse, to vacate and remand for further proceedings. It often explains its order in an accompanying opinion. Most of the edited opinions civil procedure students read are appellate rather than trial court opinions.

[2] *See, e.g.,* Fed. R. Civ. P. 1, which provides that the federal rules of civil procedure "shall be construed and administered to secure the just, speedy, and inexpensive determination of every action." Hereinafter we will cite to a Federal Rule of Civil Procedure as "Rule—."

[3] *Hanna v. Plumer,* 380 U.S. 460, 475 (1965) (Harlan, J., concurring).

Roughly speaking, substantive rules of decision control conduct outside the courtroom, and procedural rules control conduct within.[4]

The latter determine in what courts lawyers file lawsuits, how they frame claims, denials and defenses, how the lawsuits progress from commencement to judgment, and the effect judgments have on subsequent lawsuits.

[3]　Civil Procedure in the United States

Civil procedure in the United States has three distinctive features. First, it follows an adversarial model of dispute resolution. Parties initiate and propel litigation in this model, and the judge, historically and at least in theory, plays the relatively passive role of umpire. The burden is on the parties to present their grievances and defenses. Unlike in so-called *inquisitorial* models of dispute resolution,[5] the judge rarely makes independent inquiries. The burden is also on the parties to prosecute their grievances and defenses; litigation stops unless the parties pursue it. Indeed, some scholars have argued that recent procedural rule changes have "undermined judicial evaluation of the merits of lawsuits and thereby vastly expanded attorneys' opportunities to twist procedure and substance on behalf of their clients."[6] These characteristics of our system of dispute resolution place on lawyers a heavy responsibility for assuring justice and mastering civil procedure.

Second, civil procedure in the United States is dominated by *positive law:* codified rules enacted by legislatures or their delegates. In contrast, the substantive rules of decision taught in the other traditional first year courses are more often doctrinal: declared by courts as part of the *common law.*

One difference between positive and common law lies in the materials containing the legal rules. The common-law materials are almost entirely judicial opinions, and the appropriate inquiry is: what rule best fits the case? In contrast, positive law materials are enacted laws or procedural rules and their legislative history. Emphasis in administering the latter is on legislative intent, in recognition of the superior lawmaking authority of legislatures and their delegates.

It is not always easy for the first year student to subordinate the comparatively freewheeling policy-oriented analysis of common law taught in many substantive courses to the plain language of positive law, principles of statutory construction and reading of legislative history. But mastery of the latter lays the groundwork not just for understanding much of civil procedure, but also for understanding upper level law courses. Significantly,

---

[4] For a detailed and illuminating discussion of distinctions between the two, *see* Cook, *"Substance" and "Procedure" in the Conflict of Laws,* 42 Yale L.J. 333 (1933).

[5] *See, e.g.,* Langbein, *The German Advantage in Civil Procedure,* 52 U. Chi. L. Rev. 823 (1985).

[6] Molot, *How Changes in the Legal Profession Reflect Changes in Civil Procedure,* 84 Va. L. Rev. 955, 958 (1998).

practicing lawyers rank "knowledge of statutory law" as the most important knowledge for practice, just ahead of "knowledge of procedural rules."[7]

Finally, the purpose of civil procedure is, as the Federal Rules of Civil Procedure state, "to secure the just, speedy, and inexpensive determination of every action."[8] Presumably, decisions are more likely to be just when they reach the merits. But the adversarial character of civil dispute resolution in the United States, the number of lawyers, and perhaps a national tendency to look too readily for judicial resolution of matters that other societies settle politically, administratively or privately,[9] have made the goals of "speedy and inexpensive" determinations increasingly difficult to attain.[10] As a result, there is constant pressure for more active judicial management of litigation and for judicial intervention to dispose of the litigation without trial, if possible. Thus, the 1993 amendment to Rule 1 requires the rules to be "administered" — as well as "construed" (the original term) — "to secure just, speedy, and inexpensive determination of every action." No one foresees the replacement of our adversarial model by the inquisitorial model of dispute resolution, yet the former is undergoing significant change in response to widespread criticisms of the cost and efficiency of civil litigation.

[4] Some Common Misperceptions of Civil Procedure

The study of civil procedure is often impeded by misperceptions formed before law school or by comparison of civil procedure with the substantive first year courses.

One is that civil procedure is, as scholars once labeled it, strictly *adjective* law that "exists for the sake of something else."[11] However, while it is true

---

[7] Baird, *A Survey of the Relevance of Legal Training to Law School Graduates*, 29 J. Legal Educ. 264, 273 (1978) (explaining that knowledge of common law, constitutional law, ethics, and regulations were all ranked lower by practitioners).

[8] Rule 1.

[9] *See* W. Olson, *The Litigation Explosion: What Happened When America Unleashed the Lawsuit* (1991); M. Marks, *The Suing of America: Why and How We Take Each Other to Court* (1981); J. Lieberman, *The Litigious Society* (1983).

[10] *See, e.g.,* Trubek, *et al., The Costs of Ordinary Litigation*, 31 U.C.L.A. 72 (1983); Miller, *The Adversary System: Dinosaur or Phoenix,* 69 Minn. L. Rev. 1 (1984); Rand Inst., *The Costs of Asbestos Litigation* (1983), excerpted in *Legal Times of Washington,* Aug. 8, 1983, at 26, Table 6.2 (reporting that of every dollar expended per claim, 37 cents were attributable to defendant's litigation expenses, 26 cents attributable to plaintiff's litigation expenses, and 37 cents attributable to net compensation to plaintiffs). Litigation delays vary tremendously between courts. In federal trial courts, the median time between commencement of civil litigation and disposition at trial was 8.2 months, with 2% of the dispositions at trial taking more than 20 months. 2000 Admin. Office U.S. Courts Annual Report of the Dir., Table C-5, at 208.

[11] C. Hepburn, *The Historical Development of Code Pleading in America and England with Special Reference to the Codes of New York, Missouri, California, Kentucky, Iowa, Minnesota, Indiana, Ohio, Oregon, Washington, Nebraska, Wisconsin, Kansas, Nevada, North Dakota, South Dakota, Idaho, Montana, Arizona, North Carolina, South Carolina, Arkansas, Wyoming, Utah, Colorado, Connecticut, and Oklahoma* (1897).

that civil procedure is not an end in itself,[12] it does not follow that procedural law is less significant than substantive law. At least one federal appellate court has suggested that procedures can have value independent of the merits, such that a lawyer's negligent waiver of the procedure may give rise to malpractice liability even when the procedure would not necessarily have improved the outcome.[13] The appellate cases (the chief vehicle by which substantive law is taught in law school) all reach courts by procedural initiatives, and the procedural posture in which the issues were presented to the appellate court often determines how much attention they will receive.[14] Moreover, courts sometimes rely on procedure to reach "just" results without changing inhospitable substantive law.[15] Procedure also interacts with substantive law outside the courtroom, as illustrated by the effect of the procedural device of class actions[16] on the substantive elements of securities fraud claims,[17] and the effect of the procedural requirement that plaintiffs pay for notice to class members on the effective enforcement of consumer laws.[18] Law has not escaped "the tendency of all modern scientific and philosophic thought . . . to emphasize the importance of method, process, or procedure."[19]

Another common misperception is that civil procedure is nothing more than the unimaginative and routine application of black-letter law to dry procedural issues. This may be a law student's initial reaction to the positive law materials from which civil procedure is primarily taught.[20] Yet positive law is more dynamic than the black letter of a rule or statute might indicate. Moreover, important parts of civil procedure, including personal jurisdiction (court's power to bind particular defendants) and *res judicata* (the effect of prior judgments on subsequent litigation), are based primarily on judicial doctrine.

---

[12] *See* § 1.01[1], *supra.*

[13] *Jones Motor Co. v. Holtkamp, Liese, Beckmeier & Childress P.C.*, 197 F.3d 1190 (7th Cir. 1999) (asserting that failure to perfect jury demand may be such a procedure, but affirming judgement for malpractice defendant because plaintiffs had not proven resulting damages to a reasonable certainty).

[14] *See* §§ 13.08 & 13.09 (scope and intensity of review), *infra.*

[15] F. James *et al., Civil Procedure* § 1.1 (4th ed. 1992) (quotation marks supplied). *See* Cover, *For James Wm. Moore: Some Reflections on a Reading of the Rules,* 84 Yale L.J. 718 (1975).

[16] Suits which may be brought by representative parties on behalf of a defined class of members who are not themselves participants in the litigation but may be bound by its outcome. *See* § 9.09 (class actions), *infra.*

[17] *See* Scott, *The Impact of Class Actions on Rule 10b-5,* 38 U. Chi. L. Rev. 337, 338 (1971) (arguing that class actions permit some class members to recover who would fail to satisfy reliance and materiality requirements in individual actions for securities fraud).

[18] *See* Scott, *Two Models of the Civil Process,* 27 Stan. L. Rev. 937, 944 (1975) (noting that the expense of such notice dooms most consumer actions because the expense of individual lawsuits exceeds the benefits that they could confer on individual plaintiffs).

[19] M. Cohen, "The Process of Judicial Legislation" in *Law and the Social Order: Essays in Legal Philosophy* (1994).

[20] *See* § 1.01[2], *supra.*

It is important to understand that statutes or codified rules governing most procedural questions are not self-applying. Problems often elude solution by plain-language tests or application of simple canons of statutory construction. Statutes over time acquire their own judicial gloss. The legislative product may be inarticulate, forcing courts to finish the lawmaking process. Or the legislature may deliberately create a rule that can never be completed in the abstract. Rules of the latter kind place courts at procedural crossroads, supplying general criteria for decision and leaving the result to courts' appreciation of the facts in particular cases.[21]

Furthermore, many, if not most, procedural questions are susceptible to more than one answer. Civil procedure, hence effective litigation, consists less of finding black-letter answers than of choices among tactical options. These choices turn not just on the rules and procedural posture of litigation, but also on the relative strengths and attitudes of the parties, the relationships between lawyers and judge, and all the other subtle factors that make lawyering an art as well as a profession.

A third misperception is that civil procedure is trial practice.[22] This may cause some law students who cannot picture themselves as trial lawyers to approach their civil procedure course with less enthusiasm. But even a brief glance at litigation statistics refutes this perception. For example, of all the federal civil actions terminated in the year ending Sept. 30, 2000, 72% ended before the pretrial conference that often precedes trial in federal court[23] (one in four of these ended without court action of any kind), 8% ended during or after pretrial, and only 2% lasted through trial.[24] More than half of those were tried to a judge rather than a jury,[25] calling upon far different lawyering skills than jury trial practice. State civil disposition statistics[26] send the same message: civil procedure is not about trial. Litigation in the United States is predominantly *pretrial* practice. In this phase of litigation, it is not theatrics, charisma or trial tactics that carry the day, but mastery of pretrial procedure, the ability to communicate effectively to the court, and a command of the details of the lawsuit.

---

[21] *See e.g.* § 9.05 (discussing Federal Rules 19 and 20 dealing with compulsory and permissive joinder) *infra.*

[22] For treatment of trial practice (jury selection, opening statements, presentation of evidence, closing argument, jury deliberation, and preservation of points for appeal), see Thomas A. Mauet, *Fundamentals of Trial Techniques* (3d ed. 1992); J. Jeans, *Trial Advocacy* (1975).

[23] *See* § 12.03 (pretrial conference), *infra.*

[24] 2000 *Admin. Office U.S. Courts Annual report of the Dir.*, note 9, *supra*, Table C-4A, at 205.

[25] *Id.*

[26] Only 2% of tort, contract, and real property cases in the nation's 75 largest counties were tried to a jury in 1992. Bureau of Justice statistics, U.S. Dept. of Justice (last modified Mar. 4, 1999) type = "http"address = "www.ojp.usdoj.gov/bjs/civil.htm">http://www.ojp.usdoj.gov/bjs/civil.htm

§ 1.02 Sources of Civil Procedure

Constitutional law sets the outer limits of civil procedure. The United States Constitution limits the subject matter of the cases that federal courts may hear,[27] determines the effect courts of one state must give to the judgments of another,[28] and preserves the right to jury trial in certain categories of cases in federal court.[29] In addition, the Due Process Clause of the Fifth Amendment to the United States Constitution guarantees minimal due process to litigants in federal courts, and the Due Process Clause of the Fourteenth Amendment gives a comparable guarantee to litigants in state courts. Due process has helped shape procedural requirements for personal jurisdiction (judicial power to enter binding judgments with respect to particular defendants or property),[30] notice, and the opportunity to be heard in litigation.[31] Given their potential procedural reach, in fact, it is curious perhaps that the due process clauses have not been invoked more frequently as sources of procedure.[32]

Statutes are a second source of positive procedural law. In both the federal and state systems, they define the power of various courts to hear particular cases[33] and the convenient forums for litigation.[34] In all states, statutes also help define the personal jurisdiction of state courts.[35] In addition, a declining minority of states[36] have enacted statutory procedural codes.[37]

The most important sources of positive procedural law, however, are formally adopted rules of civil procedure. The federal courts and forty states have adopted them, usually by a judicial rulemaking process authorized by a statute.[38] Although these rules systems differ from state to state, as of 1986 twenty-three states had copied, with minor modifications, the Federal Rules of Civil Procedure.[39] As a result, almost all first year civil

---

[27] U.S. Const. art. III. *See* Ch. 5 (subject matter jurisdiction), *infra.*

[28] U.S. Const. art. IV. *See* §§ 15.10-15.11 (inter-system preclusion and full faith and credit), *infra.*

[29] U.S. Const. amend. VII. *See* § 12.07[1] (right to a jury), *infra.* Most state constitutions have analogous procedural provisions governing state courts.

[30] *See* Ch. 3 (personal jurisdiction), *infra.*

[31] *See* Ch. 4 (notice and opportunity to be heard) & § 9.09[2][b] (due process requirements in class actions), *infra.*

[32] *See* Leubsdorf, *Constitutional Civil Procedure,* 63 Tex. L. Rev. 579 (1984).

[33] *See* §§ 5.10[2] (citing federal statutes illustratively), 13.02-13.04 (federal appeals), *infra.*

[34] *See* Ch. 5 (venue), *infra.*

[35] *See* § 3.07[1] (long-arm statutes), *infra.*

[36] *See* Oakley & Coon, *The Federal Rules in State Courts: A Survey of State Court Systems of Civil Procedure,* 61 Wash. L. Rev. 1367, 1378 (1986) (listing California, Connecticut, Georgia, Illinois, Kansas, Louisiana, Nebraska, New York, North Carolina, and Oklahoma as the then remaining states with procedural codes).

[37] *See* § 8.03 (history and problems of code pleading), *infra.*

[38] *Oakley & Coon,* note 10, *supra,* at 1378.

[39] *Id.* at 1377 (listing Alabama, Alaska, Arizona, Colorado, District of Columbia, Hawaii,

procedure courses and casebooks focus primarily on the federal rules, as
we will here.

Some understanding of the federal rulemaking process[40] is essential to
understanding the effect of the Federal Rules of Civil Procedure in federal
courts. The Rules Enabling Act delegates lawmaking authority to the
Supreme Court to make rules governing "general rules of practice and
procedure" for cases in the federal courts.[41] The Judicial Conference of the
United States, comprised of the Chief Justice of the Supreme Court and
designated judges from other federal courts, oversees the rulemaking
process. The Advisory Committee on Civil Rules to the Judicial Conference's
Standing Committee on Rules of Practice and Procedure is charged with
the actual work of drafting and recommending rules of civil procedure. The
Advisory Committee is comprised of judges, practitioners and law professors. The Chief Justice appoints a Reporter who monitors developments in
the field and aids the Advisory Committee.

Federal procedural rulemaking typically begins when the Advisory
Committee notes a procedural need or problem. If the Committee so directs,
the Reporter prepares a preliminary draft of responsive rule changes with
"committee notes" explaining their purpose. The Committee meets and
revises these materials and then reports them to the Standing Committee.
If the Standing Committee approves the draft for publication, it is published
in the *Federal Register* and the federal reporters for public comment. In
addition, the Advisory Committee usually holds public hearings on the draft
in diverse locations. After reviewing public comments, the Committee may
make revisions and then submit the proposed rule changes and final comments[42] to the Standing Committee of the Judicial Conference. The latter
reviews and ultimately forwards the proposal, revised if necessary, to the
members of the Judicial Conference.

Indiana, Kentucky, Maine, Massachusetts, Minnesota, Montana, New Mexico, North Dakota,
Ohio, Rhode Island, South Dakota, Tennessee, Utah, Vermont, Washington, West Virginia,
and Wyoming). This statement tends to understate the influence of the federal rules, because
four of the states with statutory procedural codes have codified versions of the federal rules
(Georgia, Kansas, North Carolina, and Oklahoma), and three other states have rules that
"show strong affinity to the content and organization of the Federal Rules. . . ." (Idaho,
Michigan, and Nevada). *Id.* at 1377-1378. *See* Graham, *State Adaptation of the Federal Rules:
The Pros and Cons*, 43 Okla. L. Rev. 293 (1990).

[40] *See generally* Walker, *A Comprehensive Reform for Federal Civil Rulemaking*, 61 Geo.
Wash. L. Rev. 455 (1993); Baker, *An Introduction to Federal Court Rulemaking Procedure*,
22 Tex. Tech. L. Rev. 323 (1991); Brown, *Federal Rulemaking: Problems and Possibilities*
(Federal Judicial Center 1981); Kaplan, *Amendments of the Federal Rules of Civil Procedure
1961-1963 (1)*, 77 Harv. L. Rev. 601, 601–602 (1964).

[41] 28 U.S.C. §§ 2071-2074. *See generally* Burbank, *The Rules Enabling Act of 1934*, 130 U.
Pa. L. Rev. 1015 (1982). The Act expressly mandates that such rules "shall not abridge, enlarge
or modify any substantive right," thus reserving substantive lawmaking to the Congress and
to the state legislatures within their proper spheres. *See generally* §§ 7.01-7.04 (the laws
applied in federal courts and the applicability of federal procedural rules), *infra. See also*
Carrington, *"Substance" and "Procedure" in the Rules Enabling Act*, 1989 Duke L.J. 281 (1989).

[42] When rule changes are adopted, the advisory committee's notes become an important
source of legislative history for construing the changes. They are published in the Federal Rules
Decisions, the principal civil procedure treatises, and in many rulebooks.

CIV PRO

If the Conference approves the proposal, it sends the rule changes to the Supreme Court. In theory, the Supreme Court conducts a substantive review of the change. In fact, the Justices have differed about their true role. Justice Douglas, for example, described it as "merely perfunctory" and the Court as "a mere conduit" for transmittal of the rules to Congress.[43] Individual justices may make statements concerning the rule changes. The Court then transmits the changes to Congress no later than May 1 of the year in which they are to become effective. The change becomes effective no earlier than December 1 of that year, unless Congress by statute modifies or rejects the rule.[44]

However, not all written rules governing federal practice are promulgated in this fashion. Rule 83 authorizes a majority of the judges of each district court to promulgate local rules "not inconsistent" with the formal federal rules of civil procedure. Many district courts have exercised this authority to issue housekeeping rules governing the length of briefs and the availability of oral hearings, attorney admissions, procedures for submitting requests for attorneys fees and other matters.[45]

The Civil Justice Reform Act of 1990 (CJRA) complicates matters further. There Congress authorized a nationwide rulemaking experiment to reduce expense and delay in the district courts.[46] The CJRA directed all district courts to appoint advisory groups to analyze their dockets and make cost- and delay-reducing recommendations. Selected courts put some of these recommendations into effect provisionally. Experimental recommendations under the CJRA need not be consistent with the Federal Rules of Civil Procedure.[47]

---

[43] See Statement of Douglas, 409 U.S. 1132 (1972) (Douglas, J., dissenting). More recently, Justice White has said that the Court's role "is to transmit the Judicial Conference's recommendations without change and without careful study, as long as there is no suggestion that the committee system has not operated with integrity." Statement of J. White, 113 S. Ct. CCC, CCCIV (1993).

[44] Except for rules affecting an evidentiary privilege, Section 2074 contemplates (but does not require) a passive role for Congress; "[i]nertia means approval." Siegel, 28 U.S.C.A. § 2074 commentary (1988). Congress usually remains silent, but has shown a greater tendency to become active in recent years. Cf. Ely, *The Irrepressible Myth of Erie*, 87 Harv. L. Rev. 693, 693-694 (1974) (describing congressional resistance to the Court's proposed federal rules of evidence), and § 4.03[1] (describing congressional substitution of its own enactment for the Court's proposed amendment to Rule 4), *infra*. Congress's constitutional authority to change the rules is not undisputed. *Compare* Mullinex, *Judicial Power and the Rules Enabling Act*, 46 Mercer L. Rev. 733 (1995) (questioning such authority to supercede procedural rulemaking by the judiciary) *with* Redish, *Federal Judicial Independence: Constitutional and Political Perspectives*, 46 Mercer L. Rev. 697 (1995) (supporting such authority on majoritarian principles).

[45] *See* Wright & Miller, *Federal Practice and Procedure* § 3154 (giving examples). The scope of local rulemaking authority is a matter of continuing debate. *See, e.g.*, Levin, *Local Rules as Experiments: A Study in the Division of Power*, 139 U. Pa. L. Rev. 1567 (1991); Flanders, *Local Rules in Federal District Courts: Usurpation, Legislation, or Information?*, 14 Loy. L.A.L. Rev. 213 (1981). In 1988, Congress acted to subject such rulemaking to closer scrutiny. *See* 28 U.S.C. § 2071 and Siegel, 28 U.S.C.A. § 2071 commentary (1988).

[46] Codified at 28 U.S.C. §§ 471-482. *See generally* Tobias, *Judicial Oversight of Civil Justice Reform*, 140 F.R.D. 49 (1992).

[47] Some may not be. *See* Tobias, note 46, *supra*, at 51-52.

Individual judges may also establish rules governing procedures for scheduling and argument in their courtrooms. Rule 83 expressly provides that "[i]n all cases not provided for by rule, the district judges and magistrates may regulate their practice in any manner not inconsistent with these rules or those of the district in which they act."[48] Furthermore, judges always have what has been called "individual calendar" discretion over scheduling and hearing practice in a particular case.[49]

The parties themselves can also be an important source of procedural rules often overlooked by law students. A few federal rules expressly authorize parties themselves to stipulate to departures from the rules,[50] and parties can make other agreements that supplement and sometimes modify positive procedural law. They often agree by contract, for example, to the appropriate forum for litigation under the contract, the mode of service of the complaint and summons, or the applicable substantive law for such litigation, superseding the otherwise applicable law.[51] At a more mundane level, litigation counsel schedule many pretrial activities among themselves.

Finally, ethical rules bearing on civil litigation are promulgated as codes of professional responsibility or rules of the bar by courts acting in conjunction with bar associations. The American Bar Association's *Model Rules of Professional Conduct*,[52] substantially adopted by the majority of the states,[53] contain several rules concerning the zeal with which a lawyer may represent a client in litigation.[54] Although historically there have been serious doubts concerning the organized bar's capacity for self-enforcement of such rules,[55] it is probable that the majority of lawyers abide them. Moreover, several Federal Rules of Civil Procedure underscore professional responsibilities in federal courts and may become a vehicle for enforcement of some of the ethical rules adopted by the bar.[56]

---

[48] *See, e.g.,* Schwarzer (J., N.D. Cal.), *Guidelines for Discovery, Motion Practice and Trial,* 117 F.R.D. 273 (1987). Judge Schwarzer's *Guidelines* admonish counsel to observe not only the Federal Rules of Civil Procedure and the District Court's Local Rules, but also "the rules and practices of the particular judge to whom the case is assigned." The latter are available "[b]y obtaining from the judge's courtroom deputy copies of the standing orders used by that judge; and [b]y inquiring of the deputy (not the law clerks) how the judge wants things done." *Id.* at 273.

[49] Siegel, 28 U.S.C.A. § 2077 commentary (1988).

[50] *See* Rules 15(a) (stipulation in lieu of court permission to amend pleadings), 26(f) (changes in discovery limitations), and Rule 29 (stipulation of discovery procedure).

[51] *See, e.g., National Equip. Rental v. Szukhent,* 375 U.S. 311 (1964) (enforcing contract that designated agent to receive service).

[52] American Bar Ass'n, *Model Rules of Professional Conduct and Code of Judicial Conduct* (1992).

[53] 56 U.S.L.W. 2466 (Feb. 23, 1988).

[54] *See, e.g.,* Model Rules 3.1-3.4, note 26, *supra.*

[55] American Bar Ass'n, Special Committee on Evaluation and Disciplinary Enforcement, *Problems and Recommendations on Disciplinary Enforcement* 1 (final draft, 1970).

[56] *See* Rule 11, *discussed in* § 8.05[2] *infra,* and Rule 26(g), *discussed in* § 10.13[1] *infra.*

§ 1.03   Briefing a Civil Procedure Case

The primary vehicles for class discussion in most civil procedure courses are assigned cases. These are judicial opinions, usually written by judges to accompany their orders (rulings) on civil procedure motions. An *order* may dispose of the lawsuit or simply resolve a skirmish between the litigants and leave the lawsuit to continue. Typically, the order simply says who won — for example: "Plaintiff's motion for summary judgment is granted [denied]." The *opinion* is written by the judge to accompany the order and to explain why the judge decided to rule in favor of the prevailing party (or, in appellate opinions, why the ruling below was reversed or affirmed).

Virtually all the orders in cases we consider were on contested matters. That is to say, the parties urged upon the court opposing choices of judicial conduct before the court decided how to rule in the order. Not all orders are accompanied by opinions, and not all opinions are designated by the court for publication. Opinions are most likely to accompany orders which settle contested matters, because judges feel greater pressure to justify what they have done under such circumstances. In this sense, judges are advocates, too. The judicial opinions we will read are the judges' means of arguing that their orders reflect decisions most likely to advance the rule and logic of civil procedure and to do justice in the individual case.

The central purpose of case briefing is to enable students to get the most out of class. Briefing helps students prepare by giving structure to their consideration of cases before class begins. It also provides a working paper during class, making it easier for students to follow developments and to advance the discussion when called upon by the professor. On the other hand, briefs may not be terribly useful tools for course review. This is because they are made before class, before thoughts about the material have matured. Comments and addenda students make on their briefs during and after classroom discussion of the case are likely to be far more useful for exam study.

Casebooks and study aids suggest how to brief a case, and many students are taught briefing in first semester orientation lectures or legal methods classes. Our concern here is to explain how the generic briefing technique should be adapted for civil procedure cases.

Most briefs and many reported judicial opinions begin with a *recitation of the pre-litigation facts* which gave rise to the claims or defenses in the litigation. These are always important, if for no other reason than to remind the reader of the real world, flesh-and-blood implications of the legal issues put by the case. But they are often of less significance in civil procedure decisions than in those focusing on points of substantive law.

Instead, the crucial facts for us are *procedural facts:* what happened to the case after it was filed. The chronology of procedural steps taken by the litigants and the court is often important. For example, the pattern might be commencement of the litigation by the filing of a complaint, defendant's filing of a motion to dismiss the complaint for some reason, argument on the motion leading to its denial, fact-finding by the parties, trial, judgment for the plaintiff, and appeal by defendant (raising, among others, the same issue presented previously by motion). Retracing procedural steps is essential to understanding who's who, what has happened in the case, and how ripe procedural rulings are for review. It is also important to an appreciation of tactical aspects of litigation.[57] It facilitates reconstruction of the alternatives available to the parties as the litigation progresses.

Thus, while an elaborate general fact description may be unnecessary in briefing most civil procedure cases, students should include a full statement of facts setting the *procedural posture* of the case. This statement should ordinarily indicate who is suing whom, facts which may be easier to diagram in the margin of the brief or the casebook itself. The student might use arrows to represent claims (and sometimes defenses) instead of describing the process narratively. Here is an illustration.

Figure 1-1

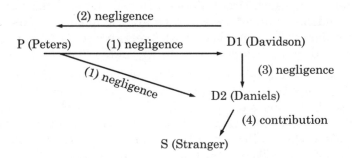

(Diagram shows that (1) Peters sued Davidson and Daniels for negligence, whereupon (2) Davidson counterclaimed against Peters and (3) cross-claimed against Daniels for negligence, and (4) Daniels impleaded Stranger on a theory of contribution.)

The chronology of procedural facts can be suggested by numbering the facts in the brief (as illustrated above) or in the case excerpt itself.

Next, it is useful to *identify the statutes or rules involved in the case.* Many study aids omit this step in briefing because they are geared primarily to briefing cases applying common law, not positive law (statutes or codified rules of procedure).[58]

---

[57] *See* § 1.01[3], *supra.*

[58] Since procedural decisions often turn on rules of positive law, a routine search for this material is a good briefing step. Note, on the other hand, that it is not useful and may even be harmful to attempt to paraphrase applicable positive law. Here there simply is no substitute for the actual language of the statute or rule. Nor is it enough to consider this kind of material in the abstract or in bulk at sporadic intervals during the semester. Students can best learn and understand statutes and rules of procedure in the context of particular case applications. It goes without saying that cases must be read with the rulebook close at hand.

For example, when you encounter positive federal law, consider the following approach. Read the cited statute or rule carefully, going to your rulebook if the text is not reproduced in the case itself. Is it clear from a reading of the provision how Congress intended to apply it to the case at hand? If so, has the court's decision given it that application? If it is not clear from a reading of the provision how Congress intended it to apply to the case at hand, has the court resolved the provision's ambiguity in a satisfactory way?

Third, the brief should *frame the issues presented by the case.* Many opinions do this expressly, but when the opinion is unclear, framing the issue is often the crucial step towards understanding the court's decision and its reasoning.

Fourth, the brief should *describe the court's decision on the issue at two levels.* The court will both supply an *answer* to the issue put by the case and make a formal *disposition* of the case, as noted often in the final paragraph. For example, when the issue is whether the plaintiff's complaint has stated a claim upon which relief can be granted, the court may decide that it does not and then grant the motion to dismiss and enter an order of dismissal. But this latter disposition — an order of dismissal — need not go hand-in-hand with the decision of the issue. The court might instead grant the motion to dismiss with leave to plaintiff to amend his complaint.

Fifth, the brief should *describe and critique the reasoning articulated for the decision.* In describing the reasoning, the student should take full advantage of dissenting and concurring opinions, sometimes expressly written to limit the applicability of the court's reasoning. Presumptuous as it might seem at first, you must also evaluate the court's reasoning. This may take some effort, since students often arrive at law school believing that the laws they will study exist as part of a static natural order — like laws of physics. Unfortunately, this attitude permits no more than a superficial grasp of the law in civil procedure or other courses. It makes the student easy prey for the rhetoric in many judicial opinions that the result reached by the court is obvious. On the contrary, many cases — particularly those selected for casebook treatment — pose close and difficult questions. Great jurists may produce illuminating opinions, but they cannot make hard cases easy. What one often finds is "not a matter of right against wrong, but of right against right."[59]

This critical side of analysis and discussion is a good deal of what makes the course (and the professor) tick. Civil procedure professors strive to illustrate and teach the proposition that civil procedure involves hard choices. In turn, answers to examination questions must reflect judgment seasoned by an appreciation of both sides of the issue.[60] To respond, students cannot afford a passive approach to assigned materials.

---

[59] Rosenberg, *Devising Procedures That Are Civil to Promote Justice That Is Civilized,* 69 Mich. L. Rev. 797 (1971).

[60] Contrary to what beginning students might assume, outright mistakes by students are

The critique of the court's reasoning will be the most ambitious portion of your brief, the part most likely to require revision during and after civil procedure class. Don't worry. As noted earlier, unrevised case briefs are ultimately unreliable, anyway. The purpose of briefing is to enable you to get the most out of class and to stimulate (and ultimately reward) your critical thought. A marked up brief is evidence that the purpose was accomplished.

§ 1.04 Research and Drafting in Civil Procedure

The starting point for research on any legal problem is to frame the issue tentatively, something that students rehearse in their preparation of case briefs.[61] For law students and beginning lawyers, even this step will sometimes prove difficult. When it does, it may be helpful to consult a civil procedure treatise like this one to frame the issue correctly and to identify relevant statutes or rules.

The second step is to read carefully any statutes or rules of procedure involved in your problem, noting when necessary any time frame for acting under them. It is difficult to overstate the importance of rereading the text of a rule or statute with each succeeding problem. This is because these provisions are drafted to cover a variety of situations arising in cases. A subsequent case thus may be governed by the same rule of procedure, yet the demands of the new controversy may illuminate a different portion of the text. As a result, even experienced lawyers take the trouble to reread carefully rules and statutes.

For federal civil procedure problems, the third step is to consult the two federal practice treatises: *Moore's Federal Practice* (Matthew Bender) and C. Wright & A. Miller, *et al., Federal Practice and Procedure* (West). Both are organized primarily by federal rule number, providing easy access when the problem involves the federal rules.[62] Both also reproduce the Advisory Committee's notes that accompanied the rule and represent most of its legislative history. Federal courts often cite analyses and conclusions from these treatises, in recognition of their thoroughness and quality. Finally, both supply voluminous case citations, updated in pocket parts or inserts. Coverage overlaps considerably; yet style, analysis and case coverage in the two are sufficiently distinct to justify examination of both in researching the typical problem of federal civil procedure.

Treatises on state procedural law also exist, although they tend to be less thorough and to be updated less frequently. When state statutes bear on

---

fairly uncommon, at least in essay examinations. The difference between an "A" and a "C" examination more often lies in the imagination and agility demonstrated in applying course rules and concepts in a new setting, rather than in differences in bottom line conclusions. This demonstration is possible only with an approach to civil procedure that is both descriptive *and* critical.

[61] *See* § 1.03, *supra.*

[62] These treatises also cover some statutory issues of federal procedure, including, notably, jurisdiction.

the issue, one can review annotations to the relevant statutory code.[63] These steps will help reframe the problem, suggest a more or less detailed analysis, and generate lists of possibly relevant cases for further research.[64] Another method of locating recent case authority for federal civil procedural rules is to use the *Federal Rules Service* (Callaghan), which digests cases by rule number.

With the development of computerized law research, however, the best way to generate a current case list and to review it is to use *Lexis* or *Westlaw*. Civil procedure problems that turn on statutes or rules are particularly well-suited to computer research, because it is easy to frame a search request around the statute or rule number. Students are cautioned, however, that there is no uniformity in judicial citation to such procedural law, and a complete search request must include in the alternative all of the likely variants. With regard to the Federal Rules of Civil Procedure, for example, these variants include at least "FRCP," "F. R. C. P.," "Fed. R. Civ. P.," "Rule," and "R." with the relevant number, and, ideally, some generic phrase to help exclude like-numbered federal rules of appellate or criminal procedure from the search.

For drafting problems involving the Federal Rules of Civil Procedure, students should consult the official appendix of forms immediately following the rules. These forms have been declared sufficient in federal practice by Rule 84. Students may also wish to examine unofficial forms. These may offer guidance in both state and federal practice.[65] They are collections of prior pleadings, motions or discovery requests. Most have passed muster at some time in a relevant court and may therefore serve as a form for current papers of the same kind.

For several reasons, such form books must be used with extreme caution and a heavy dose of common sense. First, unlike those in the official appendix to the federal rules, most published forms do not carry the imprimatur of any court system. All that stands behind many items memorialized as forms is that they worked once in a case. Close perusal of the fine print in the form books that give citations may reveal that the most recent approval of a particular form came in the nineteenth century. Arcane and dated wording in forms provides another danger signal. Second, because forms were originally created to meet the facts and demands of a different case, substantial adaptation is often necessary to make forms

---

[63] Annotations for federal rules of procedure and federal procedural statutes may also be helpful. Most can be found in Title 28 of the *United States Code Annotated*.

[64] For the typical federal procedural issue, it is rarely wise to go to the cases directly without reading the relevant sections of the treatises. Their unusual thoroughness and authority sometimes supplies an answer without need of additional case research, and they will at least focus the case search and thus ultimately save time for the issues that they address.

[65] *See, e.g., American Jurisprudence Pleading and Practice Forms Annotated* (Lawyers Co-op.); L. Frumer & I. Hill, *et al. Bender's Federal Practice Forms* (Matthew Bender); *Bender's Forms of Discovery* (Matthew Bender); *Nichols Cyclopedia of Federal Procedure Forms* (Callaghan); *Federal Procedural Forms Lawyers Edition* (Lawyers Co-op); *West's Federal Forms* (West).

usable. Finally, a form may not have been selected for its brilliance, but for its (one-time) sufficiency. It may represent no more than the lowest common denominator. Yet form books (and, particularly in large law firms today, internally-generated forms and prior papers) are often a helpful starting point for procedural drafting.

§ 1.05 Civil Procedure Bibliography and Short Form Citations

We cite in footnotes to the textbooks and articles on civil procedure that are useful sources for further reading. Several are cited often enough to warrant use of a short form citation. The following list gives the full citation for each such work, followed by the manner in which we cite it. We supply only the section numbers for these sources because the page numbers vary with succeeding editions.

I. *Hornbooks*

J. Friedenthal, M. Kane & A. Miller, *Civil Procedure* (West 3d ed. 1999) (*Friedenthal, Kane & Miller*).

F. James, J. Leubsdorf, & G. Hazard, *Civil Procedure* (Little Brown 4th ed. 1992) (*James, Hazard & Leubsdorf*).

L. Teply & R. Whitten, *Civil Procedure* (Foundation Press 2000) (*Teply & Whitten*).

C. Wright, *Hornbook on Federal Courts* (West 5th ed. 1994) (*Wright*).

II. *Treatises*

C. Wright & A. Miller, *Federal Practice and Procedure* (West) (*Wright & Miller;* volume number omitted because section numbers are unique).

J. Moore, *Moore's Federal Practice* (Matthew Bender 3d ed. 2000) (*Moore;* volume number omitted where section number is keyed to a Federal Rule of Civil Procedure). In rare cases where quoted material is taken from the second edition of *Moore*, we have left a full citation.

CHAPTER 2
UNDERSTANDING CONTRACTS

By

Jeffrey Ferriell

Professor of Law
Capital University Law School

Professor Michael Navin

Former Professor of Law
Pennsylvania State University
Dickinson School of Law

Chapter 2

Introduction

§ 1.01 The Meaning of Contract

Studying the law of contracts involves studying the law of broken promises.

A contract is nothing more than a promise that the law will enforce.[1] Though this statement appears simple, in the real world it is quite complex. The variety of situations in our society in which promises are made and broken, combined with the complexity of the public policies which might affect the enforceability of a particular promise, sometimes makes the question of whether the law will enforce a promise particularly challenging. When we say that a contract is a promise that the law will enforce, we are also implicitly saying that there must be at least some promises that the law will not enforce. As will be seen, a great deal of contract law deals with the distinctions between agreements or promises that the law will enforce and those which, for various reasons, will not be enforced.

[A] Enforcement of Promises[2]

One of the most important themes associated with the meaning of contract deals with the concept of the "enforcement" of a promise. If a contract is a promise the law will enforce, it is critical to an understanding of contract law to have an understanding of the mechanism our society uses to "enforce" a promise. The nature and extent of the legal and equitable remedies available to enforce promises are not just an important part of contract law, they are viewed by many as the central point.

If promises were enforced by the threat of a term in prison, breaking a promise would be far more serious than if enforcement were accomplished by a stern lecture. The threat of prison would probably go a long way toward discouraging breach, but it might also discourage parties from entering into contracts in the first place, unless they were supremely confident of their ability to perform. The threat of a stern lecture might leave people far too willing to breach and unwilling to place much stock in the meaning of the

---

[1] Restatement (Second) of Contracts § 1 (1981) ("contract is a promise . . . for the breach of which the law gives a remedy . . . .").

[2] Oliver Wendell Holmes, *The Path of the Law*, 10 Harv. L. Rev. 457, 462 (1897) ("The duty to keep a contract at common law means a prediction that you must pay damages if you do not keep it — and nothing else.") (Reprinted in Oliver Wendell Holmes, Collected Legal Papers 174 (1920)). Later, however, he seemed to recant: "Breaching of a legal contract without excuse is wrong . . . and if a State adds to civil liability a criminal liability to fine, it simply intensifies the legal motive for doing right . . . ." Gaily v. Alabama, 219 U.S. 219, 246 (1911) (dissent).

promise. Neither remedy would do much good for an injured party who had changed its plans in reliance on obtaining the benefits of performance of the contract.

In a market economy, promises are meaningful only if they can be relied upon by others. Promises can only be relied upon if the state's willingness to provide a remedy for nonperformance is meaningful to the injured party. In a vitally important sense, the entire meaning of a contract depends on the remedy that can be obtained for a breach of a contract.

Only in rare cases will our law compel the breaching party to perform its promise. While "specific performance" is occasionally available, the normal remedy for breach of contract is a court-sanctioned award of money damages. The amount of damages awarded for a breach of contract is based on an attempt to place the injured party in the same economic position it would have been in if the contract had been fully performed.[3] However, in some cases this will not be possible and the court's award of damages may have to be limited to those necessary to restore the injured party to the position it was in before the contract was ever made,[4] or at least to the extent necessary to ensure that the breaching party is not unjustly enriched as a result of its failure to perform.[5] These three methods of calculating damages coincide with three key interests associated with contract law: expectation, reliance, and restitution. Money damages will nearly always be based on one of these three different interests.[6]

An understanding of the law of contract remedies will be crucial in obtaining a fuller understanding of contract law generally. Without understanding of the consequences of a breach of contract it is impossible to understand the meaning of a contract in the first place.[7]

[B] Which Promises to Enforce

A second important feature of contract law is the distinction it makes between promises which the law will enforce and those which it will not. Promises which are a part of an exchange, of the type that typically occur in the marketplace, are generally presumed to be enforceable, while promises which consist of nothing more than a commitment to make a gift are presumed not to be enforceable.[8]

Our free market economy depends on the predictable enforceability of promises that are based on agreed exchanges. Thus, ordinary exchange transactions, such as a promise to work in exchange for a salary, a promise

---

[3] *See* U.C.C. § 1-305(a) (2001) (formerly UCC § 1-106); Restatement (Second) of Contracts §§ 344(a) & 347 (1981).

[4] *See* Restatement (Second) of Contracts §§ 344(b) & 349 (1981).

[5] Restatement (Second) of Contracts § 344(c) (1981).

[6] *See generally* Lon L. Fuller & Robert Perdue, *The Reliance Interest in Contract Damages (pts 1 & 2)*, 46 Yale L.J. 52, 373 (1936 & 1937).

[7] *See* Chapters 14–17, *supra*.

[8] *See* Chapter 3, *supra*.

to sell a house in exchange for a promise to pay a certain price, or even an exchange of services bartered for something else desired by the provider, must be predictably enforceable in order for a market economy to function.[9] Promises to make gifts, while of great concern to the one who will receive the gift, are of lesser importance to the functioning of a vital economy. For this and other reasons, contract law draws a sharp dividing line between promises made as part of an exchange and promises as an intended gift.[10]

Still, there will be circumstances where the exchange between the parties is tainted somehow, either due to the mental incapacity of one of the parties, or to the unfair or overbearing conduct of one of them, which permits the presumption of enforcement of the exchange to be rebutted.[11] In addition, people sometimes take meaningful action in reliance on a promise, even though it is nothing more than an otherwise legally unenforceable promise to make a gift.[12] In other situations, gift promises might be motivated by a desire to achieve some intangible business purpose, which relates to the functioning of the economy. In these situations the presumption that a promise to make a gift is not legally enforceable can also be rebutted.[13] Thus, although the general rule is that promises which are part of an exchange will be enforced and that promises to make a gift will not be enforced, there are many situations where a promise will not be enforced even though it is part of an exchange and may situations where a promise will be enforced even though it is not a part of an exchange.

[C] Controlling (or at least Predicting) the Future

Another key aspect of contract law is the role of contracts in assisting members of society in attempting to control, or at least to predict, the future. Our simple definition of a contract as a promise that the law will enforce makes this clear — a contract always involves a promise, and a promise is always a commitment about something which will happen in the future.

A person who makes a promise expresses a willingness to act (or to not act) in some specific way in the future.[14] If Sam promises Barb that he will sell her his BMW if she pays him $20,000, Sam has made a statement about future action that he is willing to take. He is also saying something about what he would like, in the future, to receive.

Of course in this situation, involving a contract between Sam and Barb for the sale and purchase of Sam's BMW, the contract is likely to be fully performed by the parties, in the near future. However, many contracts

---

[9] *See* § 3.03 The Essence of Consideration — the Bargained-for Exchange, *supra.*

[10] *See* § 3.04 Consideration at the Margins of Contract Law — Promises to make a Gift.

[11] *See* Chapter 12 Defenses to Breach of Contract: Illegality, Lack of Capacity & Improper Means of Obtaining Consent; Unconscionability, *supra.*

[12] *See* Chapter 4 Promissory Estoppel, *supra.*

[13] *See* § 8.02 Consideration Requirement for Modifications, *supra.*

[14] Restatement (Second) of Contracts § 2(1) (1981).

involve long-term commitments which may last for months, years, or even decades. If Karen enters into a contract to sell her house to Phil, performance is likely to occur within a month or two of the time the contract was made. But, it is likely to effect the parties' futures for a relatively long time. Having promised to sell her house to Phil, Karen has possibly given up forever the opportunity to remain living in her current home. And Phil has made a substantial commitment, which will probably prevent him from purchasing an alternative house, even if he finds one he likes better than Karen's, the day after he entered into the agreement to purchase her house.

Although most employees are merely "employees at will" who can either be fired or who can resign at any time without breach of either party's obligations, many contracts are for a much longer duration. Actors often enter into agreements to appear in movies and thus tie up their schedules for the duration of the time it takes to complete the filming of the project. In doing so, they not only make commitments about how they will spend their future time, they necessarily forego the opportunity to take on another, perhaps more promising project, which would require their participation at the same time. And, the filmmaker, by engaging a particular actor, may be making a commitment upon which the filmmaker's future reputation will depend.

In more conventional businesses, an electric producing power plant may enter into a contract to purchase a substantial quantity of coal for an entire generation.[15] This type of contract represents the parties' hopes and expectations for the long-term future, not just with respect to the demand for electricity, but with respect to environmental regulations concerning the use of coal and the price and availability of alternative sources of fuel. With such a contract, the seller assures itself of a guaranteed market at a predictable price, and the buyer assures itself of a readily available source of a supply at prices it can reliably predict and use as the basis for a steady rate structure for the electricity-consuming public.

In all of these situations the legal enforceability of the promises made by the parties permits them to provide some assurances against an uncertain future. Sam can be sure that he has found someone to purchase his car and can confidently go ahead with his plans to buy a different vehicle knowing how much money he will have to spend. Barb, for her part, will be assured of reliable transportation and can quit spending her time car shopping. In the transaction between Karen and Phil, Phil can be confident that he will have a place to live and Karen can set aside her fears of what might happen if she is forced to leave town for that new job, still saddled with the responsibility of owning her existing home. And, both the coal mine and the public utility can make plans for the future, knowing that they need not worry about a volatile market for the price of coal.

---

[15] *E.g.,* Northern Indiana Public Service Co. v. Carbon County Coal Co., 799 F.2d 265 (7th Cir. 1986) (contract for sale and purchase of 1.5 million tons of coal every year for 20 years); Aluminum Co. of America v. Essex Group, Inc., 499 F. Supp. 53 (W.D. Pa. 1980) (21 year contract for purchase of "alumina").

In each of these situations the parties have used a contract to minimize their concerns about an uncertain future. [16] Contract law thus deals with our use of promises to limit the degree of doubt that we all face in our lives. In this regard, contracts play a major role in helping us plan for the future. If promises were not enforceable in some way it would be much more difficult to plan around many of the risks inherent in life. Without contracts, life itself would be less certain.

[D] Obligations Voluntarily Assumed

Another critical theme in contract law is the voluntary nature of the obligations a contract imposes. To the extent that there are legal consequences that follow from making or breaking a promise, they are the result of the parties' voluntary decisions to enter into the contract. Contracts are obligations which are voluntarily assumed — they are not imposed by society. In this respect, contract law makes it possible for us to transform our intentions into legally binding obligations as an extension of the voluntary expression of our free will. [17] Contract law is thus fundamentally different from the law of torts, which deals with obligations that are imposed on us externally by society. Obligations in contracts are those which are voluntarily assumed.

The voluntary nature of contract liability has implications for many subtopics of contract law. If the law determines that a party's promise was not truly a voluntary act, the promise will not usually be enforced. For example: a promise made by a minor, (a 17 year old's promise to pay for a car, for example) [18] or one made under the a threat of violence, [19] will not be enforceable because our society chooses not to conclude that such obligations were not voluntarily undertaken. Minors are deemed incapable of undertaking the responsibility of a contractual obligation. Individuals who make commitments "with a gun to their head" should not be bound to perform when their agreement was made pursuant to compulsion.

Other examples where promises may not be enforced include those induced by fraud [20] or undue influence, [21] where truly voluntary consent is missing. Likewise, unusually one-sided obligations may not be enforceable

---

[16] The Restatement (Second) of Contracts defines a promise as "a manifestation of intention to act or refrain from acting in a specified way, so made as to justify a promissee in understanding that a commitment has been made." Restatement (Second) of Contracts § 2 (1981).

[17] *See generally* J. Willard Hurst, Law and the Conditions of Freedom in the Nineteenth Century United States (1968); James Gordley, *Contract Property, and the Will — The Civil Law and Common Law Traditions,* in The State and Freedom of Contract 66, 79–83 (H. Scheiber ed. 1998).

[18] *See* § 12.03[A] Minors, *supra.*

[19] *See* § 12.04[C] Improper Threats, *supra.*

[20] *See* § 12.04 [B] Fraud, Misrepresentation, and Non-Disclosure, *supra.*

[21] *See* § 12.04[D] Undue Influence, *supra.*

due to unconscionability where there was a gross disparity in the bargaining power between the parties at the time the agreement was made.[22]

[E] Contracts based on Outward Manifestations of Intent

By their very nature as well, promises are outwardly manifested expressions of intent that usually involve words that may either be spoken, written or both.[23] Contract law includes an extensive set of rules that are used to assist courts in determining the meaning and legal effect of what we say and do. Some of these rules deal with whether words or actions are properly even considered promises — whether they can be reasonably interpreted by others as commitments about the future.[24] Many of them deal with the offer and acceptance process that is the principal touchstone in contract law for determining whether there has been mutual assent between the parties.[25] Other rules are designed to assist in the interpretation of the language used by the parties.[26] Similarly, the "parol evidence rule" facilitates the enforceability of written contracts by imposing restrictions on the evidence a party can use to attempt to contradict the terms of a written contract intended by the parties to be the final expression of the terms of their agreement.[27]

[F] Significance of Reliance

Another key theme in contract law deals with the likelihood that promises will be relied upon by others. The recipient of a promise often relies on what has been said. This reliance takes the form of a change in plans or in expenses incurred on the faith that a promise will be performed. Likewise, people sometimes refrain from doing something they otherwise might have done because of their confidence that a promise will be performed, or at least that the law will enforce it.[28]

Many common examples exist: a prospective employee may quit her current job in reliance of a promise of a new one; an employee may decide to retire in reliance on a promise of a pension to be paid; a homeowner might quit making calls in search of a favorable interest rate in reliance on a mortgage broker's promise to make a loan to refinance her home; a college might make plans for the future development of its programs or facilities in reliance on promises from donors even before it has the donations in

[22] See § 12.05 Unconscionability, *supra*.

[23] See § 5.02 Objective Theory of Contract Formation, *supra*.

[24] See § 5.03 Determining Whether an Offer has been Made, *supra*.

[25] See § 5.01 Introduction to Mutual Assent, *supra*.

[26] See § 6.01 Determining the Terms of a Contract, *supra*.

[27] See § 6.05 The Parol Evidence Rule, *supra*.

[28] Sidney W. DeLong, *The New Requirement of Search Term Begin Enforcement Reliance Search Term End in Commercial Promissory Estoppel: Section 90 as Catch 22*, 1997 Wis. L. Rev. 943, 1016 (1997).

hand. As we will see later, each of these situations presents a serious question about whether a contract has been formed and whether the promises made should be enforced. Given the devastating consequences of the failure by these promisors to perform, it is not surprising to learn that a significant portion of contract law deals with efforts to protect those who have taken some action in reliance on the promises of others, even though a complete contract may not have been made.[29]

The fact that people are likely to rely on promises made by others plays an important role in contract law. In the view of many, promises are enforceable primarily because they are relied upon — or at least because of the foreseeable likelihood that they may be relied upon by others. In another sense, it may be possible to justify enforcing promises because the reliance on them is based on an assumption that the promise is enforceable in a court of law (this is the standard contract situation). If it turns out that reliance was not justified, such as where the defendant's promise was procured through duress, enforcement is not warranted. Thus, reasonable and foreseeable reliance on a promise may serve to make a promise enforceable even though the promise might not otherwise satisfy all of the requirements that would cause it to be part of a "contract" and therefore enforceable.

[G] Freedom of Contract

Finally, and perhaps most importantly, the "freedom of contract" is one of the large themes associated with contract law. As Sir Henry Maine famously noted in 1861 "the movement of the progressive societies has hitherto been a movement from Status to Contract."[30] Because legally enforceable promises are voluntarily made based on our outward expressions of our free will, we are generally free to enter into contracts on any terms we wish, with the confidence that the contract and its terms will be enforced.[31] This freedom, based on the economic principle that each individual is in the best position to know what is in his or her own best interest, and should be free to pursue that interest, has been the great engine of commerce in the western world.

Still, much of contract law deals with the extent of societal limitations on the freedom of contract. The doctrine of consideration, which generally

---

[29] *See* Chapter 4 Promissory Estoppel, *supra*.

[30] Henry Maine, Ancient Law 182 (Sir Frederick Pollock ed., 1930); *see also* Friedrich Kessler, *Contracts of Adhesion—Some Thoughts About Freedom of Contract*, 43 Colum. L. Rev. 629, 641 (1943) (on the return to the significance of status).

[31] P.S. Atiyah, The Rise and Fall of Freedom of Contract (1979) Michael J. Trebilcock, The Limits of Freedom of Contract (1993); Harold C. Havighurst, *Limitations upon Freedom of Contract*, 1979 Ariz. St. L.J. 167; Friedrich Kessler & Edith Fine, Culpa in Contrahendo, *Bargaining in Good Faith, and Freedom of Contract: A Comparative Study*, 77 Harv. L. Rev. 401, 407–09 (1964); Friedrich Kessler, *Contracts of Adhesion—Some Thoughts About Freedom of Contract*, 43 Colum. L. Rev. 629, 641 (1943); *See* Mark Pettit, Jr., *Freedom, Freedom of Contract, and the "Rise and Fall"*, 79 B.U. L. Rev. 263, 265 (1999); Samuel Williston, *Freedom of Contract*, 6 Cornell L.Q. 365, 379 (1921).

prevents promises to make gifts enforceable, imposes a significant limit on our freedom to make certain types of legally binding promises. Members of society can freely enter into nearly every imaginable type of exchange transaction; they can make a present gift of whatever property they own, so long as it does not harm their creditors,[32] but promises to make a gift in the future are generally not enforceable absent some reasonable and foreseeable reliance on the promise.[33] Likewise, public policy regulates the form in which contracts are created by requiring certain types of particularly important contracts to be in writing.[34] Other public policies regulate the manner in which warranties may be disclaimed,[35] the extent to which remedies may be limited,[36] and the ability of parties to specify the amount of damages that will be owed for a breach of contract.[37] Still other public policies are likely to intervene, depending on the subject matter of the contract, such as those relating to family relationships,[38] those dealing with employment,[39] or those involving consumers.[40]

Further, although the doctrine of consideration enhances freedom of contract by generally refusing to inquire into the adequacy of the amount of consideration given for a promise,[41] the doctrine of "unconscionability" sometimes intervenes to prevent enforcement of a contract where the terms are "unfair" and when there was some flaw in the bargaining process that led to the formation of the contract.[42]

Nearly every sub-topic of contract law involves some balancing of the principle supporting freedom of contract and societal restraints on that same very freedom.[43]

§ 1.02 Types of Contracts

Contracts can be classified in many different and sometimes overlapping ways. Contracts are sometimes characterized as express or implied, as bilateral or unilateral, as void or voidable, or as executory. These characterizations are frequently helpful in resolving issues related to the characterizations.

---

[32] Unif. Fraudulent Transfer Act §§ 4–5 (1984).

[33] *See* § 3.04 Consideration at the Margins off Contract Law — Promises to Make a Gift, *supra.*

[34] *See* Chapter 7, Is a Writing Required? — The Statute of Frauds, *supra.*

[35] *See* U.C.C. § 2-316 (2001); § 9.07 Disclaimers of Warranties, *supra.*

[36] *See* U.C.C. § 2-719 (2001); § 9.07[C] Limited Remedies, *supra.*

[37] *See* U.C.C. § 2-718 (2001); Restatement (Second) of Contracts § 356 (1981); § 16.03 Liquidated Damages, *supra.*

[38] *See* § 12.02 Contracts Affecting Family Relationships, *supra.*

[39] *See* § 17.04 Balancing the Equities: Practicality and Fairness, *supra.*

[40] *See* § 1.02[G][2] Rules Governing Transactions with Consumers, *supra.*

[41] *See* § 3.05 The Insignificance of the Relative Values of a Bargained-For Exchange, *supra.*

[42] *See* § 12.05 Unconscionability, *supra;* Melvin Aron Eisenberg, *The Bargain Principle and Its Limits,*, 95 Harv. L. Rev. 741 (1982).

[43] Anthony T. Kronman, *Paternalism and the Law of Contracts*, 92 Yale L.J. 763 (1983).

[A] Express and Implied Contracts[44]

Courts sometimes characterize contracts as "express" or "implied." Implied contracts are sometimes further characterized as implied "in fact" or implied "in law."

If a contract is made in express oral or written terms it is sometimes said to be an "express contract." Express contracts take many forms, ranging from a detailed multi-page contract negotiated over many months, for the sale of a large business[45] to a simple agreement for the sale of a used car concluded with a handshake. On the other hand, contracts "implied in fact" are created far more informally, perhaps through nothing more than a nod of the head or a wave of the hand. A patron in a bar might, for example, hold up two fingers, indicating to the bartender that he wants to purchase another round of drinks for him and his companion, thus implying his agreement to pay the standard price for the drinks. As one court explained:

A contract implied in fact is not created or evidenced by explicit agreement of the parties, but is inferred as a matter of reason or justice from the acts or conduct of the parties. However, all of the elements of an express contract must be shown by the facts or circumstances surrounding the transaction-mutuality of intent, offer and acceptance, authority to contract-so that it is reasonable, or even necessary, for the court to assume that the parties intended to be bound.[46]

There is no legal difference between an express contract and a contract implied in fact.[47] Both are true contracts, based upon the expressed intentions of the parties to enter into a voluntary obligation. The only distinction between the two is the manner in which the parties' intent is expressed.

A contract "implied in law" on the other hand, is not really a contract at all.[48] A contract implied in law, or a "quasi-contract" as it is sometimes called, ss based on the law of restitution.[49] The law of restitution seeks

---

[44] Willard L. Boyd III and Robert K. Huffman, *the Treatment of Implied-in-law and Implied-in-fact Contracts and Promissory Estoppel in the United States Claims Court*, 40 Cath. U. L. Rev. 605, 629 (1991).

[45] *E.g.,* Empro Mfg. Co. v. Ball-Co Mfg., Inc., 870 F.2d 423 (7th Cir. 1989).

[46] Prudential Ins. Co. v. United States, 801 F.2d 1295, 1297 (Fed. Cir. 1986), cert. denied, 479 U.S. 1086 (1987); *see also* Baltimore & O.R. Co. v. United States, 261 U.S. 592, 597 (1923) where the United States Supreme Court said:

The "implied[-in-fact] agreement" . . . is not an agreement "implied in law," more aptly termed a constructive or quasi contract, where, by fiction of law, a promise is imputed to perform a legal duty, as to repay money obtained by fraud or duress, but an agreement "implied in fact," founded upon a meeting of minds, which, although not embodied in an express contract, is inferred, as a fact, from conduct of the parties showing, in the light of the surrounding circumstances, their tacit understanding.

[47] Arthur Linton Corbin, 1 Corbin on Contracts §§ 1.19 (1993).

[48] *See* Martin v. Little, Brown and Co., 450 A.2d 984, 988 (Pa. Super. Ct. 1981); Continental Forest Prods v. Chandler Supply Co., 518 P.2d 1201, 1205 (Idaho 1974).

[49] *See* Callano v. Oakwood Park Homes Corp., 219 A.2d 332 (N.J. Super. Ct. 1966).

to prevent "unjust enrichment" and thus does not depend on the voluntary consent of the parties.

A clear example of this is found in *Cotnam v. Wisdom*. [50] The plaintiffs were surgeons who performed emergency surgery on Mr. A.M. Harrison, who hit his head when he was thrown from a street car. Mr. Harrison never became conscious and was never able to express his willingness to pay for the emergency medical services rendered by the plaintiffs in an effort to save Mr. Harrison's life. Mr. Harrison's estate was nevertheless liable, on a theory of quasi-contract for the value of the benefit received by Mr. Harrison, as a result of the doctor's efforts, even though there was no agreement between the parties and thus no real contract.

When the parties are both conscious, and capable of expressing their consent, the distinction between a contract implied in law and a contract implied in fact is more difficult to draw. When the owner of a house undergoing renovation asks the contractor to make a change or makes a request for additional work, it might be unclear whether the contractor's claim for payment for the extra work is based on the unjust enrichment to the owner that would otherwise occur or on the owner's implied consent to pay for the additional work. [51] Not only may the remedy be slightly different, but, he existence of an express contract dealing with the project might impose a barrier to recovery based on a contract implied in law. [52]

Other cases are more clearly based on unjust enrichment and not the parties' informal expressions of assent. In *Schott v. Westinghouse Electric Corp.,* [53] an employee submitted a suggestion to his employer pursuant to a company program which encouraged employees to make suggestions by holding out the possibility of a cash award. The suggestion form signed by the employee contained an express disclaimer of contractual liability, making it clear that there was no agreement by the employer to pay for the suggestion. Thus, the only possible basis for the employee's recovery was on a theory of quasi-contract based on any unjust enrichment of the employer who used the suggestion to its benefit.

Another important distinction between express contracts, contracts implied in fact on the one hand, and contracts implied in law on the other, is the remedy provided. In a true contract, based on the voluntary assent of the parties, remedies are based on the injured party's expectations. [54] When the court finds a quasi-contract the remedy is based on the value of the benefit conferred on the party who was enriched, in an effort to prevent any enrichment which otherwise would be unjust. [55]

---

[50] 104 S.W.164 (Ark. 1907).

[51] *See* Associated Builders, Inc. v. Oczkowski, 801 A.2d 1008 (Me. 2002).

[52] Hall Contracting Corp. v. Entergy Services, Inc., 309 F.3d 468 (8th Cir. 2002).

[53] 259 A.2d 443 (Pa. 1969).

[54] *See* § 14.02. Damages based on the Injured Party's Expectations, *supra.*

[55] *See,* § 14.01[B] Purposes of Contract Remedies: Expectation, Reliance, & Restitution, *supra.*

[B] Formal and Informal Contracts

The distinction between "formal" and "informal" contracts has two meanings. The traditional distinction was based on whether the formation of the contract adhered to certain ritualistic formalities[56] such as the impression of melted wax on a written contract with an impression known as a "seal."[57] In this sense the term "formal contract" was used to refer to the form of the agreement and played a critical element in its enforceability or other attributes.[58] Modern examples are negotiable instruments, negotiable documents, and letters of credit, all of which are governed by special provisions of the Uniform Commercial Code.[59] In this traditional sense, the term "informal contract" was used to refer to all other contracts, regardless of whether they were written or oral, or whether they were simple or complex.[60]

In the more modern sense a formal contract is one which is in a carefully negotiated and expressed in a final written document.[61] An informal contract is one formed more casually, possibly not bothering with any kind of a writing.[62] Thus, when one of your authors hired a local home renovation construction firm to build an addition to his house he signed an elaborate printed contract providing for a wide variety of possible contingencies and allocating responsibilities between the parties with respect to many details associated with the project. On the other hand, the agreement he made with his landscaper to install an array of perennial flowers, shrubs, and trees, consisted of little more than a drawing with a price scribbled in the corner. And, his wife's agreement (she is also an attorney) to pay a caterer for a large private party was even more informal: they settled on a date, a time, a place, a menu, the number of people who would be attending, and a price. The differences in the degrees of formality do not effect the enforceability of the agreement, though, as will be seen, they may have a bearing on the admissibility of evidence of promises which were never incorporated into any final written version of the parties' agreement.[63]

---

[56] See, e.g., Harold D. Hazeltine, The Formal Contract of Early English Law, 10 Colum. L. Rev. 806 (1910).

[57] See Restatement (Second) of Contracts § 6(a) (1981).

[58] See Arthur Linton Corbin, 1 Corbin on Contracts § 1.5 (1993); Peter Linzer, Rough Justice: A Theory of Restitution and Reliance, Contracts and Torts, 2001 Wis. L. Rev. 695, 696 n. 5.

[59] See Restatement (Second) of Contracts § 6 (1981).

[60] Peter Linzer, Rough Justice: A Theory of Restitution and Reliance, Contracts and Torts, 2001 Wis. L. Rev. 695.

[61] See Willliam C. Whitford, The Role of the Jury (and the Fact/Law Distinction) in the Interpretation of Written Contracts, 2001 Wis. L. Rev. 931, 938.

[62] See Robert Childres & Stephen J. Spitz, Status in the Law of Contracts, 47 N.Y.U.L. Rev. 1, 4 (1972); Wendell H. Holmes, The Freedom Not to Contract, 60 Tul. L. Rev. 751, 790 (1986).

[63] See Robert Childres & Stephen J. Spitz, Status in the Law of Contracts, 47 N.Y.U.L. Rev. 1 (1972).

[C]   Bilateral and Unilateral Contracts

Contract law sometimes distinguishes between "bilateral" and "unilateral" contracts.[64] A bilateral contract involves two promises; a unilateral contract involves only one. The distinction was abandoned by the Restatement (Second) of Contracts,[65] and was never found in the Uniform Commercial Code. Though of questionable utility, the distinction is still sometimes drawn.[66]

Its most common use is in connection with the manner in which a contract is created. In a bilateral contract, a contract is formed through an exchange of promises. Thus, when Ron's Roofing promises to install a new roof on Julie's house, in exchange for the Julie's promise to pay for the work, a bilateral contract is formed. The contract exists as soon as the parties' promises are exchanged for one another. Both parties have made an enforceable promise: Ron's Roofing will be liable to Julie if Ron fails to perform the promised work and Julie will owe a debt to Ron's Roofing if she fails to make timely payment for the work.

In a unilateral contract, only one of the parties makes an offer which can only be accepted by performance: "If you find my lost cat, and return him to me safely, I'll pay you $100." The owner of the cat has made a promise, but has not sought a return promise in exchange. The contract is not concluded by an exchange of promises. Instead, it is concluded when the requested performance is complete — when the cat is found and safely returned. Until the cat is found, there is no binding contract.[67] Thus, the offeree is free to abandon his search for the missing cat at any time, without liability for breach.

Modern decisions treat the distinction primarily as a question of the manner in which acceptance is made. If the offer does not invite acceptance in the form of a return promise, but instead insists on performance as the exclusive manner of acceptance, the contract is not generally regarded as formed until completion of the requested performance.[68] Still, as will be seen, a promisee who begins performance in reliance on the promise may be prevented from attempting to revoke the promise, until a reasonable time for completion has passed.[69]

---

[64] Restatement of Contracts § 12 (1932).

[65] See Restatement (Second) of Contracts § 1 (1981).

[66] Brannan & Guy, P.C. v. City of Montgomery, 828 So.2d 914, 921 (Ala. 2002); D.L. Peoples Group, Inc. v. Hawley, 804 So.2d 56 (Fla. Ct. App. 2002); Dahl v. HEM Pharmaceuticals Corp., 7 F.3d 1399 (9th Cir. 1993).

[67] See, e.g., Dahl v. HEM Pharmaceuticals Corp., 7 F.3d 1399 (9th Cir. 1993); Hamer v. Sidway, 27 N.E. 256 (N.Y. 1891).

[68] See Restatement (Second) of Contracts § 32 cmt. b (1981).

[69] See Restatement (Second) of Contracts § 45(1) (1981); see generally. § 5.05[B][3] Acceptance by Performance Without a Return Promise — Unilateral Contracts, supra.

[D] Executory Contracts

An "executory contract" is one that has not yet been substantially performed.[70] An "executed contract" on the other hand, is one in which the obligations have been at least substantially if not fully performed.[71] If Karen and Phil enter into an agreement that Phil will purchase Karen's home for $225,000, the contract is still fully "executory" during the time between the creation of the contract and the "closing" when Karen delivers a deed to the house to Phil and where Phil pays Karen the promised sum of money.

A contract may be fully executory, with both parties having substantial duties remaining to be performed, or it might be fully performed by one party with the other having duties remaining to be performed. Thus, if Sam promises to sell his auto to Barb, for a price of $20,000, Sam may have delivered the goods on Monday and waited for Barb to pay him for the car on Tuesday.[72] Likewise, a construction company may have completed work on the owner's house, but not yet received payment for its work.

Whether a contract remains fully or partially executory is relevant to several issues including the enforceability of a modification made without consideration,[73] the avoidance of a contract entered into by a party who is intoxicated[74] or affected by a mental disability,[75] and whether the contract can be rescinded[76] or modified after it has been assigned.[77] Whether the contract remains fully executory also affects the doctrine of anticipatory repudiation.[78]

Courts sometimes also refer to the "execution" of a written contract to refer to whether the contract has been signed, using "executed" as synonymous with "signed" or "authenticated."[79]

[E] Adhesion Contracts

Adhesion contracts are those in which one of parties has little or no opportunity to bargain over the specific terms of the agreement.[80] Instead,

---

[70] *E.g.,* Gaugert v. Duve, 579 N.W.2d 746 (Wis. App. 1998).

[71] Smith v. Allen, 436 P.2d 65 (Cal.1968).

[72] As Wimpy from "Popeye" used to say. "I will gladly pay you Tuesday, for a hamburger today."

[73] *See* Restatement (Second) of Contracts § 89 (1981).

[74] *See* Restatement (Second) of Contracts § 16 cmt. b (1981).

[75] *See* Restatement (Second) of Contracts § 15(2) (1981).

[76] Restatement (Second) of Contracts § 148 (1981).

[77] *See* Restatement (Second) of Contracts § 338 cmt. f (1981).

[78] *See* Restatement (Second) of Contracts § 253 cmt. c (1981); *see also* § 11.06 Anticipatory Repudiation, *supra.*

[79] *See also* U.C.C. § 9-102(a)(7) (2001).

[80] *See generally* Robert A. Hillman & Jeffrey J. Rachlinski, *Standard-Form Contracting in the Electronic Age,* 77 N.Y.U. L. Rev. 429 (2002); Todd D. Rakoff, *Contracts of Adhesion: An Essay in Reconstruction,* 96 Harv. L. Rev. 1173 (1983); Edwin Patterson, *The Delivery of a Life Insurance Policy,* 33 Harv. L. Rev. 198, 222 (1919).

the party who has drafted the contract presents it on a "take-it-or-leave-it" basis, leaving the other party with the choice of entering into the contract as written, or walking away from the transaction completely. Such contracts are usually in a "standardized form" with the same terms offered to every customer.

Insurance policies are good examples of adhesion contracts. The insured has a choice of whether to agree to the terms of the policy or to shop around for a better deal from someone other insurance company. Apart from the availability of a limited number of standardized additional protections or "riders," the purchaser is not usually able to negotiate over the specific terms of the protection offered by the policy. Likewise, many employment contracts are contracts of adhesion, with the employee bound by the terms supplied by the employer to all of its employees, and not usually susceptible to negotiation by the employee.[81]

When the terms of a contract of adhesion are oppressive or overly one-sided, they are sometimes unenforceable under the doctrine of "unconscionability." In *Henningsen v. Bloomfield Motors, Inc.*[82] terms purporting to limit the liability of the seller of a defective automobile, contained in a form contract with terms standardized throughout the automobile industry, were held unenforceable due to their oppressive nature and the gross inequality in bargaining power between the parties.[83]

Despite decisions like *Henningsen*, life would be both difficult and expensive if all contracts of adhesion were unenforceable.[84] The use of standardized form simplifies the contracting process by reducing the transaction costs associated with creating the contract. Likewise, they permit institutional parties who enter into many similar transactions with a wide variety of customers to plan the delivery of the goods and services they provide. Tailoring the terms of each individual transaction to the particular and sometimes idiosyncratic desires of every customer would make the process of entering into contracts cumbersome and the process of fulfilling the terms of those contracts extraordinarily difficult. This is particularly true when most customers desire essentially the same terms. The costs savings experienced as a result of the advantages of employing standardized terms will be passed on, at least in a competitive market, to customers in the form of lower prices.[85] Accordingly, most contracts of adhesion are fully enforceable.

---

[81] *E.g.,* Fittante v. Palm Springs Motors, Inc., 29 Cal.Rptr.2d 659 (Cal. 2003). Your own agreement with your law school is just such a contract. You are not able to negotiate over which courses you will take, at least during your first year; nor are you likely to find the school's tuition structure subject to negotiation — apart, at least from whatever financial aid award you have received.

[82] 161 A.2d 69 (N.J. 1960).

[83] *Id.* at 75; *see generally* § 12.05 Unconscionability, *supra.*

[84] Michael I. Meyerson, *The Reunification of Contract Law: The Objective Theory of Consumer Form Contracts,* 47 U. Miami L. Rev. 1263, 1269–70, 1275 (1993).

[85] *See* Carnival Cruise Lines v. Shute, 499 U.S. 585, 594 (1991).

Although most adhesive contracts are not unconscionable, they are nevertheless subject to closer scrutiny than contracts in which all or most of the terms have been separately negotiated by the parties. For example, ambiguities in contracts of adhesion are usually construed against the party who drafted the unclear language.[86] Likewise, courts might insist that adequate notice be provided with respect to particularly one-side or otherwise onerous terms, such as a forum selection clause which would force the party lacking any bargaining power to pursue any litigation in a distant and inconvenient forum.[87] However, despite these occasional limitations, adhesive contracts are generally fully enforceable according to their terms.

[F] Void, Voidable and Unenforceable Contracts

Some contracts are illegal.[88] Moreover, otherwise legal contracts are sometimes tainted by the lack of capacity of the parties, due either to their age or mental condition,[89] or because of the use of improper means of obtaining consent, including fraud, duress, undue influence, or unconscionability.[90] On other occasions performance is excused due to mistake, impossibility, or frustration of purpose.[91]

These circumstances may either make the contract "void ab initio" (void from the outset) and thus completely invalid, or, on the other hand, merely "voidable" at the election of one of the parties.[92] When a contract is said to be "unenforceable" it means that there is no remedy for breach, but that the existence of the contract may be recognized in some other way,[93] such as the basis for an action in tort for interference with a contractual relationship.[94]

When the agreement between the parties is completely illegal, such as an agreement to commit a crime or a tort, the agreement is "void."[95] There might have been an agreement, but there was ever a "contract." Neither party can enforce the agreement and there is nothing the parties can do

---

[86] E.g., Grinnell Mut. Reinsurance Co. v. Jungling, 654 N.W.2d 530, 536 (Iowa 2002); Howard v. Federal Crop Insurance Corp. 540 F.2d 695 (4th Cir. 1976).

[87] See, e.g., Hunt v. Superior Court, 97 Cal.Rptr.2d 215 (Cal. Ct. App. 2000); see also Carnival Cruise Lines, Inc. v. Shute, 499 U.S. 585 (1991).

[88] See Chapter 12.02 — Contracts Unenforceable due to Conflict with Public Policy; Illegal Contracts, supra.

[89] See Chapter 12.03 — Incapacity, supra.

[90] See Chapter 12.04 — Obtaining Assent Improperly: Fraud, Duress, and Undue Influence, supra.

[91] Restatement (Second) of Contracts § 7 cmt. b (1981); see Chapter 13 — Excuse: Mistake and Change of Circumstances, supra.

[92] Restatement (Second) of Contracts § 7 (1981).

[93] See Restatement (Second) of Contracts § 8 (1981)

[94] See Daugherty v. Kessler, 286 A.2d 95, 97 (Md. 1972); Arthur Linton Corbin, 1 Corbin on Contracts §§ 1.6, 1.7, & 1.8 (Interim ed. 1993); Abraham M. Levin, The Varying Meaning and Legal Effect of the Word "Void," 32 Mich. L. Rev. 1088 (1933).

[95] See § 12.02 Contracts Unenforceable due to Confict with Public Policy; Illegal Contracts, supra.

to make the agreement valid. Such agreements are sometimes referred to as "void contracts." And, because a contract is an agreement the law will enforce, the term "void contract" is a bit of a misnomer.

When there is some other problem with the agreement, but it is still enforceable by one of the parties, the contract is said to be "voidable." However, until the party with the right to either enforce or disaffirm the contract to exercise its right, the contract remains valid. And, the party with the right to disaffirm the contract might, seeing advantages in the deal, decide to ratify the contract and go ahead with its performance.

A good example of a contract which is voidable at the election of one of the parties is an agreement with someone who, like a child or a person suffering from a mental disability, lacked the legal capacity to enter into the contract.[96] Thus, the court-appointed guardian of an Alzheimer's patient may seek to disaffirm a contract the patient previously entered into with a nursing home, on the grounds that the patient was not capable of understanding the nature of the agreement she made.

On the other hand, there may be no reason to disaffirm the contract. If the nursing home is providing the patient with good care at a reasonable price it may make more sense to leave the contract in place. Likewise, a 17 year old, who is satisfied with the car he contracted to buy, may want to keep it despite his legal power to disaffirm the deal and give the car back to the seller. In these situations, where the contract is merely voidable, not void, the party suffering from the lack of contractual capacity will have the option of disaffirming the contract or enforcing it. If the party lacking capacity wants to enforce the contract, the other party remains bound.

[G] Contracts involving "Merchants" and those for "Consumer Goods or Services"

The law of contracts does not apply uniformly to everyone. Article 2 of the Uniform Commercial Code in particular, frequently draws distinctions between contracts involving one or more business professionals, or "merchants," and those lacking any particular business expertise. In addition, special statutory provisions or common law rules are frequently applicable to transactions involving consumers.

[1] Rules Applicable to Merchants[97]

Special rules apply to merchants because of their expertise in connection with either the subject matter of the transaction or with the practices involved in the transaction. U.C.C. § 2-104 defines a merchant as

> a person who deals in goods of the kind or otherwise by his occupation holds himself out as having knowledge or skill peculiar

---

[96] *See* § 12.03[B] Mental Incapacity, *supra.*

[97] Zipporah Batshaw Wiseman, *The Limits of Vision: Karl Llewellyn and the Merchant Rules,* 100 Harv. L. Rev. 465 (1987); John F. Dolan, *The Merchant Class of Article 2: Farmers, Doctors, and Others,* 1977 Wash. U.L.Q. 1.

to the practices or goods involved in the transaction or to whom such knowledge or skill may be attributed by his employment of an agent or broker or other intermediary who by his occupation holds himself out as having such knowledge or skill. [98]

Thus, a person may acquire the status of a merchant due to knowledge or skill he has which is particular to the goods involved in the transaction. Likewise, depending on the context, a person may be a merchant because of his expertise in connection with the business practices involved in the transaction, even though these are general business practices which would be familiar to anyone in business. [99] Moreover, an unsophisticated person, without expertise, may be saddled with the responsibilities of a merchant by representing himself as a person with special knowledge or skill. One's occupation alone may be sufficient for this purpose. Finally, a person may be treated as a merchant if he engages an employee or other agent who represents himself as having specialized knowledge or skill relevant to the transaction.

Where applicable, these specialized rules rest on the premise that greater reliance is usually placed on a person who either has expertise or who represents themselves as having expertise related to the transaction.

Whether someone is a merchant sometimes depends on the context in which the issue arises. The Official Comments to U.C.C. § 2-104 point out three separate contexts in which designating someone as a merchant may be important. [100] The definition of a merchant applies somewhat differently to each transaction.

Although Article 2 of the U.C.C. generally governs all contracts for the sale of goods, several provisions of Article 2 of the U.C.C. impose special rules governing the contract formation process when one or both of the parties qualifies as a merchant. These rules include the statute of frauds, [101] rules relating to firm or irrevocable offers, [102] the "battle of the forms," [103] and modifications of contracts. [104] All of these rules require little expertise beyond that which would normally be expected of anyone who is in business, such as the usual business practice of responding to mail. [105]

A second context in which a person's status as a merchant is important is in connection to the implied warranty that goods will be of merchantable

---

[98] U.C.C. § 2-104(1) (2001).

[99] U.C.C. § 2-104 cmt. 2 (2001).

[100] Id.

[101] U.C.C. § 2-201 (2001); see § 7.06[B] Confirmatory Memorandum Between Merchants, supra.

[102] U.C.C. § 2-205 (2001); see § 5.09[D] Firm Offers Under U.C.C. § 2-205, supra.

[103] U.C.C. § 2-207 (2001); see § 5.09 Mirror-Image Rule and the Battle of the Forms Under U.C.C. § 2-207, supra.

[104] U.C.C. § 2-209(2) (2001); see § 8.04[B] Agreements that Modifications Must Be Written, supra.

[105] U.C.C. § 2-104 cmt. 2 (2001).

quality.[106] The warranty applies only if the seller is not only a merchant, but if the seller is a "merchant with respect to goods of [the] kind" involved in the transaction.[107]

A third set of rules impose slightly elevated responsibilities on merchants in a variety of general and specialized settings, ranging from overall duty of good faith[108] to the specific duties imposed on a merchant to follow the seller's instructions with respect to defective goods in the merchant buyer's possession.[109] When used in these and other contexts, the more general or specific sense of the definition of merchant can apply.[110]

[2] Rules Governing Transactions with Consumers

[a] Consumer Protection Legislation

Special rules sometimes also apply to transactions with consumers. Most of these rules are not part of the general law of contracts. Instead, they are found in a myriad of state and federal legislative and regulatory provisions which afford greater protections to consumers than are available under the common law of contracts. Foremost among these rules are those found in federal Consumer Credit Protection Act, which includes provisions related to consumer loan transactions,[111] credit reporting,[112] debt collection practices,[113] and electronic funds transfers.[114] The federal Magnuson-Moss Warranty Act is responsible for the form in which many consumer product warranties appear.[115] Many of these statutes are accompanied by complex administrative regulations.[116]

Likewise, the Federal Trade Commission (FTC) has adopted myriad trade regulation rules pursuant to its authority under the Federal Trade Commission Act.[117] The FTC's Regulations for Sales Made at Homes[118] are particularly important. They give consumers the right to rescind a sale made at the consumer's home if the consumer cancels the transaction within three business days after the contract is made.[119] This three-day

---

[106] U.C.C. § 2-314 (2001); *see* § 9.03 Implied Warranty of Merchantability, *supra.*

[107] U.C.C. § 2-314 (2001); *see* § 9.03[A] Seller a Merchant with Respect to Goods of the Kind, *supra.*

[108] U.C.C. § 2-103(1)(b) (2001).

[109] U.C.C. § 2-104 cmt. 2 (2001).

[110] *Id.*

[111] The Truth in Lending Act, 15 U.S.C. §§ 1601–1667f (2000).

[112] The Fair Credit Reporting Act, 15 U.S.C. § 1681–1681u (2000).

[113] The Fair Debt Collection Practices Act, 15 U.S.C. § 1692–1692o (2000).

[114] Electronic Funds Transfer Act, 15 U.S.C. § 1693–1693r (2000).

[115] 15 U.S.C. §§ 2301–2312 (2000).

[116] *See generally* Howard J. Alperin & Roland F. Chase, Consumer Law (1986).

[117] 15 U.S.C. § 45 (2000).

[118] 16 C.F.R. 429.0–429.3 (2002).

[119] 16 C.F.R. § 429.1 (2002).

right of rescission, applicable only to sales concluded in the consumer's home, is the source of the common misconception that any consumer transaction can be rescinded within a three-day period.[120] A similar three-day cooling-off period is available for certain home equity mortgage loan transactions.[121]

In addition, there are many special state consumer protection statues covering a wide variety of topics such as home renovation contracts,[122] automobile repairs,[123] consumer loans[124] to name a few. These statutes vary considerably state to state. The most important of these statutes are the Uniform Consumer Credit Code,[125] adopted in seven states,[126] and the Uniform Consumer Sales Practices Act,[127] adopted in only three states.[128]

With minor variations, the scopes of these various statutes are quite similar. They apply to agreements which are primarily intended for personal, family, or household purposes.[129] Thus, it is not the nature of the goods which controls whether consumer protection law applies to the transaction. Instead, it is the purpose of the agreement. For example, the purchase of a computer at an electronics store, for installation in the buyer's home to be used to play games, keep track of the family checking account, and to surf the Internet for fun and amusement would be for personal, family, or household purposes and would be subject to most consumer protection laws. The purchase of an identical computer for use in a home office for exclusively business purposes, would not be covered by most of these statutes.[130]

An important exception is the Magnuson-Moss Consumer Warranty Act.[131] Most of its provisions apply to transactions involving products "*normally used* for personal family or household purposes . . . ."[132] Thus, because

---

[120] Nearly every year one of my Contracts students approaches one of your authors seeking information "for a friend" about the friend's ability to rescind a contract for the purchase of an automobile.

[121] Truth in Lending Act § 125, 15 U.S.C. § 1635 (2000).

[122] *E.g.,* Ohio Rev. Code Ann. 1345.21–1345.28 (Anderson 2002); FTC Door-to-Doore Sales Regulatioins 16 C.F.R. §§ 429.0–429.3 (2003).

[123] *E.g.,* 107 Ohio Admin. Code § 109:4-3-13 (2001).

[124] *See,* Elizabeth R. Schiltz, *the Amazing, Elastic, Ever-expanding Exportation Doctrine and its Effect on Predatory Lending Regulation,* 88 Minn. L. Rev. 518 (2004).

[125] *See, e.g.,* Colo. Rev. Stat. Ann. §§ 5-1-101 to 5-9-103 (LexisNexis 2003).

[126] States adopting the act are Colorado, Idaho, Indiana, Iowa, Kansas, Maine, Oklahoma, South Carolina, Utah, Wisconsin, and Wyoming. It has also been enacted in Guam.

[127] *See, e.g.,* Ohio Rev. Code §§ 1345.01 — 1345.51 (Anderson 2002).

[128] Ohio, Kansas, and Utah have adopted the Uniform Consumer Sales Practices Act. *E.g.,* Ohio Rev. Code Ann. §§ 1345.01–1345.50 (Anderson 2002).

[129] *E.g.,* Truth in Lending Act § 103(h), 15 U.S.C. § 1602 (2000).

[130] An important exception is the Magnuson-Moss Consumer Warranty Act, 15 U.S.C. §§ 2301–2312 (2000). It applies to transactions involving products "normally used for personal family or household purposes . . . ." 15 U.S.C. § 2301(1) (2000).

[131] 15 U.S.C. §§ 2301–2312 (2000).

[132] 15 U.S.C. § 2301(1) (2000) (emphasis added).

personal computers are "normally used" for personal, family, or household purposes, the sale of a computer for use in either a home office, or a conventional office located at a business, would be governed by the Act.

[b] Consumer Contracts

The 2003 revisions to Article 2 of the Uniform Commercial Code added a new set of rules regarding "consumer contracts." A consumer contract is a contract between a "merchant seller" and a "consumer."[133] Thus, Article 2's new provisions governing consumer contracts only apply when the seller is a merchant[134] and the buyer is a consumer. Transactions between merchants and transactions between consumers are not governed by these new provisions.

Among the new provisions governing consumer contracts are those specifying the manner of disclaiming warranties,[135] those limiting a seller's right to cure after the buyer justifiably revokes acceptance,[136] those protecting a consumer buyer from liability for any consequential damages suffered by a merchant seller,[137] and a provision preventing sellers from limiting the duration of the limitations period in such contracts.[138]

[c] Unconscionability

Apart from these types of statutory and regulatory provisions, contract law usually applies uniformly to consumers and non-consumers. A possible important exception is the law of "unconscionability."[139] A contract or one of its terms may be unenforceable due to unconscionability if the terms of the agreement unreasonably favor one party and if, due to an inequality in bargaining power or other flaws in the bargaining process, the other party was unable to make a reasonable choice about entering into the transaction.[140]

Although this doctrine is not strictly limited to transactions involving consumers[141] it is most frequently applied to transactions with individuals

---

[133] Revised U.C.C. § 2-103(1)(d) (2003).

[134] U.C.C. § 2-104 (2003); see § 1.02[G] Contracts involving "Merchants and those for "Consumer Goods or Services", supra.

[135] Revised U.C.C. § 2-316(2) (2001); see Linda J. Rusch, Is the Saga of the Uniform Commercial Code Article 2 Revisions Over? A Brief Look at What NCCUSL Finally Approved, 6 Del. L. Rev. 41, 69 (2003).

[136] Revised U.C.C. § 2-508 (2003); see Linda J. Rusch, Is the Saga of the Uniform Commercial Code Article 2 Revisions Over? A Brief Look at What NCCUSL Finally Approved, 6 Del. L. Rev. 41, 74–75 (2003).

[137] Revised U.C.C. § 2-710 (2003); see Linda J. Rusch, Is the Saga of the Uniform Commercial Code Article 2 Revisions Over? A Brief Look at What NCCUSL Finally Approved, 6 Del. L. Rev. 41, 86 (2003).

[138] Revised U.C.C. § 2-725(1) (2001); see Linda J. Rusch, Is the Saga of the Uniform Commercial Code Article 2 Revisions Over? A Brief Look at What NCCUSL Finally Approved, 6 Del. L. Rev. 41, 89 (2003).

[139] See § 12.05 Unconscionability, supra.

[140] See Williams v. Walker-Thomas Furniture Co., 350 F.2d 445 (D.C. Cir. 1965).

[141] See Campbell Soup Co. v. Wentz, 172 F.2d 80 (3d Cir. 1948).

for personal, family, or household purposes.[142] Further, many courts have been unwilling to apply the unconscionability doctrine to contracts between businesses.[143]

§ 1.03　History of Contract Law[144]

An entire history of the law of contracts is far too detailed and complex to be covered in more than a cursory fashion here. However, a basic understanding of the origins and development of contract law in England and the United States, will be of help to those attempting to learn its intricacies today.

[A]　Roman Law of Contracts

The Roman law of contracts, like all contract law, distinguished between promises which were legally enforceable and those which were not. However, Rome never developed a comprehensive set of rules governing contracts.[145] Instead, Rome had a wide variety of doctrines which made promises of various types enforceable.

One of the most important was "stipulatio," or in modern parlance, "stipulation." Stipulatio was a type of unilateral contract. It imposed an obligation on one party and created a corresponding right in favor of the other party. It was created by exchanging a precise series of formal questions and answers,[146] similar in fashion to the manner in which very traditional Christian baptismal ceremonies are still performed.[147] What we would recognize today as a bilateral contract could only be accomplished only through an exchange of two separate sets of questions and answers with each party taking his turn in making a reciprocal "stipulationes."[148]

Roman Law also provided for a number of so-called "real" contracts: mutuum, commodatum, depositum, and pignus.[149] They are referred to as

---

[142] See generally Jane P. Mallor, Unconscionability in Contracts Between Merchants, 50 Sw. L.J. 1065 (1986).

[143] E.g., Zapatha v. Dairy Mart, Inc., 408 N.E.2d 1370 (Mass. 1980); but see A & M Produce Co. v. FMC Corp., 186 Cal. Rptr. 114 (Ct. App. 1982).

[144] P. Atiyah, The Rise and Fall of Freedom of Contract (1979); E. Allan Farnsworth, The Past of Promise: An Historical Introduction to Contract, 69 Colum. L. Rev. 570 (1969); Grant Gilmore, The Death of Contract (1974); W.S. Holdsworth, Debt, Assumpsit, And Consideration, 11 Mich. L. Rev. 347 (1913); Morton Horwitz, The Historical Foundations of Modern Contract Law, 87 Harv. L. Rev. 917 (1974); A.W.B. Simpson, The Horowitz Thesis and the History of Contracts, 46 U. Chi. L. Rev. 533 (1979); A.W.B. Simpson, A History of the Common Law of Contract (1987); Tony Weir, Contracts in Rome and England, 66 Tul. L. Rev. 1615, 1620 (1992).

[145] Russ Versteeg, Law in the Ancient World 349 (2002).

[146] W.W. Buckland & Arnold D. McNair, Roman Law and Common Law 194–95 (2d ed.1965); see also Robert W. Lee, the Elements of Roman Law 345–46 (1956).

[147] Tony Weir, Contracts in Rome and England, 66 Tul. L. Rev. 1615, 1620 (1992).

[148] W.W. Buckland & Arnold D. Mcnair, Roman Law and Common Law 195 (2d ed. 1965); Parviz Owisa, The Notion and Function of Offer and Acceptance Under French and English Law, 66 Tul. L. Rev. 871, 874 n.3 (1992).

[149] Russ Versteeg, Law in the Ancient World 351 (2002); Alan Watson, The Law of Obligations in the Later Roman Republic 157, 167, 179 (1984).

"real" because they were based on the delivery of a thing or a "res" and thus the obligation to return the thing or its value.[150] "Mutuum" involved the delivery of money goods and the corresponding obligation to deliver an equivalent quantity (but not necessarily the same items) of money, or goods of the same kind, at a later date. "Commodatum" was akin to a bailment or lease of goods, with the bailee required to return the specific goods that had been delivered.[151] "Depositum" on the other hand was more akin to a modern bailment, or even, as the name suggests, a deposit in a bank account, where the res was delivered for safekeeping.[152] Finally, "pignus" was similar to the modern possessory security interest or "pledge," with the creditor's obligation to return the goods dependent on the debtor's payment or performance of an obligation.[153]

The Romans also recognized a variety of more informal consensual contracts that resembled many modern transactions, including contracts for the sale of goods (emptio venditio), agreements for the lease of land or goods (locatio conductio rei), contracts for the completion of a specific task, such as construction of a building (locatio operus faciendi), or for more unskilled tasks (locatio conductio operarum).[154] This category included partnership agreements or joint ventures (societas).[155]

There were, as well, a variety of unnamed or "innominate" contracts, which were enforceable, so long as one of the parties had already performed its side of the bargain.[156] However, these more informal obligations never expanded to make a simple exchange of executory promises legally enforceable.[157]

[B] Limitations of the Early English Writs to Enforce Executory Promises

One might have thought that English law would have picked up where Roman law left off. This, however, did not occur.[158] Instead, the English system developed along a different track.

The early English common law writ system was not particularly hospitable to the enforcement of promises. To obtain relief from the common law courts, a plaintiff had no alternative but to frame his complaint within the

---

[150] E. Allen Farnsworth, *The Past of Promise: An Historical Introduction to Contract*, 69 Colum. L. Rev. 576, 589 (1969).

[151] Russ Versteeg, Law in the Ancient World, 352 (2002).

[152] Russ Versteeg, Law in the Ancient World 352 (2002); W.W. Buckland & Arnold D. McNair, Roman Law and Common Law 277 (2d ed.1965).

[153] W.W. Buckland & Arnold D. McNair, Roman Law and Common Law 314 (2d ed.1965).

[154] Russ Versteeg, Law in the Ancient World, 352 (2002).

[155] *Id.* at 353.

[156] W.W. Buckland & Arnold D. McNair, Roman Law and Common Law 310 (2d ed.1965).

[157] E. Allen Farnsworth, *The Past of Promise: An Historical Introduction to Contract*, 69 Colum. L. Rev. 576, 590 (1969).

[158] *Id.* at 591.

scope of one of the available forms of action. If the wrong the plaintiff had suffered did not fit within one of the available writs, relief was not available. Accordingly, much of the history of the development of the our modern law of contracts is the history of the stretching and manipulation of the forms of action that existed in England in the fifteenth and sixteenth centuries to accommodate the needs of society for a general theoretical foundation for enforcing promises.

The principal difficulty encountered by the forms of action was that none of the existing writs fit the common modern circumstances of breach of an unperformed executory exchange of promises. An owner of goods who had promised to sell them to a buyer simply had no recourse if the buyer reneged on his promise to pay for them when the time for delivery arrived.[159]

The common law writ of "covenant" made the parties' promises enforceable, but only if they were made in a writing to which the promisor had affixed his wax "seal."[160] Physical production of the sealed document eventually became a necessity, thus limiting the general utility of the writ of covenant for more informal promises.[161] Furthermore, like the Roman sitpulatio, the form of the promise completely governed its substance.[162]

The writ of "debt" was also available to enforce a promise to repay a loan of a specific sum of money. However, it was not available if the sum of money owed was uncertain. Moreover, liability was based more on the injustice that would result if the debtor were permitted to retain the value of the money loaned than on the debtor's liability for breach of his promise to pay. While it was useful for creditors attempting to collect loans they had made, or for sellers attempting to collect the price of goods which had been sold and already delivered,[163] "debt" was simply unavailable to enforce an executory exchange of promises where neither party had yet performed.[164]

The writ of "detinue" was available in even more limited circumstances, to recover goods which had been delivered to a bailee and then wrongfully withheld.[165] A buyer who had paid the price of goods, but had not yet received them from the seller had an action in "debt," not "detinue." The rigidity of the common law writ system would not permit even this degree of flexibility.

The ultimate problem with all of these forms of action was that none of them provided relief for breach of an informal bilateral contract involving

---

[159] See, e.g., Neri v. Retail Marine Corp., 285 N.E.2d 311 (N.Y. 1972).

[160] E. Allen Farnsworth, *The Past of Promise: An Historical Introduction to Contract*, 69 Colum. L. Rev. 576, 593 (1969).

[161] See John H. Langbein, *Historical Foundations of the Law of Evidence: A Vew from the Ryder Sources*, 96 Colum. L. Rev. 1168, 1183 (1986).

[162] See Lon Fuller, *Consideration and Form*, 41 Colum. L. Rev. 799 (1941)

[163] F.B. Ames, *Parol Contract Prior to Assumpsit*, 8 Harv. L. Rev. 252, 260–61 (1894).

[164] W.S. Holdsworth, *Debt, Assumpsit, And Consideration*, 11 Mich. L. Rev. 347, 348 (1913).

[165] B. Shipman, Handbook of Common Law Pleading 114–17 (3d ed. 1923).

purely executory promises. Covenant was available only if the contract was in the form of a sealed writing. Detinue permitted recovery only to recover chattels previously delivered to a bailee. And, debt was available only to recover a fixed sum owed to a plaintiff who had already fully performed. If neither party had yet performed, the law provided no relief.

Apart from these structural limits, the writ system suffered from a more serious failing. The defendant could successfully avoid liability, regardless of the weight of the evidence, by utilizing the procedure of "wager of law."[166] If the defendant could find twelve individuals to swear (truthfully or not) that they believed the defendant's version of the facts, the defendant would prevail.[167]

These limitations were ultimately surmounted largely as a result of the success of the common law courts in their competition with the ecclesiastical[168] and the chancery courts[169] for the lion's share of jurisdiction.[170]

[C] Contract from the Law of Torts — the Writ of Assumpsit

The first word of the first case in Prof. Lon Fuller's original Contracts casebook,[171] at the beginning of *Hawkins v. McGee*[172] foretells, for first year law students, the entire history of the modern law of contracts: "Assumpsit." Assumpsit developed not from the early law of contracts, but instead from the law of torts.

The early common law of torts distinguished between "trespass," which was available for wrongs involving some actual or implied physical force, such as assault, battery, false imprisonment, abduction, or physical injury to land or goods;[173] and "trespass on the case," which was available for injuries not involving any kind of force,[174] including defamation, or breach of warranty.[175]

An action for trespass on the case could be brought against someone who undertook to render a performance and then performed it badly. The classic example, drawn from an early case involved a promise by a carpenter who made a promise to build a house "good and strong and of a certain form,

---

[166] John H. Baker, An Introduction to English Legal History 64–65, 265, 268 (2d ed. 1979).

[167] *See* F. Maitland, The Forms of Action at Common Law 34 (1909).

[168] E. Allen Farnsworth, *Parables About Promises: Religious Ethics and Contract Enforceability,* 71 Fordham L. Rev. 695, 702 (2002).

[169] *See generally* Timonty S. Haskett, *The Medieval English Court of Chancery*, 14 Law & Hist. Rev. 245 (1996).

[170] W.S. Holdsworth, *Debt, Assumpsit, and Consideration*, 11 Mich. L. Rev. 347, 349 (1913),

[171] Lon L. Fuller, Basic Contract Law 1 (1947).

[172] Hawkins v. McGee, 146 A. 641 (N.H. 1929).

[173] *See* Benjamin J. Shipman, Handbook of Common-Law Pleading 68 (3d ed. 1923).

[174] *Id.* at 83; *See* James B. Ames, *The History of Assumpsit*, 2 Harv. L. Rev. 1, 8 (1888).

[175] Benjamin J. Shipman, Handbook of Common-Law Pleading 95 (3d ed. 1923).

and yet [made] a house which is weak and bad and of another form . . .".[176] The analogy to the modern construction contract, involving defective work, is readily apparent.[177] Thus, a subcategory of trespass on the case, known as "special assumpsit" became available for breach of a promise by poor performance or "misfeasance."[178]

In cases involving non-performance, or "nonfeasance," rather than poor performance, or misfeasance an action for special assumpsit was not at first available, or in the language of the day, "would not lie,"[179] unless one of the parties had already performed.[180] The earlier misfeasance cases were based on the premise that the promisee had suffered a detriment in reliance on the promise.[181] This made it easy to draw an analogy, in cases where no performance had been rendered, permitting enforcement of the promise where the promisee had changed his or her position in reliance on the promise.[182] By the end of the sixteenth century the necessity of detrimental reliance had disappeared and an action in assumpsit was available merely as a result of an exchange of promises, on the theory that the promise made by the plaintiff was a sufficient detriment to make the promisor's promise enforceable.[183]

At the outset of the seventeenth century, when Elizabeth I was Queen, an action could be brought to recover damages for breach of a simple contract even though neither party had yet performed.[184] Thus, the owner of a house could sue a contractor for the contractor's failure to commence the promised work even though no payment had been made by the homeowner and was not yet due.

The final ascent of the writ of assumpsit occurred in *Slade's Case* in 1602.[185] *Slade's case* established that an action could be brought in assumpsit, with its attendant right to a jury trial, to recover an obligation to pay a previously liquidated sum.[186] Such an action could previously only have been brought as an action under the writ of "debt" in which the defendant could avoid liability through "wager of law" with its

---

[176] Y.B. 14 Hy 6 [1679 ed],at 18 (1436), 3 Holdsworth, History of English Law 430 4th ed. 1935); see E. Allen Farnsworth, *The Past of Promise: An Historical Introduction to Contract*, 69 Colum. L. Rev. 576, 594 (1969).

[177] *See, e.g.*, K & G Constr. Co. v. Harris, 164 A.2d 451 (Md. Ct. App. 1960).

[178] James B. Ames, *The History of Assumpsit*, 2 Harv. L. Rev. 1, 5 (1888).

[179] E. Allen Farnsworth, *The Past of Promise: An Historical Introduction to Contract*, 69 Colum. L. Rev. 576, 595 (1969).

[180] James B. Ames, *The History of Assumpsit*, 2 Harv. L. Rev. 1, 13 (1888).

[181] *Id.*

[182] *Id.*

[183] *Id.* at 596.

[184] *E.g.*, Strangeborough v. Waener, 74 Eng. Rep. 686 (Q.B. 1588).

[185] Slade's Case, 76 Eng. Rep. 1074 (1602); *see* See 3 William Holdsworth, A History of English Law 451 (7th ed. 1965).

[186] A.W.B. Simpson, *The Place of Slade's Case in the History of Contracts*, 74 Law. Q. Rev. 381 (1958).

accompanying risk of perjury.[187] Thus, the writ of "indebitatus assumpsit" or "general assumpsit" was available for the recovery of debts in an action in which a jury would serve as the finder of fact.[188] The right to a jury trial resulted in a shift away from the merchants courts and to the common law courts, jurisdiction over disputes in cases involving what we would today recognize as a commercial contract.[189]

Between the time of *Slade's Case* and today, the law of the contracts grew and prospered with the market economy that developed during the last 400 years. The industrial revolution necessitated its further development and expansion. A clear set of rules helps facilitate economic development through private exchanges. Accordingly, the law must change when business and society changes. Thus, although it sometimes may seem as if contract law is difficult to adjust, the Internet and the information revolution of today spurs its continued adaptation to a constantly changing world.

---

[187] Andrew N. Adler, *Can Formalistm Convey Justice? — Oaths, "Deeds," & Other Legal Speech Acts in Four English Renaissance Plays,* 72 St. John's L. Rev. 237, 238–39 (1998).

[188] *See* Val D. Ricks, *The Sophisticated Doctrine of Consideration,* 9 Geo. Mason L. Rev. 99, 101 n. 11 (2000).

[189] Michael E. Tigar, Address, *Litigators' Ethics,* 67 Tenn. L. Rev. 409, 410 (2000).

CHAPTER 3
UNDERSTANDING PROPERTY
LAW

By

John G. Sprankling

Associate Dean & Distinguished Professor and Scholar
McGeorge School of Law
University of the Pacific

Chapter 3

WHAT IS "PROPERTY"?

§ 1.01   An "Unanswerable" Question?

What is "property?"[1] The term is extraordinarily difficult to define. One of America's foremost property law scholars even asserts that "[t]he question is unanswerable."[2] The problem arises because the legal meaning of "property" is quite different from the common meaning of the term. The ordinary person defines property as *things*, while the attorney views property as *rights*.

Most people share an understanding that property means: "*things* that are *owned* by persons."[3] For example, consider the book you are now

---

[1] *See generally* John E. Cribbet, *Concepts in Transition: The Search for a New Definition of Property*, 1986 U. Ill. L. Rev. 1; Francis S. Philbrick, *Changing Conceptions of Property in Law*, 86 U. Pa. L. Rev. 691 (1938); Charles A. Reich, *The New Property*, 73 Yale L.J. 733 (1964); Joseph L. Sax, *Some Thoughts on the Decline of Private Property*, 58 Wash. L. Rev. 481 (1983); Jeremy Waldron, *What Is Private Property?*, 5 Oxford J. Legal Stud. 313 (1985).

[2] John E. Cribbet, *Concepts in Transition: The Search for a New Definition of Property*, 1986 U. Ill. L. Rev. 1, 1.

[3] Thomas C. Grey, *The Disintegration of Property, in* Nomos XXII 69, 69 (J. Roland Pennock & John W. Chapman eds., 1980).

reading. The book is a "thing." And if you acquired the book by purchase or gift, you presumably consider it to be "owned" by you. If not, it is probably "owned" by someone else. Under this common usage, the book is "property."

In general, the law defines property as rights[4] among people[5] that concern things. In other words, property consists of a package of legally-recognized rights held by one person in relationship to others with respect to some thing or other object. For example, if you purchased this book, you might reasonably believe that you own "the book." But a law professor would explain that technically you own legally-enforceable rights concerning the book.[6] For example, the law will protect your right to prevent others from reading this particular copy of the book.

Notice that the legal definition of "property" above has two parts: (1) *rights* among people (2) that concern *things*. The difficulty of defining "property" in a short, pithy sentence is now more apparent. Both parts of the definition are quite vague. What are the possible *rights* that might arise concerning things? Suppose, for example, that A "owns" a 100-acre tract of forest land. What does it mean to say that A "owns" this land? Exactly what are A's rights with respect to the land? The second part of the definition is equally troublesome. What are the *things* that rights may permissibly concern? For example, could A own legal rights in the airspace above the land, in the wild animals roaming across the land, or in the particular genetic code of the rare trees growing on the land? Indeed, can A own rights in an idea, in a graduate degree, in a job, or in a human kidney? In a sense, this entire book is devoted to answering these and similar questions.

§ 1.02 Property and Law

[A] Legal Positivism

Law is the foundation of property rights in the United States. Property rights exist only if and to the extent they are recognized by our legal system. As Jeremy Bentham observed: "Property and law are born together, and die together. Before laws were made there was no property; take away laws, and property ceases."[7] Professor Felix Cohen expressed the same thought more directly: "That is property to which the following label can be attached. To the world: Keep off X unless you have my permission, which I may grant or withhold. Signed: Private citizen. Endorsed: The state."[8] This view that

---

[4] While property is commonly discussed in terms of "rights," perhaps "relationships" would be a better term. *See* § 1.03[C].

[5] "People" is used here in a broad sense to include business and governmental entities as well as individuals.

[6] Still, even attorneys and legal scholars loosely refer to someone "owning" a particular parcel of land or other thing if the person owns *all* the legal rights to it. While convenient, this shorthand adds to the semantic confusion.

[7] Jeremy Bentham, The Theory of Legislation 69 (Oceana Publications, Inc. 1975) (1690).

[8] Felix S. Cohen, *Dialogue on Private Property*, 9 Rutgers L. Rev. 357, 374 (1954).

rights, including property rights, arise only through government is known as *legal positivism*.

[B]　An Illustration: *Johnson v. M'Intosh*

The Supreme Court's 1823 decision in *Johnson v. M'Intosh*[9] reflects this approach. Two Native American tribes sold a huge parcel of wilderness land to a group of private buyers for $55,000. The federal government later conveyed part of this property to one M'Intosh, who took possession of the land. Representatives of the first buyer group leased the tract to tenants, and the tenants sued in federal court to eject M'Intosh from the land. The case revolved around a single issue: did Native Americans have the power to convey title that would be recognized by the federal courts? The Court held the tribes lacked this power and ruled in favor of M'Intosh.

Writing for the Court, Chief Justice Marshall stressed that under the laws of the United States, only the federal government held title to the land before the conveyance to M'Intosh, while the Native Americans merely held a "right of occupancy" that the federal government could extinguish. The title to lands, he explained, "must be admitted to depend entirely on the law of the nation in which they lie."[10] The Court's decision could not rely merely on "principles of abstract justice" or on Native American law, but rather must rest upon the principles "which our own government has adopted in the particular case, and given us as the rule for our decision."[11] In short, under the laws established by the United States, must a United States court hold that the United States owned the land? For Marshall, the answer was easy: "Conquest gives a title which the Courts of the conqueror cannot deny."[12] Property rights, in short, are defined by law.

[C]　Natural Law Theory

In contrast to legal positivism, *natural law theory* posits that rights arise in nature as a matter of fundamental justice, independent of government. As John Locke observed, "[t]he Law of Nature stands as an Eternal Rule to all Men, *Legislators* as well as others."[13] The role of government, Locke argued, was to enforce natural law, not to invent new law. Natural law was a central strand in European philosophy for millennia, linking together Aristotle, Christian theorists, and ultimately Locke, and heavily influencing American political thought during the eighteenth century. As the Declaration of Independence recited, the "unalienable Rights" of "Life, Liberty, and

---

[9] 21 U.S. (8 Wheat.) 543 (1823). *See also Tee-Hit-Ton Indians v. United States,* 348 U.S. 272 (1955) (holding federal government was not obligated to pay for removal of timber from lands claimed by Native Americans).

[10] *Johnson v. M'Intosh,* 21 U.S. (8 Wheat.) 543, 572 (1823).

[11] *Johnson v. M'Intosh,* 21 U.S. (8 Wheat.) 543, 572 (1823).

[12] *Johnson v. M'Intosh,* 21 U.S. (8 Wheat.) 543, 588 (1823).

[13] John Locke, Two Treatises of Government 358 (Peter Laslett ed., student ed. 1988) (3d ed. 1698).

the Pursuit of Happiness" were endowed upon humans "by their Creator"; governments exist merely "to secure these rights."

The Declaration of Independence was the high-water mark of natural law theory in the United States. The Constitution firmly directed the young American legal system toward legal positivism, subject only to the Ninth Amendment's vague assurance that certain rights are "retained by the people." The influence of natural law theory steadily diminished thereafter. By 1823, when deciding *Johnson v. M'Intosh,*[14] *the Supreme Court could easily dismiss the natural law argument that "abstract justice" required recognition of Native American land titles.*

§ 1.03 Defining Property: What Types of "Rights" Among People?

[A] Scope of Property Rights

Suppose that O "owns" a house commonly known as Redacre. If we asked an ordinary person what O can legally do with Redacre, the response might be something like this: "O can do anything he wants. After all, it's *his* property. A person's home is his castle." This simplistic view that property rights are *absolute*—that an owner can do "anything he wants" with "his" property—is fundamentally incorrect.

Under our legal system, property rights are the product of human invention. As one court explained: "Property rights serve human values. They are recognized to that end, and are limited by it."[15] Thus, property rights are inherently *limited* in our system. They exist *only to the extent* that they serve a socially-acceptable justification.

As discussed in Chapter 2, the existence of private property rights is supported by a diverse blend of justifications. These justifications share two key characteristics. Each recognizes the value of granting broad decision-making authority to the owner. Under our system, a high degree of owner autonomy is both desirable and inevitable. But none of these justifications supports unfettered, absolute property rights. On the contrary, each requires clear limits on the scope of owner autonomy. Indeed, in a sense we can view property law as a process for reconciling the competing goals of individual owners and society in general. Society's concerns for free alienation of land, stability of land title, productive use of land, and related policy themes sometimes outweigh the owner's personal desires.

---

[14] 21 U.S. (8 Wheat.) 543 (1823).

[15] *State v. Shack,* 277 A.2d 369, 372 (N.J. 1971).

[B] Property As a "Bundle of Rights"

[1] Overview

It is common to describe property as a "bundle of rights"[16] in relation to things. But which "sticks" make up the metaphorical bundle? We traditionally label these sticks according to the *nature* of the right involved. Under this approach, the most important sticks in the bundle are:

(1) the right to exclude;

(2) the right to transfer; and

(3) the right to possess and use.

The rights in the bundle can also be divided in other ways, notably by *time* and by *person*. For example, consider how we could subdivide the right to possess and use based on time (*see* Chapters 8–9, 12–14). Tenant T might have the right to use and possess Greenacre for one year, while landlord L is entitled to use and possession when the year ends. Or we could split up the same right based on the identity of the holders (*see* Chapters 10–11). Co-owners A, B, and C might all hold an equal right to simultaneously use and possess all of Blueacre.

[2] Right to Exclude

One stick in the metaphorical bundle is the right to exclude others from the use or occupancy of the particular "thing." If O "owns" Redacre, O is generally entitled to prevent neighbors or strangers from trespassing (*see* Chapter 30). In the same manner, if you "own" an apple, you can preclude others from eating it. Of course, the right to exclude is not absolute. For example, police officers may enter Redacre in pursuit of fleeing criminals; and O probably cannot bar entry to medical or legal personnel who provide services to farm workers who reside on Redacre.[17]

Is the right to exclude a necessary component of property? Not at all. O might own title to Redacre subject to an easement that gives others the legal right to cross or otherwise use the land (*see* Chapter 32). Or O might lease Redacre to a tenant for a term of years (*see* Chapter 15), thus surron dering the right to exclude. Similarly, a local rent control law might prevent O from ever evicting his tenant from Redacre, absent good cause (*see* § 16.03[B][2]).

[3] Right to Transfer

A second stick in the "bundle of rights" is the right to transfer the holder's property rights to others. O, our hypothetical owner of Redacre, has broad power to transfer his rights either during his lifetime or at death. For

---

[16] *See, e.g., Kaiser Aetna v. United States,* 444 U.S. 164, 176 (1979) (referring to the "bundle of rights that are commonly characterized as property").

[17] *State v. Shack,* 277 A.2d 369 (N.J. 1971).

example, O might sell his rights in Redacre to a buyer, donate them to a charity, or devise them to his family upon his death. In our market economy, it is crucial that owners like O can transfer their rights freely (*see* § 9.08[A]).

But the law imposes various restrictions on this right. For example, O cannot transfer title to Redacre for the purpose of avoiding creditors' claims. Nor is O free to impose any condition he wishes incident to the transfer; thus, a conveyance "to my daughter D on condition that she never sell the land" imposes an invalid condition (*see* § 9.08[B]). Similarly, for example, O cannot refuse to sell his rights in Redacre because of the buyer's race, color, national origin or gender (*see* § 20.01).[18] Some types of property are *market-inalienable*,[19] essentially meaning that they cannot be sold at all (e.g., human body organs),[20] while other types of property cannot be transferred at death (e.g., a life estate).

Is the right to transfer essential? No. For example, although certain pension rights and spendthrift trust interests cannot be transferred, they are still property.[21]

[4] Right to Possess and Use

A third stick is the right to possess and use. As owner of Redacre, O has broad discretion to determine how the land will be used. For example, he might live in the house, plant a garden in the backyard, play tag on the front lawn, install a satellite dish on the roof, and host weekly parties for his friends, all without any intervention by the law. Similarly, if you "own" an apple, you can eat it fresh, bake it in a pie, or simply let it rot.

Traditional English common law generally recognized the right of an owner to use his land in any way he wished, as long as (a) the use was not a nuisance (*see* Chapter 29) and (b) no other person held an interest in the land (*see* Chapters 8–19, 32–34). Today, however, virtually all land in the United States is subject to statutes, ordinances, and other laws that substantially restrict its use (*see* Chapter 36).[22] For example, local ordinances typically provide that only certain uses are permitted on a particular parcel; if Redacre is located in a residential zone, O cannot operate a store or factory there. If the Redacre home is a historic structure, the local historic preservation ordinance may bar O from destroying the building or even altering its appearance.[23] Similarly, Redacre might be subject to private

---

[18] *See also Jones v. Alfred H. Mayer Co.,* 392 U.S. 409 (1968) (upholding constitutionality of statute prohibiting racial discrimination in sale or other transfer of property).

[19] *See* Margaret J. Radin, *Market-Inalienability*, 100 Harv. L. Rev. 1849 (1987).

[20] *See also Andrus v. Allard,* 444 U.S. 51 (1979) (upholding constitutionality of statute prohibiting sale of endangered species).

[21] *See, e.g., Broadway Nat'l Bank v. Adams,* 133 Mass. 170 (1882) (holding beneficiary's interest in spendthrift trust was not transferable).

[22] *See also Schild v. Rubin,* 283 Cal. Rptr. 533 (Ct. App. 1991) (overturning trial court decision that enjoined neighbors from playing basketball during specified hours).

[23] *See also Eyerman v. Mercantile Trust Co.,* 524 S.W.2d 210 (Mo. Ct. App. 1975) (refusing to enforce instructions in decedent's will that her home be destroyed).

environmental concerns continue, disputes about property rights in our finite land supply will escalate.

[C] Personal Property

[1] Chattels

Items of tangible, visible personal property—such as jewelry, livestock, airplanes, coins, rings, cars, and books—are called *chattels*. Virtually all of the personal property in feudal England fell into this category. Today, property rights can exist in almost any tangible, visible "thing." Thus, almost every moveable thing around you now is a chattel owned by someone. There are two particularly prominent exceptions to this general observation. Even though human kidneys, fingers, ova, sperm, blood cells, and other body parts might be characterized as "tangible, visible things," most courts and legislatures have proven reluctant to extend property rights this far (*see* Chapter 6). Similarly, deer, foxes, whales, and other wild animals in their natural habitats are deemed unowned (*see* Chapter 3).

[2] Intangible Personal Property

Rights in intangible, invisible "things" are classified as intangible personal property. Stocks, bonds, patents,[27] trademarks, copyrights, trade secrets, debts, franchises, licenses, and other contract rights are all examples of this form of property.[28] The importance of intangible personal property skyrocketed during the twentieth century, posing new challenges that our property law system was poorly equipped to handle.[29]

What are the other intangible "things" in which property rights may exist? The answer to this question is changing quickly. Consider the example of a person's name. Traditionally, property rights could not exist in a name, unless it was used in a special manner (e.g., as a trademark). Today, however, the law protects a celebrity's "right of publicity"—the right to the exclusive use of the celebrity's name and likeness for commercial gain (*see* § 7.05[F]).[30] But the answers to other questions are less clear. If spouse A works to finance spouse B's law school education, is B's law degree deemed marital "property" such that A is entitled to a share when he and B divorce? If A works for C for 30 years, does A have a property right in his job?[31]

---

[27] *See, e.g., Hughes Aircraft Co. v. United States,* 717 F.2d 1351 (Fed. Cir. 1983).

[28] The fact that intangible personal property is sometimes evidenced by a document (e.g., a stock certificate or promissory note) does not convert it into a chattel.

[29] For example, can property rights exist in computer time? *See Lund v. Commonwealth,* 232 S.E.2d 745 (Va. 1977) (overturning defendant's conviction for larceny on the basis that computer time is not a "good" or "chattel").

[30] *See, e.g., Midler v. Ford Motor Co.,* 849 F.2d 460 (9th Cir. 1988).

[31] *See, e.g., Perry v. Sindermann,* 408 U.S. 593 (1972); *Local* 1330, United Steel Workers v. United States Steel Corp., 631 F.2d 1264 (6th Cir. 1980); *see generally* Joseph W. Singer, *The Reliance Interest in Property,* 40 Stan. L. Rev. 614 (1988).

Upon retirement, does A have a property right in social security benefits?[32] The universe of intangible things is seemingly endless, and the law in this area will continue to evolve rapidly.

---

[32] See Flemming v. Nestor, 363 U.S. 603 (1960) (finding no property right in social security benefits for purposes of Due Process Clause); but cf. Joy v. Daniels, 479 F.2d 1236 (4th Cir. 1973) (holding tenant in federally-subsidized apartment had property right to continue occupancy, absent good cause for eviction, for purposes of Due Process Clause).

CHAPTER 4
UNDERSTANDING TORTS

By

John L. Diamond

Professor of Law
University of California,
Hastings College of the Law

Lawrence C. Levine

Professor of Law
University of the Pacific,
McGeorge School of Law

M. Stuart Madden

Distinguished Professor of Law
Pace Law School

Chapter 4
INTENTIONAL INTERFERENCE WITH PERSONS AND PROPERTY

SYNOPSIS

TORTS

61

§ 1.01 INTENT

[A] *Overview and Definition*

Intentional torts share the requirement that the defendant intentionally commit the elements that define the tort.[1] Intent is a term of art. Most contemporary courts adhere to the *Restatement* definition, which defines intent to mean either that the defendant desires the result or knows to a substantial certainty that it will occur.[2] The definition is in the alternative and is subjective. The defendant must, in her mind, exhibit desire or substantial certainty. The fact that a reasonable person would have been substantially certain is not dispositive, but only evidentiary in determining whether the defendant actually had the requisite mental state.

---

[1] *See generally* David J. Jung & David I. Levine, *Whence Knowledge Intent? Whither Knowledge Intent?*, 20 U.C. Davis L. Rev. 551 (1987); Richard A. Posner, Economic Analysis of Law § 6.15 (4th Ed. 1992); William L. Prosser, *Transferred Intent*, 45 Tex. L. Rev. 650 (1967).

[2] Restatement § 8A.

[B] *Intent as "Desire"*

Intent is satisfied if the defendant desires the consequences of her acts. This becomes legally relevant if those desired consequences constitute a tort.[3] For example, if A desires to pick up a concrete block and then inadvertently drops it on B's foot, A has not desired to cause harmful or offensive contact on B, and therefore is not liable for intentional battery.[4] The injury is unintentional, and any potential liability depends on proving negligence. In many instances, A will not confess to having desired consequences resulting in a tort. In those cases, the finder of fact must consider whether circumstantial evidence justifies concluding that A desired the tort. For example, if A loads a gun and then shoots directly at B, the court will almost inevitably conclude that A desired to cause B consequences which constitute battery. However, the test is subjective, meaning that the court must conclude that A in her own mind did in fact desire consequences constituting the tort.

[C] *Intent as "Substantial Certainty"*

Intent is usually also satisfied when the defendant is substantially certain that her acts will cause the elements of the tort to occur. If A blows up a stagecoach, knowing D is on the coach, A has intentionally injured B, even if A had no desire to injure B.[5] The substantial certainty test is subjective. The defendant must actually in her own mind know the results that constitute the tort will occur.

Substantial certainty should not be confused with reckless conduct. The defendant is reckless when she takes a substantial, unreasonable risk that the elements of the tort will occur, such as when A drives at a very excessive speed, risking a collision. Intentional conduct requires a showing that the actor either desires or knows with substantial certainty the tortious result will occur as a result of her conduct.[6]

[D] *Transferred Intent*

Historically, the transferred intent doctrine has been applied to five intentional torts.[7] The five torts are battery, assault, false imprisonment,

---

[3] *See Lambertson v. United States*, 528 F.2d 441 (2d Cir. 1976) (intent to cause contact constituted a battery and not negligence).

[4] *See* § 1.02, *below*, for definition of battery.

[5] *Cf. Garratt v. Dailey*, 279 P.2d 1091 (Wash. 1955), where the court remanded to the trial court the issue of whether a five-year-old boy was substantially certain the victim would fall while attempting to sit on a chair the boy had moved.

[6] *See, e.g., Vogel v. Grant-Lafayette Electric Cooperative*, 548 N.W.2d 829, 836–837 (Wis. 1996), holding that electric cooperative was not "substantially certain" stray electrical current would cause injury and therefore did not "intentionally" interfere with use and enjoyment of dairy farmer's property. *But see also Bohrman v. Main Yankee Atomic Power Co.*, 926 F. Supp. 211 (D. Me. 1996), holding several university students could claim damages for an "intentional" battery because the nuclear power plant they were touring was allegedly "substantially certain" the students would be exposed to excessive doses of radiation.

[7] *See* William L. Prosser, *Transferred Intent*, 45 Tex. L. Rev. 650 (1967).

trespass to chattel, and trespass to land. Under transferred intent, if the defendant intends any of these five torts, but her acts, instead or in addition, result in any of the other five intentional torts, the defendant is liable, even though she did not intend the other tort. For example, if A intends to assault B, but accidentally commits battery against B or another party C, A is liable for the battery.[8] As the example illustrates, not only does the intent to commit one tort satisfy the intent requirement for the other tort, but the intent to commit a tort against one victim can transfer to any other victim.[9]

The transferred intent rule may have emerged because these five torts were historically associated with a single action for trespass. The concept of trespass was not limited to the contemporary meaning of trespass to land, but embodied many types of direct injuries. It is important, consequently, to recognize that courts have applied the concept only to these five intentional torts.[10]

The Restatement does not adopt transferred intent generally. It does accept, however, transferred intent between battery and assault. The Restatement allows the intent to commit a battery or assault to satisfy the requisite intent required under the definitions for both torts.[11]

Transferred intent can be criticized for blurring the concept of intent. The intent to injure property is very different from the intent to injure a person, and yet the doctrine permits the intent requirement of one to satisfy the intent requirement of the other. The concept of transferred intent also can run counter to notions of proximate cause which, in negligence, generally impose liability only for foreseeable risks.[12] On the other hand, the intentional tortfeasor is arguably more deserving to bear the risk of a different kind of tortious injury than is an innocent victim.

[E] *The Mistake Doctrine*

Under the mistake doctrine, if a defendant intends to do acts which would constitute a tort, it is no defense that the defendant mistakes, even reasonably, the identity of the property or person he acts upon or believes incorrectly there is a privilege. If, for example, A shoots B's dog, reasonably believing it is a wolf, A is liable to B, assuming B has not wrongfully induced the mistake.[13] Similarly, if A enters B's land, believing reasonably it is A's

---

[8] *See Etcher v. Blitch,* 381 So. 2d 1119 (Fla. Ct. App. 1979), where defendant intended to frighten the plaintiff by shooting at him, but the bullet, in fact, struck the plaintiff.

[9] *See Talmage v. Smith,* 59 N.W. 656 (Mich. 1894). *See also Manning v. Grimsley,* 643 F.2d 20 (1st Cir. 1981), where a professional baseball player threw a ball into the crowd intending to hit a heckler, but instead struck another spectator.

[10] Transferred intent is not applicable even to other similar torts. For example, although conversion is very similar to trespass to chattel, transferred intent doesn't apply to conversion. *See* § 1.05[C], *below.*

[11] *See* Restatement §§ 13, 21.

[12] For a discussion of proximate cause in the context of intentional torts, *see* § 12.01, *below.*

[13] *See Ranson v. Kitner,* 31 Ill. App. 241 (1889).

land, A is liable to B for trespass to land.[14] So long as the defendant intends to enter the property, the fact that she mistook the identity of the property or other circumstances is irrelevant.

Courts have applied the mistake doctrine to a variety of intentional torts.[15] Nevertheless, in many instances actors benefit from specific privileges,[16] such as self-defense,[17] which protect the defendant from liability for reasonable mistakes, notwithstanding the mistake doctrine.

Is the mistake doctrine appropriate? While a principle applied to intentional torts, it effectively imposes strict liability on a defendant who interferes with another's property or person by mistaking the object's identity or other circumstances that would justify interference. From a moral perspective, the defendant may not be at fault. From a deterrent perspective, the mistake doctrine, by not exonerating reasonable mistakes, can excessively discourage reasonable risks by a potential defendant. On the other hand, in the context of property loss, the defendant might gain an unjust enrichment if she, for example, mistakenly consumes A's corn without having to compensate A. This may justify the use of the doctrine in the context of injury to or loss of property.

[F] Insanity and Infancy

Unlike in criminal law, neither insanity nor infancy are defenses for intentional torts.[18] However, intent is subjective and requires that the defendant actually desires or be substantially certain the elements of the tort will occur. Consequently, if the defendant is extremely mentally impaired or very young, she may not actually possess the requisite intent. For example, if A, a one-year-old, pulls the trigger of a gun, she may intend to pull the trigger, but not intend a battery and for that reason not be liable. The child or the insane person need not, however, appreciate the significance or wrongness of their act. If a child knows an adult will fall when he pulls a chair from under her, he intends wrongful contact and consequently a battery, without the need to prove the child intended serious harm.[19]

From a moral perspective, it would appear questionable to impose liability on individuals too immature or mentally impaired to know right

---

[14] See Perry v. Jefferies, 39 S.E. 515 (S.C. 1901), where defendant was held liable for removing trees from the plaintiff's own land although defendant believed the land to be his own.

[15] The Restatement specifically endorses the mistake doctrine in § 164 for trespass to land and in § 244 for trespass to chattel and conversion.

[16] See Chapter 2, below.

[17] See § 2.02, below.

[18] See Curran, Tort Liability of the Mentally Ill and Mentally Deficient, 21 Ohio St. L.J. 52 (1960). See also Colman v. Notre Dame Convalescent Home, Inc., 968 F. Supp. 809, 811 (D. Conn. 1997) (patient suffering from senile dementia could be held liable for battery); McGuire v. Almy, 8 N.E.2d 760 (Mass. 1937) (insane person intended harmful contact). For a discussion of the impact of insanity and infancy on negligence, see §§ 3.04 and 3.05, below.

[19] See note 5, above. See also In re Cornell, 42 B.R. 860 (1984) (bankruptcy court holds seven-year-old capable of forming intent for arson).

from wrong. On the other hand, the law of torts is not criminal law and does not condemn, but only shifts the economic burdens of loss. Should the victim bear the loss when the insane or juvenile defendant has assets to pay for the loss inflicted by their conduct? From an accident avoidance perspective, one can argue that liability encourages those responsible for preserving the insane or juvenile's assets to control the risks presented by such defendants. Such arguments, however, ignore the proposition that the guardians themselves may, in many instances, be personally liable for their negligent failure to adequately supervise juveniles or the insane.

§ 1.02   BATTERY

[A]   Overview and Definition

Battery[20] occurs when the defendant's acts intentionally cause harmful or offensive contact with the victim's person.[21] Battery in tort law, unlike criminal law, is exclusively an intentional tort. Accidental contact, in contrast, must be analyzed under negligence or strict liability.

Battery has historically compensated not only harmful contact but also offensive contact. Hence, the tort from its earliest origin in English common law has recognized the validity of compensating psychological as well as physical injury. Indeed, by grouping offensive and harmful contact together as one tort, the tort declines to delineate what many even today would argue are at least two distinct kinds of wrongs.

[B]   Intent Requirement

While battery requires intent, the prevailing tort definition does not require an intent to harm. It is only necessary that the defendant intend to cause either harmful or offensive contact. As the ancient case of *Cole v. Turner*[22] held, "the least touching of another in anger is battery." Once the defendant intends and accomplishes the offensive or harmful touching, she is responsible for harm caused by the battery even if minimal or no physical harm was actually intended. Consequently, where a school boy playfully but without privilege slightly kicks a classmate without intending harm, he is responsible for the unexpected serious illness which resulted.[23]

---

[20] *See generally* Osborne M. Reynolds, Jr., *Tortious Battery: Is "I Didn't Mean Any Harm" Relevant?*, 37 Okla. L. Rev. 717 (1984).

[21] *See* Restatement §§ 13, 16, and 18.

[22] 90 Eng. Rep. 958 (Nisi Prius 1704). *See also Leichtman v. WLW Jacor Communications, Inc.*, 634 N.E.2d 697, 699 (Ohio Ct. App. 1994), holding cigarette smoke purposely directed at plaintiff can constitute battery. *But see Shaw v. Brown & Williamson Tobacco Corp.*, 973 F. Supp. 539, 548 (D. Md. 1997), holding secondhand smoke was not an intentional battery based on the smoker's "substantial certainty" the smoke would touch the plaintiff. Whether secondhand smoke should constitute a battery is controversial. *See* Rimer, *Secondhand Smoke Damages: Extending a Cause of Action for Battery Against a Tobacco Manufacturer*, 24 Sw. U.L. Rev. 1237 (1995).

[23] *Vosburg v. Putney*, 50 N.W. 403 (Wis. 1891). The touching must, however, be unlawful.

Furthermore, where a physician performs a medical procedure without the patient's consent, thereby constituting a battery, regardless of her good intentions, she is responsible for all consequential harm even if the procedure was performed competently.[24]

The preceding illustrations demonstrate how, once the defendant has engaged in even a mere technical battery against the plaintiff, the risk of unforeseen harm arising from the battery is borne by the defendant.[25] Consequently, the defendant can be liable for far greater damages than she may have intended. Since battery is one of five intentional torts between which there is transferred intent,[26] the risk of unforeseen liability can be extended much further. If, for example, A intends to deface B's book (trespass to chattel) by throwing ink at it, but in the attempt inadvertently misses and hits either B or bystander C in the eye causing a serious injury, A is liable for the unintended battery against B or C.

[C] Harmful or Offensive Contact

Battery encompasses either harmful or offensive contact. As such, the tort compensates for psychological affronts where even trivial physical contact has occurred. The offensive contact need not even physically touch the body. In *Fisher v. Carrousel Motor Hotel, Inc.*,[27] plaintiff recovered for the aggressive and demeaning grabbing of a plate the plaintiff was holding.[28] The cause of action in battery clearly protects not only injurious physical intrusions, but personal autonomy as well.

There is no requirement that the victim be conscious of either the contact or its harmful or offensive nature at the time of the intrusion. Consequently, if A, without consent or privilege, kisses B while she is asleep, A is still

---

In *Vosburg*, the kick was not in the context of athletic play, but during class period. *See* James A. Henderson, Jr., *Why Vosburg Comes First?*, 1992 Wis. L. Rev. 853. *See also Lambertson v. United States*, 528 F.2d 441 (2d Cir. 1976), where unconsented horseplay resulted in the victim being impaled on a meathook.

[24] *See Mohr v. Williams*, 104 N.W. 12 (Minn. 1905), where a physician operated on the patient's left ear when consent was only given for operating on the right ear. For a discussion contrasting unconsented medical procedures constituting battery with negligent informed consent, *see* § 7.03, *below*.

[25] Implicit in this liability, but generally not discussed by courts in the context of intentional torts, is when, if ever, rules requiring proximate causation limit liability, particularly for unexpected consequences. *See* § 12.01, *below*.

[26] The transferred intent doctrine historically transferred intent between battery, assault, false imprisonment, trespass to land, and trespass to chattel. The *Restatement* adopts transferred intent between battery and assault by defining the requisite intent for the two torts to include either the intent to commit a battery or assault. *See* Restatement §§ 13, 21. *See* § 1.01[D], *above*.

[27] 424 S.W.2d 627 (Tex. 1967).

[28] The court concluded that "the intentional snatching of an object from one's hand is as clearly an offensive invasion of his person as would be an actual contact with the body." *Fisher v. Carrousel Motor Hotel, Inc.*, 424 S.W.2d 627, 629 (Tex. 1967). The plaintiff, a black male, was an engineer for the National Aeronautics and Space Agency who had been invited to a business luncheon and was then denied service on account of his race.

liable for battery.[29] Where A imposes an offensive or harmful contact on B, motive is irrelevant. So long as society defines the contact as harmful or offensive, A is liable for battery.[30]

Suppose A, unlike an ordinary person, would be offended by a friendly pat on the back. If B innocently pats A's back, the requisite intent to cause offensive or harmful contact is missing and there should be no liability even if A does find the contact offensive. Suppose, however, B continues to pat A in a context that most people would not find offensive, but A does. Should B's knowledge of A's hypersensitivity to contact constitute a battery? The Restatement, in a caveat, declines to decide the question, and judicial authority is sparse and ambiguous.[31] If A's hypersensitivity would result in physical injury, the tort of battery would more likely provide protection. Where only psychological injury is claimed, perhaps the courts should look to the feasibility of acquiescing to the victim's demands. Was the contact difficult to avoid in a crowded elevator or merely gratuitous?

[D] Causation

The defendant's voluntary action must be the direct or indirect legal cause of the harmful or offensive contact.[32] However, defendant need not herself actually contact the victim. For example, if A intentionally hits B with a rock, A has committed battery.

[E] Policy Rationale

Protection from unlawful contact readily appears a basic right worthy of recognition in tort law. Morally such affronts are difficult to justify. From a deterrent perspective, legal redress discourages wrongful contact and violent retaliation. The historic willingness of courts to compensate for merely offensive contacts represents an extremely early acknowledgment that psychological injury is worthy of compensation. Contemporary observers of tort law may be wary of extending compensation, however small, to trivial contacts. On the other hand, where a plaintiff's interest in vindication is sufficiently significant to justify the transactional costs of a lawsuit, the risk of alternative extralegal remedies may justify the tort remedy. For example, if A spits on B, the opportunity to sue for battery may discourage a more violent retaliation for B's psychological injury.

---

[29] See also Doe v. Johnson, 817 F. Supp. 1382 (W.D. Mich. 1993), where the victim's consent to sexual intercourse did not preclude liability for battery where the defendant knowingly did not disclose risk of transmission of AIDS virus. In contrast, assault and, generally, false imprisonment require a victim's contemporaneous awareness of tort. See §§ 1.03[B][2] and 1.04[E], below, respectively.

[30] See Clayton v. New Dreamland Roller Skating Rink, Inc., 82 A.2d 458 (N.J. Super. Ct. App. Div. 1951), where the defendant's employees, over the victim's objections, attempted with the best of intentions to treat an arm injury.

[31] Restatement § 19.

[32] See §§ 11.01 and 12.01, below.

§ 1.03 ASSAULT

[A] Overview

The ancient tort of assault represents the still controversial recognition that pure psychological injury should be compensable.[33] The historic case of *I de S et Ux v. W de S*[34] allowed the husband (the wife had no legal standing) to recover from the defendant who wielded an axe at the plaintiff's wife. The court concluded that even though the wife was not physically touched, the attack had caused her harm, the fear of imminent physical injury. Given its groundbreaking foray into the concept of purely emotional injury, it is understandable that the tort of assault is construed very narrowly. Subsequent to this early recognition of a cause of action in assault, a variety of other torts now allow compensation for emotional harm. One question for contemporary students of the law is whether, and to what degree, the fetters on assault should be lifted. Alternatively, perhaps the development of tort compensation for psychological harm only demonstrates the risks of allowing any monetary redress for emotional harm.

[B] Definition

Assault occurs when the defendant's acts intentionally cause the victim's reasonable apprehension of immediate harmful or offensive contact. The *Restatement*, unlike many courts, deletes the requirement that apprehension be "reasonable."[35] The tort definition must be contrasted with the traditional criminal common law definition of assault. Under the criminal law, assault is an attempted battery. Under the tort definition, only *apprehension* of immediate contact must be established. Furthermore, an actual attempt to commit battery, while always a criminal assault, would not constitute a tortious assault unless the victim suffered apprehension of immediate contact. Thus, a perpetrator swinging a bat at the head of one who was looking the other way would be vulnerable to a charge of criminal assault, but not the tort of assault.

[1] Intent Requirement

Assault is an intentional tort. The defendant must desire or be substantially certain that her action will cause the apprehension of immediate harmful or offensive contact. The accidental creation of such apprehension is not assault, but may constitute the much more recently created tort of negligent infliction of emotional distress.[36] If A suffers fright because B is running carelessly toward A, there is no assault. If, on the other hand,

---

[33] *See generally* Lawrence Vold, *The Legal Allocation of Risk in Assault, Battery and Imprisonment—The Prima Facie Case*, 17 Neb. L. Rev. 149 (1938).

[34] Year Book, Liben Assisarum, fol. 99, pl. 60 (1348).

[35] Restatement § 21 (*see* discussion § 1.04, *below*).

[36] *See* § 10.01, *below*.

A insists on shooting an arrow above B and A knows with a substantial certainty it will cause apprehension to B, A is liable for assault even if A does not desire to cause apprehension. The defendant's motive is irrelevant, provided she either desired or knowingly created apprehension.

Under the transferred intent doctrine, the intent to commit any of the four other intentional torts of battery, false imprisonment, trespass to chattel and trespass to land satisfies the requisite intent for assault. [37] Consequently, if A intends a battery against B, but instead assaults B or C, A is liable for assault. [38]

[2] Apprehension

The victim must perceive that harmful or offensive contact is about to happen to him. If the victim is attacked from behind or while asleep, [39] there is no apprehension prior to contact and consequently no assault. Although B may be upset at discovering, after the fact, that a rock nearly hit him, there is no assault. [40] Indeed, even if B is hit, while battery exists, assault does not without the requisite advance apprehension of contact. Apprehension can be created, however, without the actual attempt to cause contact. For example, if the defendant uses an unloaded gun but intentionally leads the victim to believe the gun *is* loaded, assault occurs if the defendant fires at the victim, even though the defendant had neither the intent nor the ability to shoot the victim. The intent to cause apprehension of imminent contact suffices to create the assault. [41]

To create the victim's apprehension, the defendant must have, however, the apparent (if not actual) ability to cause imminent harmful or offensive contact. One illustration is *Western Union Telegraph Co. v. Hill*, [42] in which the court held it was a question of fact for the jury whether the manager of a telegraph office was liable for assault when he attempted to touch plaintiff's wife and offered "to love and pet her" [43] while still behind a counter that divided him from the victim.

---

[37] *See* § 1.01[D], *above*. The *Restatement* adopts transferred intent between battery and assault by defining the requisite intent for the two torts to include the intent to commit either a battery or assault. *See* Restatement §§ 13, 21.

[38] *See Alteiri v. Colasso,* 362 A.2d 798 (Conn. 1975).

[39] *Consider e.g., McCraney v. Flanagan, 267 S.E.2d 404 (N.C. Ct. App. 1980), where the court dismissed the alleged assault because the victim, who was drunk, was not conscious at the time of the alleged assault. Note that recollection of the assault is not required if other proof establishes contemporaneous apprehension.*

[40] *See* Restatement § 22. *See also State v. Barry,* 124 P. 775 (Mont. 1912), where the plaintiff was not aware of a gun pointed at him until after the threat had passed.

[41] *See Allen v. Hannaford,* 244 P. 700 (Wash. 1926), where the defendant pointed what he knew to be an unloaded gun at the victim, who thought gun was loaded.

[42] 150 So. 709 (Ala. Ct. App. 1933).

[43] *Id.* at 710.

[3] Imminent Harmful or Offensive Contact

For assault to be actionable the victim's apprehension must be of *imminent* harmful or offensive contact. In *Cucinotti v. Ortmann*,[44] the court rejected attempts by the plaintiff to assert a claim for assault since the plaintiff failed to claim in his pleading that the defendant did anything more than verbally threaten to strike him with blackjacks. The court affirmed the traditional rule that words alone are insufficient to establish assault since the lack of an overt act in furtherance of the assault failed to establish the imminence of the attack. The *Restatement* argues against rigid acceptance of the traditional rule, and concludes that verbal statements can on occasion imply sufficient imminency.[45] Under the *Restatement* view, for example, A's announcement that B is instantly to be shot, although only verbal, can create imminent apprehension.

The *Restatement* does not challenge, however, the basic assault requirement that the victim perceive *imminent* harmful or offensive contact. Consequently, if A, with a perfect record of successfully carrying out his threat, promises to beat up B in 30 minutes, B cannot seek compensation for assault, at least until nearly 30 minutes has expired, and under traditional doctrine only after an overt act toward contact by A has commenced.[46]

The apprehension can be of either imminent harmful or offensive contact. Consequently, apprehension that A will throw a water balloon on B, or will spit on B, can, if perceived as sufficiently imminent, constitute assault even when the threatened contact is only offensive and not harmful. Such applications of assault emphasizes the tort's ability to compensate a purely psychological affront to the victim.

[4] Reasonable Apprehension

Many judicial recitations of the elements of assault require the victim to suffer "reasonable" apprehension. The *Restatement* rejects this requirement.[47] If A knows B believes, unreasonably, that a pencil is a gun and A pushes on the eraser as if to shoot B, causing B apprehension of imminent harm, the *Restatement* would characterize A's conduct as assault. Because A has intentionally created apprehension by exploiting B's unreasonable beliefs or gullibility, the *Restatement* argues that intent is still satisfied and A's intentional exploitation of B's gullibility should be compensable. The argument is most persuasive when A's intent to cause imminent apprehension is "purposeful" intent. The *Restatement* also characterizes substantial

---

[44] 159 A.2d 216 (Pa. 1960).

[45] *See* Restatement § 31.

[46] *See Dicken v. Puryear*, 276 S.E.2d 325 (N.C. 1981), where the court did not find the defendant liable for assault for a threat to kill the victim in the future if the victim didn't leave the state. *See also Castro v. Local* 1199, 964 F. Supp. 719, 732 (S.D.N.Y. 1997) (threatening an employee while slamming a table was "forward looking" and was therefore insufficiently immediate to constitute assault).

[47] *See* Restatement § 27.

certainty to cause a result as intent.[48] Consequently, the *Restatement*'s definition of assault could include the situation where A, knowing B is unreasonably intimidated by A's appearance, proceeds to enter the elevator where A is standing. The *Restatement* definition was, undoubtedly, not intended to encompass such a situation where A is privileged to act.

[5] Fear versus Apprehension

The *Restatement* and several court decisions distinguish between "fear" and "apprehension."[49] The requisite apprehension of imminent contact need not produce fear in the victim. The apprehension simply acknowledges the victim's awareness that imminent harmful or offensive contact will occur unless the victim takes effective evasive action. Consequently if A, within hitting range, strikes out at B, even though B is confident she can move to avoid A's contact, B has still suffered an assault. B's superior strength or evasive techniques do not immunize A from liability for the attack, provided B apprehends imminent contact would occur in the absence of evasive action. Furthermore, even apprehension of an offensive, but non-harmful contact, can constitute assault, even though the mere offensiveness of the imminent contact would not induce fear.

[6] Conditional Assault

An assault made conditional on the victim's noncompliance with an unlawful demand still constitutes an assault, even if the victim is confident no assault will actually occur if the victim complies with the unlawful request.[50] If A brandishes a club toward B, but offers not to strike B if he hands over his wallet, A has assaulted B. Even though B may not actually apprehend contact so long as B is prepared to submit to A's demands, courts have traditionally found A liable for assault. While an overt act by the defendant is required, such decisions do reflect an early willingness of courts to expand assault beyond the strictest requirement of actual apprehension of imminent contact.

On the other hand, if A effectively assures B that his overt menacing act will not imminently consummate in harmful or offensive contact regardless of B's actions, no assault exists. For example, if A announces that but for the presence of a police officer, A would hit B with the stick he is brandishing above B, there is no assault.[51]

[7] Source of the Contact

It is not necessary that the defendant be the perceived source of the threatened harmful or offensive contact. If A persuades B that a stick A

---

[48] *See* § 1.01, *above.*

[49] *See* Restatement § 24 cmt. b; *Coleman v. Employment Security Dep't,* 607 P.2d 1231 (Wash. Ct. App. 1980).

[50] *See Keefe v. State,* 19 Ark. 190 (1857); Restatement § 30.

[51] *See Tuberville v. Savage,* 86 Eng. Rep. 684, 1 Mod. Rep. 3 (1669), where the defendant stated, "If it were not assize [tax] time, I would not take such language from you."

has positioned next to B is actually a snake about to strike B, A has created apprehension of imminent harmful contact and is liable for assault.[52]

[C] Justifications for the Tort

[1] Moral Justifications

From a moral perspective, assault reflects a wrongful affront to the victim. On the other hand, by requiring advance apprehension of contact, it arguably is under-inclusive. An attack from behind is just, if not more, reprehensible and yet excluded from the tort definition of assault. While any attempted battery constitutes criminal assault, the tort definition of assault excludes compensation for the distress derived from a subsequent awareness that a battery was attempted. This is in contrast to the tort of battery, which allows compensation for both harmful and merely offensive contact even when the victim was not cognizant of the contact at the time. It is also possible to argue that assault is over-inclusive from a moral perspective. The act of creating apprehension of merely offensive contact, even when no contact at all is intended, constitutes tortious assault. Such behavior appears far less morally offensive than an actual attempt to seriously harm a victim, which is excluded from tortious assault if the victim was not cognizant of the attack.

[2] Compensation Rationale

From a compensation perspective, assault does introduce the concept that purely psychological injury constitutes compensable harm when it is intentionally inflicted. By excluding as compensable psychological distress prompted by future threats or awareness of a past attack, the tort is extremely restrictive in what kind of psychological stress it will allow to be compensated. While arguably perception of imminent contact reflects a special kind of psychological injury more worthy of compensation, it is hard to justify the inclusion of mental distress prompted by imminent offensive but not harmful contact, while excluding mental distress caused by threats of nonimminent but very harmful contact. On the other hand, the strict time frame does provide a bright line dividing compensable and noncompensable distress. Furthermore, as detailed in § 1.06, *below*, the newer tort of intentional infliction of mental distress does allow severe mental distress in other categories to be compensated, mitigating the exclusionary impact of limiting recovery to apprehension of imminent contact under assault.

[3] Deterrence Rationale

The tort of assault can deter violent retaliatory responses to an unlawful attack. The tort provides a legal redress to the victim when apprehension of imminent attack allows a legitimate privilege of self-defense. Nonimmediate threats or attacks that the victim does not perceive in advance

---

[52] *See* § 1.03[B][3], *above*.

neither constitute assault nor justify self-defense.[53] In short, the tort of assault correlates with the victim's privilege of self-defense. Arguably the tort discourages wrongful retaliation to an assault by providing monetary compensation which could be offset by the victim's own tortious behavior if he responded excessively to the initial attack. Such deterrence, however, depends on a potential wrongdoer's awareness that legal liability will ensue.

The tort definition of assault does not compensate, and therefore does not act to deter, a surreptitious attack in which the victim does not apprehend imminent contact. A successful attack, however, would make the aggressor liable for battery. Consequently, the assault tort, while not by itself a deterrent to many forms of initial attacks, does arguably work to encourage the victims of attacks to refrain from behavior in excess of that justified by self-defense.

§ 1.04   FALSE IMPRISONMENT

[A]   Overview and Definition

In false imprisonment, the defendant unlawfully acts to intentionally cause confinement or restraint of the victim within a bounded area.[54] Accidental confinement is not included and must be addressed under negligence or strict liability. It is generally held that the victim must be aware of the confinement at the time of the restraint.[55] False imprisonment compensates for psychological, physical and economic injury occasioned by the imprisonment. A recurring issue for courts is the often factually based distinction between wrongfully coerced confinement from confinement that is lawfully encouraged or persuaded.

[B]   Bounded Area

The victim must be confined within an area bounded in all directions. It is not false imprisonment if the victim is free to proceed in any direction, even though she is prevented from going in the direction she wants.[56] The bounded area can be, however, a large area, even an entire city.[57] A vehicle, although moving, can still constitute a bounded area.[58] Reasonable means

---

[53] For a discussion of the privilege of self-defense, *see* § 2.02, *below.*

[54] *See generally* William L. Prosser, *False Imprisonment: Consciousness of Confinement,* 55 Colum. L. Rev. 847 (1955); *see also* Restatement §§ 35–45A.

[55] *But see* Restatement § 42, discussed at § 1.04[E], *below.*

[56] *See Bird v. Jones,* 115 Eng. Rept. 668 (1845), where the court held it was not false imprisonment when part of a public highway was closed for a boat race, and the victim could not pass through but was allowed to leave.

[57] *See Allen v. Fromme,* 126 N.Y.S. 520 (1910). *Cf. Albright v. Oliver,* 975 F.2d 343 (7th Cir. 1992), indicating an entire state may be a bounded area.

[58] *See Sindle v. New York City Transit Authority,* 307 N.E.2d 245 (N.Y. 1973), acknowledging the failure of a school bus driver to release a student at a stop could constitute false imprisonment, but holding that imprisonment in this case was justified to protect persons and property; *see also Cieplinski v. Severn,* 168 N.E. 722 (Mass. 1929).

of escape precludes liability for false imprisonment. The escape is not reasonable if it requires the victim to be heroic, endure excessive embarrassment or discomfort, or if the victim is unaware of the means of escape.[59]

[C] *Means of Confinement or Restraint*

For false imprisonment to exist, the victim must be confined or restrained. The confinement may be accomplished by (1) physical barriers; (2) force or threat of immediate force against the victim, the victim's family or others in her immediate presence, or the victim's property; (3) omission where the defendant has a legal duty to act; or (4) improper assertion of legal authority.

[1] Physical Barrier

If physical barriers are utilized to restrain the victim, the barriers to constitute false imprisonment must surround the victim in all directions so that no reasonable means of escape exists.[60]

[2] Force or Threat of Immediate Force

Force or threat of immediate force can also be utilized to restrain the victim. The force may be directed at the victim, her family, companions or property. Consequently, if A wrongfully grabs B's coat and B refuses to leave without her coat, A is liable to B for false imprisonment. Although B could have left without her coat, the restraint that results from not abandoning her property constitutes imprisonment.[61] On the other hand, if A threatens B with serious injury on the following day, if B leaves the premises, A is not liable for false imprisonment, even if B remains on the premise, since no immediate force has been threatened. Presumably, in the latter instance the victim is at liberty to leave and seek protection from the threat. Furthermore, the use of threats of economic retaliation or termination of employment to coerce a victim to remain also do not constitute false imprisonment.

The tort of false imprisonment recognizes the coercive restraint of immediate force, even when only applied to personal property, but fails to recognize highly coercive but non-immediate threats. Contemporary critics may conclude that more judicial flexibility in finding coercion is warranted. Indeed, some contemporary cases, while ostensibly based on marginal

---

[59] *See Talcott v. National Exhibition Co.,* 128 N.Y.S. 1059 (1911), where the plaintiff was found reasonably unaware of a means of escape in a baseball stadium.

[60] *See Whittaker v. Sandford,* 85 A. 399 (Me. 1912), where the victim was detained on a yacht surrounded by water without access to rowboat. *See also* Restatement § 36, indicating that unreasonable means of escape includes exposure of individual, material harm to clothes, or danger of harm to another. *But see Smith v. Comair, Inc.,* 134 F.3d 254, 259–260 (4th Cir. 1998), holding that airline refusal to permit passenger to reboard flight at stopover was not false imprisonment since passenger was free to leave city by any other means.

[61] *See Fischer v. Famous-Barr Co.,* 646 S.W.2d 819 (Mo. Ct. App. 1982); *but see Marcano v. Northwestern Chrysler-Plymouth Sales, Inc.,* 550 F. Supp. 595 (N.D. Ill. 1982).

immediate physical force, appear to be influenced by the accompanying economic coercion.[62] On the other hand, the more courts depart from requiring obvious force to find false imprisonment, the more difficult it becomes to distinguish voluntary from coerced submissions. Indeed, many decisions already grapple with the subtle factual distinction between voluntary compliance with a request to stay and submission to implied threats of immediate force.[63]

[3] Omissions

False imprisonment can also result from a defendant's omission when the defendant had a legal duty to act. If A invites B out to his boat and promises to bring A ashore when requested, B's failure to do so constitutes false imprisonment.[64] Since there is no general duty to act, the plaintiff must establish that the defendant, in the specific context, does have an obligation to act.[65]

[4] Improper Assertion of Legal Authority (False Arrest)

The improper assertion of legal authority can unlawfully restrain a victim. This form of false imprisonment constitutes false arrest. The victim must submit to the arrest for it to constitute imprisonment. The arrest is improper if the actor imposing confinement is not privileged under the circumstances.[66] The applicable privileges vary for police officers and private citizens.[67] For example, if A fraudulently induces B into wrongfully believing A is a police officer and B submits to detention under circumstances where only a police officer is privileged to detain, A is liable for false arrest.[68]

---

[62] See Dupler v. Seubert, 230 N.W.2d 626 (Wis. 1975) (finding physical threats were utilized to restrain employee).

[63] See Lopez v. Winchell's Donut House, 466 N.E.2d 1309 (Ill. Ct. App. 1984), where a cashier was held to have merely complied with moral pressure when she submitted to go to a back room for an interrogation by her supervisor regarding a possible theft. See also Hardy v. LaBelle's Distributing Co., 661 P.2d 35 (Mont. 1983). Cf. Peterson v. Sorlien, 299 N.W.2d 123 (Minn. 1980), where the parents of an adult child were held to have right to place certain limits on adult child's liberty during "deprogramming" from cult faith so long as plaintiff assents at some point to the action.

[64] See Whittaker v. Sandford, 85 A. 399 (Me. 1912).

[65] See § 8.02, below.

[66] See Enright v. Groves, 560 P.2d 851 (Colo. Ct. App. 1977), where the victim was wrongfully arrested for failure to produce a driver's license while walking a dog.

[67] In general, under the common law, arrests pursuant to an apparently valid warrant are privileged. A police officer is privileged to arrest for a felony without a warrant when she reasonably suspects the other is guilty. A private citizen is only privileged when she reasonably suspects the individual arrested committed a felony and a felony in fact has taken place. This allows the private citizen a privilege to make a reasonable mistake in arresting the wrong person only if the crime actually occurred. Both police officers and private citizens are privileged to arrest for misdemeanors constituting breaches of the peace occurring in their presence. See Restatement §§ 116, 119, 121, 122.

[68] See Restatement § 41.

[D] Contrast With Malicious Prosecution and Abuse of Process

False imprisonment compensates for unlawful confinement. Confinement that is privileged[69] is not unlawful. False arrest is a form of false imprisonment where the confinement is accomplished through the unlawful assertion of legal authority. Where an arrest is privileged and therefore conforms to all requisite legal requirements to justify arrest, the possibility of liability for false arrest is precluded. An arrest pursuant to lawful procedures, and therefore not false imprisonment, if motivated by bad faith and satisfying other important elements, may constitute malicious prosecution.[70] The improper use of certain compulsory processes such as subpoenas, despite conforming to legal requirements, and therefore not false imprisonment, may be tortious as an abuse of process.[71]

[E] Consciousness of Confinement

False imprisonment requires that the victim be conscious of the confinement at the time of imprisonment.[72] The *Restatement* modifies this requirement and would find liability for false imprisonment, even when the victim is not aware of the confinement, if the victim is harmed by the confinement.[73] Thus, under the *Restatement* view, if A, an infant, is locked in a car trunk and suffers injury, B is liable for false imprisonment, even if A is unaware of the confinement. The general requirement of consciousness emphasizes that false imprisonment is a tort protecting a psychological perception of autonomy and not simply the denial of personal autonomy.

[F] No Minimum Time

False imprisonment covers even minimal lengths of detention. Thus if A is detained by B for one minute, B is liable for false imprisonment.

---

[69] *See* Chapter 2, *below* and note 66, *above*.

[70] *See* § 20.02, *below*.

[71] *See* § 20.05, *below*; *Consider e.g., Maniaci v. Marquette University,* 184 N.W.2d 168 (Wis. 1971), where the court reversed liability on a claim of false imprisonment, but held that the plaintiff alleged a proper case for abuse of process. Plaintiff, a student at Marquette University, was restrained from leaving campus by the university dean and others through wrongful use of temporary civil commitment procedures designed to determine whether the student's mental condition required imposing detention. The university officials knew the student's mental condition did not justify civil commitment, but used the procedure to temporarily detain the student until her father could be notified of her intent to withdraw from the university. The court held that the university's compliance with legal procedures precluded plaintiff's claim of false imprisonment, but that the defendant's misuse of procedure allowed liability for abuse of process.

[72] *See Parvi v. City of Kingston,* 362 N.E.2d 960 (N.Y. 1977), where the court held that partial intoxication during confinement and lack of recollection of confinement does not preclude a finding that victim was sufficiently conscious of confinement to sustain claim for false imprisonment. *But see Kajtazi v. Kajtazi,* 488 F. Supp. 15, 18–19 (E.D.N.Y. 1978), holding in contrast to *Restatement* that false imprisonment of child did not require child's awareness of confinement or proof of harm.

[73] Restatement § 42.

Obviously, however, the amount of the compensation awarded for false imprisonment will reflect the length of the detention.

[G] *Transferred Intent*

False imprisonment is one of five intentional torts[74] where intent transfers. If A intends an assault against B and either B or C is unintentionally imprisoned, A is liable for false imprisonment.

[H] *Policy Issues*

From a moral perspective, the tort of false imprisonment appropriately responds to a deprivation of individual liberty. Arguably problematic is the general requirement that the victim must be contemporaneously conscious of the restraint. Nevertheless, unknowingly being subject to restraint appears a less serious affront to the individual's autonomy.[75]

Perhaps the most difficult issue false imprisonment raises is attempting to delineate what kinds of restraints are wrongful. Traditional doctrine includes immediate force against personal chattels as a method of restraining victims who declined to leave their chattels, but excludes threats of non-immediate future violence to accomplish restraint of movement. Similarly, intense economic pressure does not constitute a method for restraint. Arguably, while such pressures are less immediate, courts should be prepared to include broader categories of wrongful coercion as potentially constituting the tort, despite the factual difficulty such inclusion might pose.

§ 1.05 TRESPASS TO CHATTEL AND CONVERSION

[A] *Overview*

Trespass to chattel and conversion are two separate intentional torts that protect personal property from wrongful interference.[76] The two torts, which overlap in part, are derived from different historical origins. In many, but not all, instances, both torts may be applicable.

Not all interference with personal property is tortious. For trespass to chattel there must be actual damage to the property, significant deprivation of use, or dispossession. Unlike trespass to land, which awards nominal

---

[74] The others include battery, assault, trespass to land and trespass to chattel. *See* § 1.01[D], *above*.

[75] The *Restatement*'s waiver of the requirement that the plaintiff be conscious of the restraint, when an injury occurs, addresses concerns that the requirement of consciousness will preclude compensation when there is a cognizable loss.

[76] *See, generally*, William L. Prosser, *The Nature of Conversion*, 42 Cornell L. Q. 168 (1957); John R. Faust, Jr., *Distinction Between Conversion and Trespass to Chattel*, 37 Or. L. Rev. 256 (1958); Jeff C. Dodd, *Rights in Information: Conversion and Misappropriate Causes of Action in Intellectual Property Cases*, 32 Hous. L. Rev. 459 (1995).

damages for technical trespass, minor intermeddling of personal property is not tortious. Conversion exists only when the damage or other interference with the personal property is sufficiently serious to justify a forced sale to the defendant. The defendant is liable for the entire market value of the chattel and not simply a smaller repair or rental cost. Consequently, conversion requires more serious interference with the chattel than might satisfy the minimal threshold for trespass to chattel. Adequate interference with property to constitute conversion does not preclude, however, liability under trespass to chattel. In such instances, the torts overlap.

[B] *Definition of Trespass to Chattel*

Trespass to chattel is the intentional interference with the right of possession of personal property. The defendant's acts must intentionally damage the chattel, deprive the possessor of its use for a substantial period of time, or totally dispossess the chattel from the victim.[77]

[1] Bad Faith Not Required

Trespass to chattel does not require that the defendant act in bad faith or intend to interfere with the rights of others. It is sufficient that the actor intends to damage or possess a chattel which in fact is properly possessed by another. In the classic case of *Ranson v. Kitner*,[78] the defendant killed the plaintiff's dog but argued that the "dog had a striking resemblance to a wolf,"[79] which the defendant could have legally hunted. The court held good faith was not a defense. So long as the defendant intended to kill the particular animal, the requisite intent is satisfied, and even a reasonable mistake as to identity or ownership, unless wrongfully induced by the victim, cannot exonerate the defendant from liability. *Ranson* is illustrative of the "mistake doctrine"[80] which applies to both trespass to chattel and conversion. In such instances, once the defendant merely intends to act upon a chattel, the concept of "intent" approaches strict liability.

[2] Actual Damage, Substantial Deprivation, or Dispossession Required

Unlike trespass to land,[81] trivial interference with another's personal chattels is not actionable in tort. If A knows that B does not want anyone touching his automobile, but A touches it anyway, there is no trespass to chattel in the absence of actual damage to the automobile. While it could be argued that torts should vindicate any intentional interference with

---

[77] *See* Restatement §§ 217, 218.

[78] 31 Ill. App. 241 (1888).

[79] *Id.* at 242.

[80] *See* § 1.01[E], *above.*

[81] *See* § 18.02, *below.*

personal property, the prevailing law does not allow such recovery, as would be granted for similar interference with real property.[82]

Depriving the possessor of the use of his chattel also constitutes trespass to chattel, provided there is significant deprivation and not mere momentary interference. For example, if A without privilege uses B's suitcase for one week, the conduct can constitute trespass to chattel. By contrast, an unauthorized one-minute use of the luggage would ordinarily not constitute the tort (unless the one minute was critical) since there is no measurable deprivation.[83]

Trespass to chattel also exists if the tortfeasor totally dispossesses the victim of his chattel, as by stealing or otherwise wrongfully asserting dominion and control over the property. Such dispossession is sufficient interference to constitute the tort even if the chattel is quickly recovered from the perpetrator. In such instances, the tortfeasor has more than used the chattel, but challenged the victim's right of possession to the property. Liability can be imposed in such instances, even when the defendant, as discussed in § 1.05[B][1], *above*, acts in a good faith but incorrect belief the chattel is his/her own.

The *Restatement* would also include as trespass to chattel interference with a chattel which results in injury to the possessor or injury to a person or thing in which the possessor has a legally protected interest.[84] Consequently, if A without privilege touches B's dog, causing the dog to bite B, A is liable for the injury to B.

[3] Transferred Intent

Historically, the doctrine of transferred intent has been applied to trespass to chattel (unlike conversion). Under the doctrine, intent for any of four other torts (battery, assault, trespass to land, or false imprisonment) can be substituted to satisfy the requisite intent for trespass to chattel.[85] If A intends to hit B with ink and misses, but hits B's or C's book, A is liable for the damage to the book under trespass to chattel. Even if the book is destroyed, conversion would not exist since the book's destruction was not intentional and transferred intent is not applicable to conversion.

[C] *Definition of Conversion*

The *Restatement* defines conversion as "an intentional exercise of dominion and control over a chattel which so seriously interferes with the right

---

[82] *See Glidden v. Szybiak,* 63 A.2d 233 (N.H. 1949), holding that pulling a dog's ears did not harm the dog and therefore did not constitute a trespass to chattel. *But consider CompuServ v. Cyber Promotions, Inc.,* 962 F. Supp. 1015, 1023–1024, 1026 (S.D. Ohio 1997), holding that unsolicited bulk e-mail advertisements can constitute trespass to chattel by consuming space on an online computer service provider's network and thereby harming its operation.

[83] *See* Restatement §§ 218, 221 ct. b.

[84] Restatement § 218.

[85] *See* § 1.01[D], *above.*

of another to control it that the actor may justly be required to pay the other the full value of the chattel."[86] It is derived from the action of trover which originally addressed the recovery of lost property. While conversion is no longer restricted to lost property, courts still generally limit protection to tangible property unless the intangible property has distinct scientific, literary or artistic value.[87]

Only very serious harm to the property or other serious interference with the right of control constitutes conversion. Damage or interference which is less serious may still constitute trespass to chattel. The *Restatement* has identified six factors in determining the seriousness of the interference:

(a)   The extent and duration of the actor's exercise of dominion or control;

(b)   The actor's intent to assert a right in fact inconsistent with the other's right of control;

(c)   The actor's good faith;

(d)   The extent and duration of the resulting interference with the other's right of control;

(e)   The harm done to the chattel;

(f)   The inconvenience and expense caused to the other.[88]

Applying these factors, there is a general agreement that if A intentionally destroys B's chattel, A is liable for conversion. If A intentionally caused minor damage to B's chattel, A would not be liable for conversion but would be liable for trespass to chattel. If A attempts to steal B's chattel, but is caught within minutes, A is liable for conversion because of the weight placed on his bad faith. If A mistakenly takes B's chattel, but returns it within minutes after realizing her error, A is not liable for conversion. If, however, A mistakenly takes B's chattel and then accidentally loses or destroys it, A's intentional taking, although in good faith, constitutes conversion since the deprivation is permanent.

Purchasing stolen property, even if the purchaser was acting in good faith and was not aware the seller did not have title, constitutes conversion by both the seller and innocent buyer. Both A's and B's acts seriously interfere with the ownership of the rightful owner.

---

[86] Restatement § 222A.

[87] *See Pearson v. Dodd,* 410 F.2d 701 (D.C. Cir. 1969), where receiving, copying, and returning the private files taken by third parties from the office of a United States Senator was held not to constitute conversion. In *Moore v. Regents of the University of California,* 793 P.2d 479 (Cal. 1990), the California Supreme Court held that a patient's cells, which were extracted by a physician and utilized to manufacture a patented cell line, were not subject to conversion because the patient did not retain ownership of the cells following their removal.

[88] Restatement § 222A.

§ 1.06 INTENTIONAL INFLICTION OF MENTAL DISTRESS

[A] Overview

The tort of intentional infliction of mental or emotional distress is relatively new, but has now gained general recognition in the latter half of this century.[89] Unlike most traditional intentional torts, the elements of intentional infliction of mental distress are far less precise. While this allows for a flexible individual approach to determination of liability, it also introduces greater uncertainty and has on some occasions collided with First Amendment values.

[B] History

While there exists some older authority in support of independent liability for mental distress,[90] general recognition of the tort was roughly commensurate with its endorsement by the *First Restatement* in 1934.[91] Indeed, the *First Restatement* only recognized the tort when the severe distress caused physical injury in the victim. Such intentional infliction of mental distress was deemed tortious by the *First Restatement* only because such extreme and outrageous conduct manifested negligence toward the physical health of the victim since it was foreseeable the victim would suffer physically from his distress.[92] Numerous cases allowing recovery by patrons for gross insults from common carriers and innkeepers, without proof the victim suffered severe distress, were viewed as a special exception.[93]

In 1947 the *Restatement* was amended to recognize the tort without requiring physical manifestation, a position subsequently adopted by a

---

[89] *See generally* David Crump, *Evaluating Independent Torts Based Upon "Intentional" or "Negligent" Infliction of Emotional Distress: How Can We Keep the Baby from Dissolving in the Bath Water?*, 34 Ariz. L. Rev. 439 (1992); Daniel Gilvelber, *The Right to Minimum Social Decency and the Limits of Evenhandedness: Intentional Infliction of Emotional Distress by Outrageous Conduct*, 82 Colum. L. Rev. 42 (1982); Calvert Magruder, *Mental and Emotional Disturbance in the Law of Torts*, 49 Harv. L. Rev. 1033 (1936); William L. Prosser, *Intentional Infliction of Mental Suffering: A New Tort*, 37 Mich. L. Rev. 874 (1939). Intentional infliction of emotional distress should be contrasted with the subsequent judicial acceptance of liability for negligent infliction of emotional distress, *see* § 10.01, *below*.

[90] *See Wilkinson v. Downton*, 2 Q.B. 57 (1897), where the defendant falsely told the plaintiff that the plaintiff's husband had been seriously injured in an accident and instructed her to retrieve him. The plaintiff, whose resulting serious shock led to physical injury, was held to warrant compensation by the court. *See also Bouillon v. Laclede Gaslight Co.*, 129 S.W. 401 (Mo. Ct. App. 1910), where the victim suffered a miscarriage when a gas company employee allegedly instigated an argument in front of victim.

[91] First Restatement § 46.

[92] *Id.*, cmt. c. For an excellent historical review, *see State Rubbish Collectors Ass'n v. Siliznoff*, 240 P.2d 282 (Cal. 1952).

[93] *See* First Restatement § 48 cmt. c; *see also* § 1.06[E], *below*.

majority of American states for intentional infliction of emotional distress.[94] In an influential decision, the California Supreme Court endorsed the 1947 *Restatement* amendment in *State Rubbish Collectors Ass'n v. Siliznoff*.[95] The recognition of intentional infliction of emotional distress in *Siliznoff* allowed plaintiff to recover for threats against himself, his property and business. In that case, the plaintiff, a garbage collector, did not comply with the association's division of customers and was subjected to an array of threatening behaviors by association representatives. The court held that liability could not be based on assault[96] since the threats of personal injury were not immediate. Rather than expand assault and other traditional torts to cover future threats of violence, the court embraced the new tort. Contemporary scholars can still debate whether this potentially massive expansion in potential liability is warranted.

[C] *Definition*

Intentional infliction of mental distress exists when the defendant, by extreme and outrageous conduct, intentionally or recklessly causes the victim severe mental distress. Most states no longer require that the victim suffer physical manifestations of the mental distress.

[1] **Extreme and Outrageous Conduct**

The *Restatement* defines extreme and outrageous conduct as behavior which is "beyond all possible bounds of decency and to be regarded as atrocious, and utterly intolerable in a civilized community."[97] While there is no objective standard, mere rudeness or callous offensiveness is insufficient. The vulnerability of the victim and the relationship of the defendant to the victim can be critical. Cruelty toward a young child or a very ill patient is more likely to be perceived as outrageous than would be comparable conduct directed towards a healthy adult.[98] The presence of a superior-subordinate relationship will also be taken into account. Accordingly, continuous mocking by an employer toward her employee or a principal to his student is more likely to be characterized as outrageous than taunting

---

[94] *See* First Restatement § 46 as amended (1947); *see also* Restatement § 46.

[95] 240 P.2d 282 (Cal. 1952).

[96] *See* § 1.03[B][2], *above*.

[97] Restatement § 46 cmt. d. *See also Field v. Philadelphia Electric Co.*, 565 A.2d 1170, 1183–1184 (Pa. Super. Ct. 1989), where alleged intentional exposure of plaintiff to high levels of radiation and subsequent efforts to conceal exposure constituted extreme and outrageous conduct.

[98] *Consider, e.g., Alabama Fuel and Iron Co. v. Baladoni*, 73 So. 205 (Ala. Ct. App. 1916), where liability was imposed when the defendant, who was aware that the plaintiff was pregnant, intentionally shot the plaintiff's pet dog, to which she was greatly attached, in her presence. The plaintiff suffered a miscarriage as a result of the mental anguish. *Consider also KOVR-TV v. Superior Court*, 37 Cal. Rptr. 2d 431, 434–435 (Ct. App. 1995), where court held television reporter's disclosure to a child that a playmate was murdered by the playmate's mother who then committed suicide constituted extreme and outrageous conduct.

among equals.[99] Knowledge of the victim's particular hypersensitivity can make otherwise non-outrageous conduct sufficiently culpable.[100]

[a] Sexual Harassment and Racial Epithets

Courts have hesitated in extending the tort of intentional infliction of emotional distress to situations involving sexual and racial harassment, based on the theory that many instances of harassment are comprised of language that might be objectionable or morally repugnant, but nevertheless fail to meet the higher standard of "extreme and outrageous conduct."[101] This undoubtedly reflects an historical societal tolerance of sexual and racial harassment which should change as society and courts become more sensitive to the extreme repugnancy of such behavior.

Isolated propositions or attempts at seduction have, traditionally, not been actionable.[102] Nor, usually, has liability been imposed in the past based solely on racial slurs.[103] However, courts have been more likely to recognize liability where a pattern of harassment is constant and on-going.[104] Additionally, corporations have been held liable for failing to respond to harassment perpetrated by employees, particularly those in supervisorial roles.[105] Most situations where liability has been imposed for racial or sexual harassment involve a combination of speech and conduct.[106] The trend towards recognizing liability should be viewed in the context of the evolution and various interpretations given to the phrase "extreme and outrageous conduct."[107]

---

[99] Cf. Harris v. Jones, 380 A.2d 611 (Md. App. 1977), where a General Motors supervisor regularly mocked an employee's stuttering and nervousness. The court found that the supervisor's conduct was extreme and outrageous, but found insufficient evidence that such conduct caused plaintiff to suffer extreme distress.

[100] Consider, e.g., Nickerson v. Hodges, 84 So. 37 (La. 1920), where the plaintiff was obsessed with finding a buried pot of gold purportedly located on land near her property. The plaintiff's neighbors, as an April Fools' Day joke, buried an iron pot filled with earth and stones where she would find it with a note instructing her to open it in front of a large crowd. Plaintiff suffered great distress, and the court awarded her heirs recovery. Consider also George v. Jordan Marsh Co., 268 N.E.2d 915 (Mass. 1971), where the plaintiff suffered a first heart attack attributed to the defendant's harassment intended to induce her to pay her son's debt. After the first heart attack and after being advised to stop bothering the victim, the defendant continued the harassment which led to a second heart attack. The court recognized potential liability.

[101] See Restatement § 46 cmt. d.

[102] See Reed v. Maley, 74 S.W. 1079 (Ky. 1903).

[103] But see, e.g., Wiggs v. Courshon, 355 F. Supp. 206 (S.D. Fla. 1973).

[104] See Hogan v. Forsyth Country Club Co., 340 S.E.2d 116 (N.C. Ct. App. 1986).

[105] See, e.g., Ford v. Revlon, Inc., 734 P.2d 580 (Ariz. 1987).

[106] See Jean C. Love, Discriminatory Speech and the Tort of Intentional Infliction of Emotional Distress, 47 Wash. & Lee L. Rev. 123 (1990). See also Johnson v. Smith, 878 F. Supp. 1150 (N.D. Ill. 1995), holding that burning of a cross in yard and throwing a brick into the home of an African American constituted extreme and outrageous conduct.

[107] Consider e.g., Wilson v. Bellamy, 414 S.E.2d 347 (N.C. Ct. App. 1992), where the defendants were found not liable for intentional infliction of emotional distress in taking advantage of a female student's intoxication and impaired consciousness by kissing and

[b] Constitutional Limits

In *Hustler Magazine v. Falwell*,[108] the United States Supreme Court held unconstitutional the determination that a parody "advertisement" in *Hustler* magazine could result in liability under intentional infliction of emotional distress. The mock advertisement, while clearly satirical, suggested Jerry Falwell, a nationally known religious and political leader of the Moral Majority, had his first sexual encounter with his mother in an outhouse. The majority held that a public figure could not recover without proving such statements were made with *New York Times* malice, *i.e.*, with "knowledge or reckless disregard toward the truth or falsity" of the assertion.[109] As the parody was never asserted to be truthful, and as it would not reasonably be interpreted as truthful by an ordinary reader, the Court found there could be no liability.

Since *New York Times* malice is required to be proved by public figures in media defamation, the Supreme Court concluded that public figure plaintiffs should not be allowed to use intentional infliction of emotional distress as an alternative tort to evade First Amendment protections afforded defendants in defamation cases. Consequently, verbal disparagement to public figures, which are not asserted as factual, would appear, however extreme and outrageous, to be protected under the First Amendment. Public figures may presumably recover for other types of outrageous conduct under the tort. Moreover, the Supreme Court did not suggest that private plaintiffs would also be precluded from seeking redress in a similar context if the publisher is not asserting fact. While the *New York Times* standard would not apply to private plaintiffs, a lesser standard requiring proof of negligence toward the truth is applied in defamation cases involving private plaintiffs in public controversies.[110] By analogy, this lesser standard could be held applicable. On the other hand, the social value of satirizing private individuals appears much less compelling. At present there are no indications courts are prepared to limit a private victim's remedy under intentional infliction of emotional distress.[111]

---

fondling her. The defendants were, however, found liable for sexual battery. Notwithstanding the decision, contemporary courts should be increasingly ready to characterize such conduct as extreme and outrageous. *See also Jones v. Clinton*, 990 F. Supp. 657, 677 (E.D. Ark. 1998), in which it was alleged that President Clinton, while Governor of Arkansas, briefly exposed himself while propositioning a state employee. The alleged conduct was sufficiently brief and without coercion so as not to be extreme and outrageous for purpose of the alleged tort. (The President's deposition in this case ultimately led to his impeachment trial in the Senate).

[108] 485 U.S. 46 (1988).

[109] *See New York Times v. Sullivan*, 376 U.S. 254 (1964). *See* § 21.03, *below*.

[110] *Gertz v. Robert Welch, Inc.*, 418 U.S. 323 (1974). *See* § 21.03[C], *below*.

[111] *See Esposito-Hilder v. SFX Broadcasting Inc.*, 665 N.Y.S.2d 697, 700 (App. Div. 1997), where court held private individual named "ugliest bride" by radio disc jockeys was not required to prove *New York Times* malice when alleging intentional infliction of mental distress.

[2] Intent or Recklessness to Cause Severe Mental Distress

For recovery under intentional infliction of emotional distress, the plaintiff must prove that the defendant intended to cause severe emotional distress or acted with reckless disregard as to whether the victim would suffer severe distress. Although characterized as an "intentional" tort, recklessness, in addition to intent, generally suffices for liability.[112] The inclusion of recklessness, which is endorsed by the *Restatement*[113] and derived from early precedent,[114] includes liability for defendant's behavior when she acts with a deliberate disregard of a high degree of probability that severe mental distress will result even when that was not the defendant's intention. The intentional (and reckless) tort must be distinguished from negligent infliction of mental distress, which evolved later.[115]

[3] Severe Mental Distress

Intentional infliction of mental distress requires proof both that the defendant intended or recklessly imposed the risk of severe mental distress and that the victim actually suffered severe mental distress. Mild distress will not suffice. Initially, physical manifestations of severe mental distress were required, but most jurisdictions no longer require physical manifestations for the intentional tort.[116] Physical manifestations can range from heart attacks to serious stomach disorders attributed to stress and shock. While physical manifestations were the original justification for compensating for intentional infliction of mental distress,[117] the requirement evolved as an ostensible mechanism for authenticating distress and discouraging fraudulent claims. The trend away from the requirement reflects recognition that the authenticity of severe distress can best be documented by the outrageousness of the wrongdoer's conduct, and that a prerequisite of often unconfirmable physical manifestations, such as stomach trouble, is more prone to fraudulent claims.

[D] *Third-Party Recovery*

Intentional infliction of mental distress is not one of the five historic intentional torts that transfers intent between these torts and between

---

[112] This is in contrast to most intentional torts where recklessness will not suffice. *See* § 1.01[C], *above*.

[113] Restatement § 46 cmt. i.

[114] *See, e.g., Boyle v. Chandler,* 138 A. 273 (Del. 1927), where a dead body was buried recklessly.

[115] *See* § 10.01, *below*.

[116] *See* § 1.06[B], *above; but see* § 10.01, *below*, where most states, in contrast, require physical manifestation. While physical manifestation is not required, proof of severe distress is required. *See, e.g., Jones v. Clinton,* 990 F. Supp. 657, 678 (E.D. Ark. 1998), holding that plaintiff in addition to not establishing extreme and outrageous conduct also failed to prove she suffered any severe mental distress as required by tort.

[117] *See* § 1.06[B], *above*.

victims.[118] However, since intent is defined to be either desire or substantial certainty,[119] if A beats up B, knowing that B's son C is present, A may be substantially certain, and therefore intend, that C will suffer severe mental distress, even if A had no specific desire to cause C mental distress.[120] Indeed, since recklessness can suffice for intentional infliction of mental distress, the defendant needs only to act with a deliberate disregard of a high degree of risk that his conduct would cause severe distress to a third party.

Courts, however, appear concerned that this encompassing definition of intent and recklessness may cover too many individuals in the context of intentional infliction of emotional distress. Consequently, courts have usually awarded a third-party victim recovery only if, in addition to proving the elements of the tort, she is (1) a close relative of the primary victim; (2) present at the scene of the outrageous conduct against the primary victim; and (3) the defendant knows the close relative is present. The *Restatement* is somewhat less restrictive, requiring only that a primary victim's immediate family members be present and can prove the elements of the tort. Non-relatives who satisfy the elements of the tort can also recover under the *Restatement* if they are present and suffer physical manifestation of severe distress.[121] The *Restatement*'s more permissive requirements have not received general explicit judicial acceptance. On the other hand, the more commonly stated requirement that the defendant knows that the third party is present appears to be anomalous in the large minority of jurisdictions which allow bystander recovery for negligent infliction of mental distress where the close relative is present and witnesses the accident. Such jurisdictions do not in negligence cases require the defendant to know the bystander is present, and presumably would not so require for the intentional tort.[122]

Indeed, the argument for restricting bystander recovery in the intentional tort has weaknesses. The defendant, having engaged in outrageous conduct, is highly culpable. Intentional torts are commonly not insurable. Consequently, there is no general imposition on the insured community. On the other hand, the reverberations of distress suffered by relatives and friends can be great, imposing enormous liability. Less persuasive for the restrictions is the rationale that the defendant will only be "substantially certain" to cause severe distress to bystander relatives who are in fact present and witness the outrageous conduct. As long as the defendant knows of the

---

[118] See § 1.01, *above.*

[119] See § 1.01, *above.*

[120] See *Taylor v. Vallelunga,* 339 P.2d 910 (Cal. Ct. App. 1959), where a daughter suffered distress from observing attack on her father.

[121] Restatement § 46 cmt. l; such restrictions on bystanders are applicable only when they are in fact third parties and not primary victims. For example, attacking a husband out of a desire to inflict pain on his wife would make the wife a primary victim. The defendant's action was directed toward the wife. Consequently, the wife could recover without being present.

[122] See § 10.01[C], *below.*

existence of the close relatives, distress for seriously harming a relative would appear certain or at least be encompassed by recklessness, which also suffices for the tort.

[E] Exception for Innkeepers, Common Carriers, and Other Public Utilities

Innkeepers, common carriers, and other public utilities (such as a telegraph company) are liable for intentional gross insults which cause patrons to suffer mental distress.[123] The requirement that the defendant behave in an extreme and outrageous manner to impose liability for intentional infliction of emotional distress is waived. The plaintiff, to benefit from this lower threshold of liability, must be a patron of the defendant, although there is no requirement that, for example, a ticket be purchased by the patron prior to the tort's occurrence. If A, a bus driver, tells B, a pedestrian crossing the street in front of the bus, that he is an odoriferous, fat slob, A is not liable unless A's knowledge of B's special hypersensitivity or other unusual circumstances makes the conduct extreme and outrageous and the victim suffers severe emotional distress. If A makes the same remark to C, a passenger preparing to board the bus, A is liable under the special exception without the need to prove extreme and outrageous circumstances or that the victim suffered severe distress.

While the exception for innkeepers, common carriers and other public utilities is supported by venerable precedent,[124] the original rationale for the exception is debatable. Common carriers have traditionally owed passengers an exceptionally high duty of care, and perhaps this heightened liability is reflected in the exception. As well, historically carriers and inns have been monopolies with out-of-town travellers circumstantially compelled to use their services. Furthermore, others have argued that the traditional exception is explained by a class attitude toward the typical common carrier employee. While some courts have extended the exception to other commercial establishments, the questionable contemporary justifications for the special rule have resulted in most courts acknowledging the exceptions, but not extending them.[125]

[F] Policy Rationales

The tort of intentional infliction of mental distress can be criticized for being too vague. While this allows individual flexibility, it also adds

---

[123] See Restatement § 48.

[124] See, e.g., Jones v. Atlantic Coast Line Railroad Co., 94 S.E. 490 (S.C. 1917).

[125] See Slocum v. Food Fair Stores of Florida, 100 So. 2d 396, 397 (Fla. 1958), where the court held, without deciding whether to generally adopt tort of intentional infliction of mental distress, that special liability for public utilities did not apply to a grocery store. A grocery clerk told a customer, "You stink to me," allegedly causing the victim a heart attack aggravated from pre-existing heart condition. There was no allegation defendant knew about the pre-existing condition. See § 1.06[C][1], above.

uncertainty as to when the tort applies. Arguably, more specific torts could be crafted for special needs in its place with less danger of chilling legitimate First Amendment speech or other non-tortuous activity. On the other hand, the requisite requirement of outrageousness limits the tort's application and allows it to address wrongdoings that more specific torts would not anticipate. The tort gives distinct recognition to the concept that mental injury is compensable. While this can be criticized, in part because it is difficult to place monetary value on such losses, it must be acknowledged that the tort is not breaking new ground in compensating mental injury. Historic torts, like assault and battery, attempt to compensate such losses and unlike intentional infliction of mental distress do not limit recovery to severe mental distress. On the other hand, intentional infliction of mental distress is much broader in its application and its boundaries await individual jury interpretation of its limits.

CHAPTER 5
UNDERSTANDING
CONSTITUTIONAL LAW

By

Norman Redlich

*Dean Emeritus and Judge Edward Weinfeld Professor of Law
Emeritus
New York University School of Law*

John Attanasio

*Dean and William Hawley Atwell Professor of Constitutional Law
Southern Methodist University*

Joel K. Goldstein

*Professor of Law
Saint Louis University School of Law*

CON LAW

Chapter 5

THE CONSTITUTION AND CONSTITUTIONAL ARGUMENT

Introduction

Understanding constitutional law is an ambitious undertaking. The subject is complex and can be viewed from different angles. An effort to understand constitutional law may profitably consider the Constitution, the events leading to it, its operation in practice, the interaction of the various institutions it created, and the rules, principles and doctrines which are known as constitutional law.

This chapter introduces the notion of a Constitution and describes in broad terms the historical events leading up to the ratification of our Constitution. It then discusses structural arrangements used to control government. Section 1.04 addresses the need for constitutional interpretation and some theories regarding it. Section 1.05 explores different types of constitutional arguments commonly employed.

§ 1.01 Constitutions

The word "constitution" is used in several different senses. At times it describes the basic rules, written and unwritten, which create and control government. Alternatively, "constitution" may denote a document which contains those rules which provide the framework for government. Both senses of the word apply to the American system. Unlike the British Constitution, ours is a written document which delegates and defines governmental power.

The Constitution's primary purpose is to create and limit national government.[1] As such, constitutional government signifies an arrangement in which institutions of state are subject to, not superior to, law. Under American constitutional assumptions, "We the People of the United States"[2] delegated power to the Constitution which allocated it among the governing institutions it created. A singular feature of our Constitution is that its text can be formally changed only with great difficulty. Formal amendment requires some super majority support and ratification by three-fourths of the states.[3] Only 27 constitutional amendments have been

---

[1] *See, e.g. Marbury v. Madison*, 5 U. S. (1 Cranch) 137, 176 (1803).

[2] U. S. CONST., pmbl.

[3] U.S. CONST. art. V.

ratified, and ten of those came in a package shortly after the Constitution itself was adopted. In essence, the Constitution's terms are placed outside the reach of normal political action.

The English scholar, Sir Kenneth C. Wheare, observed that "[i]f we investigate the origins of modern Constitutions, we find that, practically without exception, they were drawn up and adopted because people wished to make a fresh start, so far as the statement of their system of government was concerned."[4] The experience in the United States was no exception.

§ 1.02   Ratifying the Constitution

The Constitution represented a "fresh start" after the initial period under the Articles of Confederation. The thirteen colonies had ratified the Articles after the Revolutionary War concluded in 1781. The Articles created a weak national government. States retained their sovereignty and all powers not "expressly delegated" to the United States.[5] The national government consisted of Congress; there was no executive or judiciary. Congress had limited power. It could not tax or regulate interstate commerce.

With the benefits of hindsight, it is not difficult to understand the problems the new nation experienced. Without an executive and judiciary, the national government lacked any means to enforce federal law. "Congress simply could not make anyone, except soldiers, do anything," wrote historian Leonard Levy. "It acted on the states, not on people."[6] Some States adopted protectionist laws which predictably spawned retaliatory measures. These measures eroded any semblance of national unity. Shays' Rebellion in the fall-winter of 1786-87 raised the spectre of anarchy and persuaded many of the need for a stronger national government.[7]

The Constitutional Convention convened in Philadelphia on May 25, 1787, specifically to consider changes to the Articles of Confederation. Under the terms of the Articles, any change required unanimous consent. Five days later, the Convention voted to create a national government comprised of legislative, executive, and judicial branches. Thus, within a few days of gathering, the delegates decided to abandon, rather than salvage, the Articles.[8] The vote was not unanimous; Connecticut opposed the motion and New York was divided.[9] Under the terms of the Articles, the motion failed. But those who met in Philadelphia were no longer proceeding under the prior arrangement. Edwin M. Yoder, Jr., a keen

---

[4] K. C. WHEARE, MODERN CONSTITUTIONS 6 (1966).

[5] ARTICLES OF CONFEDERATION, 1777 art. II, in U.S.C. at XLVII (2000).

[6] Leonard W. Levy, Introduction: American Constitutional History, 1776–1789 in THE FRAMING AND RATIFICATION OF THE CONSTITUTION 6 (Leonard W. Levy and Dennis S. Mahoney eds., 1987).

[7] Stanley Elkins and Eric McKitrick, The Founding Fathers: Young Men of the Revolution, 76 POL. SCI. Q. 181 (1961).

[8] Levy, supra note 6, at 11.

[9] CLINTON L. ROSSITER, 1787: THE GRAND CONVENTION 172 (1987).

constitutional historian, observed, "The fifty-five framers performed radical surgery with a clearer notion of need than mandate from the constituents they represented, who in any case were not a mass electorate. They worked in the name of 'the people of the United States,' but could afford to deliberate in secret and in indifference to 'public opinion' in the modern sense."[10]

Delegates approached the Convention with different visions of the shape government should take. Virginia offered a plan for a strong national government which could regulate individuals. New Jersey, however, proposed a plan more hospitable to smaller states. It asked for a unicameral Congress in which each state would have an equal voice and for a Supreme Court which would be the only national court. Small states typically wanted equal representation in the legislature, whereas large states thought seats should be allocated based on population.

During the next four months, the delegates reached compromises regarding their competing ideals and interests. A bicameral Congress was proposed with a House of Representatives based on population and a Senate based on equal representation. Under the Madisonian Compromise, named for James Madison, the delegates agreed to create a Supreme Court but to give Congress discretion to "ordain and establish" lower federal courts.[11] The method of selecting the executive proved controversial. Some thought the President should be elected by the people; others would have assigned Congress that task. One group doubted the people had sufficient information to make the choice; the other, feared legislative selection would make the President too weak and dependent. Repeated votes failed to resolve the issue. Ultimately, the delegates compromised. Electors chosen in each state would meet solely to choose a President and Vice President. Each state would have the number of electors equal to its representatives in Congress.

The Convention adjourned on September 17, 1787 after nearly four months of deliberation. Attention then turned towards securing ratification by at least nine states as Article VII of the Constitution required. In some states the issue was hotly contested.

A collection of 85 essays advocating ratification of the Constitution were initially published separately from October 27, 1787 to August 16, 1788 in New York City newspapers under the pseudonym, Publius. Anti-federalist sentiment was strong in New York. In fact, the essays were written by Alexander Hamilton, James Madison, and John Jay, the first two of whom had served as delegates to the Convention. Subsequently assembled and published as The Federalist Papers, the collection has a threefold significance. It provides insight into the subjective understanding of at least two delegates to the Convention, Madison and Hamilton, regarding constitutional meaning and content. It provides some inkling of how the Constitution was understood by at least some people in New York who may have

CON LAW

---

[10] EDWIN M. YODER, JR., THE HISTORICAL PRESENT: USES AND ABUSES OF THE PAST 60 (1997).

[11] U.S. CONST., art. III, § 1.

read the essays before ratifying the Constitution. Finally, it is a classic American work in political theory.[12]

Ratification came easily in some small states — Delaware, New Jersey, Georgia, Connecticut, Maryland — and by a 2 to 1 margin in Pennsylvania after some sharp tactics by James Wilson and others. But Massachusetts agreed by only a 187 to 168 vote after some who initially opposed the Constitution were persuaded. Massachusetts also expressed its opinion that certain amendments, one of which was an early draft of the Tenth Amendment, would comfort concerns. South Carolina agreed by a 2 to 1 margin but with four recommendations, including an early version of the Tenth Amendment. New Hampshire became the ninth state to ratify on June 21, 1788 by a 57 to 47 vote with twelve proposed amendments. The debates in Virginia and New York, both critical states, were contentious, and ratification prevailed by narrow margins, 89-79 and 30-27 respectively.[13] North Carolina did not approve the Constitution until late 1789; Rhode Island waited until May, 1790.

The founders appreciated the fact that they had undertaken a momentous task. Alexander Hamilton wrote in the Federalist #1:[14]

"It has been frequently remarked that it seems to have been reserved to the people of this country, by their conduct and example, to decide the important question, whether societies of men are really capable or not of establishing good government from reflection and choice, or whether they are forever destined to depend for their political constitutions on accident and force. If there be any truth in the remark, the crisis at which we are arrived may with propriety be regarded as the era in which that decision is to be made; and a wrong election of the part we shall act may, in this view, deserve to be considered as the general misfortune of mankind."

§ 1.03 The Structural Constitution

The Constitution sought both to protect individual liberty from governmental tyranny and to provide a government able to respond well to public needs. The framers were well aware of the delicacy of their task. Wrote James Madison:[15]

---

[12] See THE FEDERALIST (Clinton Rossiter ed., 1961). In Cohens v. Virginia, 19 U.S. (6 Wheat.) 264, 418–19 (1821), Chief Justice John Marshall wrote: "The opinion of the Federalist has always been considered as of great authority. It is a complete commentary on our constitution; and is appealed to by all parties in the questions to which that instrument has given birth. Its intrinsic merit entitles it to this high rank; and the part two of its authors performed in framing the constitution, put it very much in their power to explain the views with which it was framed. These essays having been published while the constitution was before the nation for adoption or rejection, and having been written in answer to objections founded entirely on the extent of its powers, and on its diminution of State sovereignty, are entitled to the more consideration where they frankly avow that the power objects to is given, and defend it."

[13] See generally, ROSSITER, supra note 9, at 285–98.

[14] THE FEDERALIST NO. 1 at 33. (Alexander Hamilton) (Clinton Rossiter ed., 1961).

[15] THE FEDERALIST NO. 51, at 322 (James Madison) (Rossiter ed. 1961).

If men were angels, no government would be necessary. If angels were to govern men, neither external nor internal controls on government would be necessary. In framing a government which is to be administered by men over men, the great difficulty lies in this: You must first enable the government to control the governed; and in the next place oblige it to control itself.

But how to oblige government to control itself?

Constitutions typically employ two different strategies to restrain government from invading individual freedom. At times constitutions design their architecture to restrain government. They arrange institutions in such a manner as to divide power and introduce obstacles to governmental action. Alternatively, Constitutions often contain a Bill of Rights which place certain rights beyond the reach of government.

The American Constitution initially relied on the first strategy. "Ambition must be made to counteract ambition,"[16] prescribed Madison. Government must be designed in a way which would allow it to respond to the people's needs yet divide power to prevent tyranny. Although the original Constitution contained some specific safeguards of individual liberties,[17] the Bill of Rights was not added until 1791. In fact, at Philadelphia a proposal to add a Bill of Rights was unanimously defeated.[18]

Some Anti-Federalists insisted that a Bill of Rights would assuage their concern about the Constitution. Hamilton argued that a Bill of Rights was "unnecessary," given limitations already included in Article I, and even "dangerous." He feared that inclusion of a Bill of Rights would expand governmental powers in unanticipated directions by encouraging the argument that any powers not explicitly limited were implicitly conferred. "They would contain various exceptions to powers which are not granted; and, on this very account, would afford a colorable pretext to claim more than were granted. For why declare that things shall not be done which there is no power to do?"[19] Madison thought a Bill of Rights could not effectively control a majority intent on acting.[20] Others, including Madison, thought adding a Bill of Rights might induce states like North Carolina and Rhode Island to join the Union.[21] The first Congress proposed 12 amendments; ten were ratified by three-fourths of the state legislature in 1791.[22] To be sure, many of those amendments, as well as others adopted later, have proved the source of important rights of individuals against national or state government. Chapters 8 and on explore those issues.

---

[16] *Id.*

[17] *See, e.g.*, U. S. CONST. art. I, § 9, 10.

[18] JACK N. RAKOVE, ORIGINAL MEANINGS: POLITICS AND IDEAS IN THE MAKING OF THE CONSTITUTION, 288 (1996).

[19] THE FEDERALIST NO. 84, at 513 (Alexander Hamilton) (Clinton Rossiter ed., 1961).

[20] RAKOVE, *supra* note 18, at 332.

[21] *See* DAVID P. CURRIE, THE CONSTITUTION IN CONGRESS: THE FEDERALIST PERIOD 1789-1801, 110 (1997).

[22] AKHIL REED AMAR, THE BILL OF RIGHTS: CREATION AND RECONSTRUCTION 8 (1998).

Yet the Constitution relied primarily on various structural devices to limit governmental power.[23] "In the compound republic of America," wrote Madison, "the power surrendered by the people is first divided between two distinct governments, and then the portion allotted to each subdivided among distinct and separate departments."[24] Power was divided between Nation and State, the concept of Federalism. Congress' power was limited to that "herein granted,"[25] with the remainder residing with the States or the People.[26] On the other hand, the Supremacy Clause declared federal law supreme over state law and bound state officials to respect and enforce federal law.[27] The states were given influence in constituting the national government. State legislatures chose each state's senators and electors chosen in each state chose the President and Vice President.

The Constitution also divided power between the three branches of the federal government, the concept known as Separation of Powers. Indeed, the vesting clause of each of the first three articles suggested this division. Article I vested legislative power in a Congress, Article II vested executive power in the President, and Article III vested judicial power in a Supreme Court and such other courts Congress might choose to create. Moreover, the Constitution created various checks and balances between governmental institutions. The President could propose legislation,[28] but a bill could not become law unless both the House and the Senate passed it and the President signed it.[29] If the President chose to veto legislation, a two-thirds majority of each house was required to pass it.[30] Ultimately, the Court's power to review legislation to ascertain its constitutionality, which was implicit in the structure of the Constitution,[31] was recognized.[32]

§ 1.04 Constitutional Interpretation

The Constitution is the basic source from which government derives its authority, but it provides only an outline of the governmental system. A Constitution is a unique document, a truth implicit in Chief Justice John Marshall's admonition that "we must never forget that it is a *Constitution* we are expounding."[33] "A constitution, to contain an accurate detail of all the subdivisions of which its great powers will admit, and of all the means by which they may be carried into execution, would partake of a prolixity

---

[23] *See* JOHN HART ELY DEMOCRACY AND DISTRUST: A THEORY OF JUDICIAL REVIEW 92–93 (1980).

[24] THE FEDERALIST NO. 51, at 323.

[25] U. S. CONST. art. I, § 1.

[26] U.S. CONST. amend. X.

[27] U.S. CONST. art. VI.

[28] U.S. CONST., art. II, § 3.

[29] U.S. CONST., art. I, § 7.

[30] U.S. Const., art. I, § 7.

[31] THE FEDERALIST NO. 78 (Alexander Hamilton) (Clinton Rossiter ed., 1961).

[32] *Marbury v. Madison*, 5 U.S. (1 Cranch) 137 (1803).

[33] *McCulloch v. Maryland*, 17 U. S. (4 Wheat.) 316, 407 (1819).

of a legal code, and could scarcely be embraced by the human mind,"[34] wrote Chief Justice John Marshall. A Constitution which attempted to anticipate all contingencies would "never be understood by the public"[35] and would prove insufficiently flexible to adapt to changing circumstances. Instead, the Constitution provided a framework many details of which were left unsaid. "We do not expect to find in a constitution minute details," wrote Justice Strong in 1870. "It is necessarily brief and comprehensive."[36] The "nature" of a Constitution "requires that only its great outlines should be marked, its important objects designated"[37] and the rest left to be deduced.

Thus, the Constitution requires interpretation. To be sure, some clauses direct clear outcomes. For instance, the Constitution provides that no one is eligible to be President until they have reached age 35,[38] that each state gets two senators[39] and that conviction for treason must be based "on the testimony of two witnesses to the same overt act, or on confession in open court."[40] These provisions give relatively clear direction regarding the subjects they address. But the meaning of other constitutional provisions is less clear. The Fifth and Fourteenth Amendments protect against deprivations of "life, liberty or property without due process of law." Concepts like life, liberty and property are contestable and mean different things to different people. And what is due process of law? The Eighth Amendment proscribes "cruel and unusual punishments"; does capital punishment come within that prohibition? Does the guarantee of the Equal Protection Clause in the Fourteenth Amendment pertain to equal opportunity, equal outcome, or something else? And what is an "establishment of religion" about which Congress cannot legislate?[41]

Much of the Bill of Rights is notoriously "open textured," but the ambiguous areas do not reside simply in the Bill of Rights. The Constitution's structural clauses raise numerous question, too. What does it mean to empower Congress "[t]o regulate commerce. . . among the several states?"[42] A substantial amount of litigation has addressed that question during the twentieth century. The President can appoint officers of the United States with the advice and consent of the Senate[43] ; but suppose the President wants to remove an officer? The Constitution does not speak specifically to that contingency. The Constitution provides that the Chief Justice presides when the President is tried on impeachment.[44] Who

---

[34] *Id.* at 407.

[35] *Id.*

[36] *Legal Tender Cases*, 79 U.S. (12 Wall.) 457, 532 (1870).

[37] *McCulloch*, 17 U.S. at 407. *See also Legal Tender Cases*, 79 U.S. at 532. ("It prescribes outlines, leaving the filling up to be deduced from the outlines.").

[38] U.S. CONST., art. II, § 1, cl. 5.

[39] U.S. CONST., art. I § 3, cl. 1.

[40] U.S. CONST., art. III, § 3, cl. 1.

[41] U.S. CONST., amend. I.

[42] U.S. CONST., art. I, § 8, cl. 3.

[43] U.S. CONST., art. II, § 2, cl. 2.

[44] U. S. Const., art. I, § 3, cl. 6.

CON LAW

presides if the Vice President is impeached? Can the Vice President, as President of the Senate,[45] preside?[46] Suppose there is no Chief Justice; can someone else preside over the President's impeachment trial? If so, who? Congress can support an army[47] and provide for a navy[48] but the Constitution says nothing about an air force. Is it unconstitutional?

These examples are illustrative, not exhaustive. One can easily multiply questions to which the Constitution does not speak directly or clearly. The U. S. Reports, and constitutional law casebooks, are filled with cases addressing contested language in the Constitution. Constitutional interpretation thus becomes a necessary task of those charged with acting in accordance with the Constitution.

This raises the question regarding how one interprets and argues about the Constitution. The appropriate method of constitutional analysis is controversial. Various judges and scholars adopt different orientations concerning constitutional interpretation.[49] Some believe constitutional interpretation should focus on the text. Many text based theories call for constitutional language to be construed consistently with the original understanding.[50] Alternatively, others advocate a "living constitution." They take their inspiration in part from John Marshall's observation that the "Constitution [is] intended to endure for ages to come, and, consequently, to be adapted to the various *crises* of human affairs."[51] They advocate reading the text in accordance with contemporary, rather than original, understandings.[52] Some advocates of a "living constitution" believe legal precedent and/or ongoing practice are more important in constitutional interpretation.[53] Thus, Professor David Strauss endorses a common law approach to constitutional interpretation. He argues:[54]

"The common law tradition rejects the notion that law must be derived from some authoritative source and finds it instead in understandings

---

[45] U.S. Const., art. I, § 3, cl. 4.

[46] For different views, *see* Joel K. Goldstein, *Can the Vice President Preside at His Own Impeachment Trial? A Critique of Bare Textualism*, 44 ST. LOUIS U. L.J. 849 (2000) (no); Michael Stokes Paulsen, *Someone Should Have Told Spiro Agnew*, 14 CONST. COMMENT 245 (1997) (yes).

[47] U. S. CONST., art. I, § 8, cl. 12.

[48] U. S. Const., art. I, § 8, cl. 13.

[49] *See* Richard H. Fallon, Jr., *How to Choose a Constitutional Theory*, 87 CAL. L. REV. 535, 541–45 (1999).

[50] *See, e.g.*, ROBERT H. BORK, THE TEMPTING OF AMERICA: THE POLITICAL SEDUCTION OF THE LAW (1990).

[51] *McCulloch v. Maryland*, 17 U.S. (4 Wheat.) 316, 415 (1819). *See also Cohens v. Virginia*, 19 U.S. (6 Wheat) 264, 387 (1821) ("But a constitution is framed for ages to come, and designed to approach immortality as nearly as human institutions can approach it.").

[52] *See, e.g.*, Paul Brest, *The Misconceived Quest for the Original Understanding*, 60 B.U. L. REV. 204, 209–17 (1980).

[53] *See, e.g.*, David A. Strauss, *Common Law Constitutional Interpretation*, 63 U. CHI. L. REV. 877 (1996).

[54] *Id.* at 879.

that evolve over time. And it is the common law approach, not the approach that connects law to an authoritative text, or an authoritative decision by the Framers or by 'we the people,' that best explains, and best justifies, American constitutional law today."

Some theories are process-oriented. For instance, Professor John Hart Ely argued that the Constitution was primarily focused on assuring fair processes, not certain outcomes. Taking his cues from Justice Stone's famous footnote four in *United States v. Carolene Products Co.*,[55] he argued that other than the Constitution's clear commands, constitutional interpretation should properly focus on making sure that political processes are open to participation by all on a fair basis. Protecting decision-making processes, not producing certain substantive outcomes, was the "paramount mission of constitutional interpretation," he argued.[56] Others characterize a commitment to process-based theories as "puzzling.".[57] Professor Laurence Tribe argued, for instance, that such theories elevate one substantive value, democratic participation, beyond others, and ignore the many constitutional provisions which reflect commitments to other values. Professor Christopher Eisgruber argues that constitutional interpretation involves "principled argument about moral and political issues," particularly as it focuses on certain clauses.[58]

This synopsis of these theories neither provides an exhaustive catalogue of constitutional theories nor does it do more than provide a few sound bites from those few it includes. The literature includes numerous possible approaches and those mentioned here lend themselves to discussion (and scrutiny) in book length treatments.

§ 1.05　Constitutional Argument

If it is difficult to agree on a prescriptive theory, it is easier to describe the types of constitutional arguments which governmental officials and lawyers typically make. These modes of constitutional arguments can be divided into several categories.

[1]　Textual Argument

The text of the Constitution is a starting point for constitutional interpretation. Virtually all students of constitutional law agree that clear textual commands merit substantial deference and that even contestable provisions must be engaged rather than ignored. "Liberty" may be subject to different meanings but we must at least acknowledge that concept is under discussion. Textualism comports with a sense of law as a positive system of

---

[55] 304 U.S. 144, 152–53 n.4 (1938).

[56] ELY, DEMOCRACY AND DISTRUST, *supra* note 23.

[57] Laurence W. Tribe, *The Puzzling Persistence of Process-Based Constitutional Theories*, 59 YALE L. J. 1063 (1980).

[58] CHRISTOPHER L. EISGRUBER, CONSTITUTIONAL SELF-GOVERNMENT 6 (2001).

rules.[59] Moreover, textualism has a democratic character to it. The text is available to all. Citizens can interpret it in some fashion without recourse to the original records or philosopher's tomes more accessible to law professors and academics. Although some see the text in originalist terms, meaning forever what it meant at ratification,[60] others believe textualism allows constitutional meaning to evolve to comport with the way in which language is understood today.[61] As Professor Philip Bobbitt put it, "one power of textual argument is that it provides a valve through which contemporary values can be intermingled with the Constitution."[62] Finally, some defend textualism as a way to restrain judicial choice, to keep judges from introducing their own political and moral sensibilities into constitutional argument.

Textualism has limits, too. The Constitution often fails to resolve difficult questions, either because it does not speak directly or clearly to a problem that arises. The examples mentioned earlier are illustrative. Can the President abrogate a treaty by his own action?[63] The Constitution does not contain an explicit answer. Under the Commerce Clause Congress can regulate commerce among the states. Suppose Congress had not regulated a particular area of commercial life. Can the states regulate that matter or is the constitutional grant of power to Congress exclusive? The Constitution's text does not contain specific language to answer those questions either. Yet as Professor Bobbitt points out, "in a Constitution of limited powers what is *not* expressed must also be interpreted."[64] Constitutional interpretation must interpret textual silence, yet the silent text often leaves us scratching our heads and wondering.

At times, the Constitution uses language which is in John Hart Ely's phrase, "open-textured"[65] ; formulations so general and abstract that they invite interpretation. Does the Eighth Amendment's ban on "cruel and unusual punishments" preclude the death penalty? What is the meaning of "liberty" in the Due Process Clause of the Fifth and Fourteenth Amendments? Even if we engage the text, its open-textured language may not point in only one direction.

Finally, if we examine constitutional practice we find that the text often does not play a crucial role. On some occasions, courts decide cases based on concepts not stated in the Constitution. The Constitution's text does not explicitly confer a general right of privacy, yet decisions prohibiting states from outlawing use of contraceptives or acknowledging a woman's right to

---

[59] *See, e.g.*, ELY, *supra* note 23 at 3 (explaining basis behind textualism).

[60] *See, e.g.*, *South Carolina v. United States*, 199 U. S. 437, 448 (1905) ("The Constitution is a written instrument. As such its meaning does not alter. That which it meant when adopted, it means now.").

[61] PHILIP BOBBITT, CONSTITUTIONAL FATE 33 (1982).

[62] *Id.* at 36.

[63] *See Goldwater v. Carter*, 444 U.S. 996 (1979).

[64] BOBBITT, *supra* note 61 at 38.

[65] *See generally* ELY, *supra* note 23, at 13–14.

terminate a pregnancy rest on that concept. Even if the Equal Protection Clause provided a basis to outlaw State sponsored school segregation, as the Court held in *Brown v. Board of Education*[66] in 1954, that clause only limits action of the States. There is no such clause in the text vis a vis the Federal Government. Does that mean that the Federal Government could operate segregated schools even though the States could not? Such an outcome would seem inconceivable. The Court avoided that result by finding an equal protection component in the Due Process Clause of the Fifth Amendment.[67] But that approach created other textual anomalies. "In the important cases, reference to and analysis of the constitutional text plays a minor role,"[68] wrote Professor Thomas C. Grey in 1976.

These criticisms do not sideline textual analysis from constitutional interpretation. The text certainly does decide some issues, e.g. the age of eligibility to be President, Senator or Representative. Even when it may not be decisive, it may at least limit the terms of discussion; the Eighth Amendment applies to "punishments," the Commerce Clause allows Congress to regulate "commerce," and so forth.[69] If the text restrains judges by focusing their attention on the Constitution's language, it also empowers them by suggesting they are free to reject decades of doctrine if it is inconsistent with the text.

Because the text is often not conclusive, the judiciary has developed other modes of analysis to help give meaning to general constitutional language in specific cases. In addition to the text, several other modes of argument command widespread support.[70]

[2] Intent of the Framers

At least three types of historical arguments find their way into legal and judicial utterances. First, some view constitutional interpretation as a quest to capture and apply the intent of the framers. These originalist arguments generally seek to discover and enforce either the intent of the drafters or ratifiers of the original Constitution. Proponents of originalism often advance one or more of four justifications for giving it strong weight. First, ratification of the Constitution was the positive act which elevated it from paper to law. It was ratified by a democratic act which required supermajoritarian support. Those who ratified it presumably understood its language to achieve certain purposes. Accordingly, those understandings are what became law.[71] Second, the founding generation was a unique

---

[66] 347 U. S. 483 (1954).

[67] *Bolling v. Sharpe*, 347 U.S. 497 (1954).

[68] Thomas C. Grey, *Do We Have an Unwritten Constitution?*, 27 STAN. L. REV. 703, 707–08 (1975).

[69] *See* Richard H. Fallon, Jr., *A Constructivist Coherence Theory of Constitutional Interpretation*, 100 HARV. L. REV. 1189, 1196 (1987).

[70] *See generally* BOBBITT, *supra* note 61; CHARLES A. MILLER, THE SUPREME COURT AND THE USES OF HISTORY 14-38 (1969); FALLON, *Constructivist Coherence*, *supra* note 69.

[71] *See generally* ANTONIN SCALIA, A MATTER OF INTERPRETATION: FEDERAL COURTS AND THE LAW (1997); *See also* ELY, *supra* note 23, at 15–18 (discussing originalism).

collection of individuals acting in a time of heightened political conscious-ness. Their intent deserves deference because of their heroic and enlight-ened character. Further, originalism represents a strategy to confine the discretion allowed unelected judges. A jurist bound to apply original meaning is limited in a way that one licensed to interpret an ever evolving Constitution is not. Finally, originalism gives the Constitution some rigor. If the Constitution is viewed as being elastic enough to accommodate changing conditions it will stretch until it loses all ability to restrain.[72]

Originalism, too, poses some problems. First, can the intent of the framers or ratifiers really be fathomed? No official minutes were kept. Records of the Constitutional Convention and ratifying conventions are fragmentary. Only a fraction of what was said was preserved and some portions are cryptic.[73] The comments of a speaker may, or may not, have reflected the views or rationales of the greater number who were silent or whose thoughts were not preserved. Sources like The Federalist Papers may tell us how Hamilton, Madison, and Jay defended constitutional provisions, but their explanations may not have reflected the sentiments of other framers or those of ratifiers, most of whom were not familiar with these essays. The framers and ratifiers may not have anticipated or addressed some issues in a form that is preserved. Even when they did, it may be treacherous to ascribe to a group the articulated views of the few who may have spoken.[74] In *Brown v. Board of Education*, the Court rescheduled arguments ostensibly so the parties could brief what the original under-standing of the Fourteenth Amendment was regarding school desegrega-tion. But after many of the nation's ablest lawyers and historians labored for months to elucidate the subject, the Court concluded that the historical argument was "at best . . . inconclusive."[75]

Capturing original intent may be particularly problematic when those doing the recovery are lawyers and judges rather than historians. As Professor Charles A. Miller wrote, "historians as scholars can generally state the matter more objectively than can advocates as historians."[76] The work of a historian rests on certain assumptions which may prove contro-versial. Yet they are likely to be more trained in the historical craft than are lawyers and judges, and better able to transport themselves back into the world view of the eighteenth century agrarian society, in which the framers and ratifiers lived to recreate what they thought. Moreover, they presumably do not approach an historical issue as advocates in the same way lawyers do.

Even if we can recapture original intent, we may ask how relevant it should be. The framers lived in different times with different problems.

---

[72] *See e.g.*, SCALIA, *supra* note 71 at 47.

[73] *See, e.g.*, Yoder, *supra* note 10 at 79–80.

[74] *See, e.g.*, BREST, *supra* note 52 at 229.; Daniel A. Farber, *The Originalism Debate: A Guide for the Perplexed*, 49 OHIO ST. L. J. 1085 (1989).

[75] *Brown v. Board of Education*, 347 U. S. 483, 489 (1954).

[76] MILLER, *supra* note 70, at 157.

Moreover, as a group of white men, many of whom owned slaves, they hardly reflect the demographic reality of our times. Transformative events — westward expansion, the Civil War, immigration, two World Wars, the Great Depression, the change from an agrarian to industrial society, the civil rights movement, and many more — left us living in quite a different world from Madison, Hamilton, and Jay. Should the Constitution bind contemporary people to the specific choices of those who lived two centuries ago?[77]

Finally, originalism cannot account for numerous decisions of the Supreme Court. The First Amendment has been interpreted to protect a broad "market place of ideas" which seems to extend far beyond the view of the founders. The Equal Protection Clause outlaws racial segregation of schools and much gender discrimination which was not within the aim of those who ratified it. And it has been made applicable against the federal government, an interpretive move hard to defend on originalist grounds.[78]

[3] Ongoing Practice

A second type of historical argument involves ongoing history, or what might be termed an adverse possession theory of constitutional interpretation. These arguments rest on the premise that constitutional meaning evolves to embrace changing reality. In part, the Constitution changes in response to the accepted interpretations of government officials — Presidents, legislators, etc. — over a period of time.[79] It also responds to accommodate changes in social practice, technology and morality. Whereas original intent history seeks to confine judges to constitutional meaning at the founding, ongoing history "allows the Constitution to move with the prevailing temper of the country and may therefore be considered forward-looking."[80]

Ongoing history may allow the Constitution to change to accommodate new circumstances or to recognize traditional practice. But how does one decide which practices are significant in changing constitutional meaning and which are not? American society oppressed African-Americans and excluded women from certain preferred roles for centuries. The longevity of these practices would not seem a basis to accord them constitutional sanction. Indeed, it has not. One escape from this quandary is to admit ongoing practice to shape the meaning of provisions respecting institutional practice and behavior, but not regarding those directly impacting individual liberty. Chief Justice Marshall relied on this resolution in *McCulloch v. Maryland*.[81] There he suggested that past practice might be appropriate

---

[77] See generally RICHARD H. FALLON, JR., IMPLEMENTING THE CONSTITUTION, 13–14 (2001). William S. Brennan, Jr., *The Constitution of the United States: Contemporary Ratification*, 27 S. Tex. L. J. 433, 438 (1986).

[78] See FALLON, *supra* note 77, at 15–16.

[79] See, e.g., *McCulloch v. Maryland*, 17 U.S. (4 Wheat.) 316, 01–02 (1819).

[80] See MILLER, *supra* note 70 at 25.

[81] *McCulloch*, 17 U. S. at 401–02.

in certain cases in which "the great principles of liberty are not concerned."[82] Yet, at times, justices do look to tradition to determine whether practices like homosexuality,[83] abortion[84] and assisted suicide[85] are constitutionally protected. Moreover, accepting Chief Justice Marshall's formulation does not eliminate the difficulty but simply limits it to cases dealing with institutions. At times the Court has found past practice suggestive of constitutional meaning; at other times, not. In *Stuart v. Laird*, Justice William Patterson used ongoing practice to silence the argument that the Constitution precluded Supreme Court justices from sitting on circuit courts. He wrote:[86]

> "To this objection, which is of recent date, it is sufficient to observe, that practice and acquiescence under it for a period of several years, commencing with the organization of the judicial system, affords an irresistible answer, and has indeed fixed the construction."

Less than two decades later, Chief Justice Marshall thought the earlier decisions of the executive and legislative branches, in favor of a national bank, suggestive of its constitutionality.[87] But 164 years later, in *Immigration and Naturalization Service v. Chadha*,[88] Chief Justice Burger suggested that the increased frequency of legislative veto provisions in federal statutes "sharpened rather than blunted"[89] the judicial scrutiny.

[4] Judicial Doctrine; Precedent

A third type of historical argument relates to judicial doctrine or precedent. These distinct, yet closely related, types of constitutional arguments use judicial formulations of the past to decide new constitutional cases. According to Professor Charles A. Miller, "[c]onstitutional doctrines are formulas extracted from a combination of the constitutional text and a series of related cases. Typically stated in shorthand fashion, they may be used almost as an emendation on the constitutional text."[90] Or as Professor Charles Fried put it, "[d]octrine is the work of judges and of those who comment on and rationalize their decisions."[91] Doctrine would include the early twentieth century ideas that government could not interfere with liberty of contract,[92] that equal protection was satisfied by separate but equal facilities,[93] that government could regulate commerce directly but

---

[82] *Id.* at 401.

[83] *See, e.g., Bowers v. Hardwick*, 478 U. S. 186 (1986).

[84] *See e.g. Roe v. Wade*, 410 U. S. 113 (1973).

[85] *See, e.g., Washington v. Glucksberg*, 521 U. S. 702 (1997).

[86] *Stuart v. Laird*, 5 U.S. (1 Cranch) 299, 309 (1803).

[87] *McCulloch*, 17 U.S. at 401.

[88] 462 U. S. 919 (1983).

[89] *Id.* at 944.

[90] MILLER, *supra* note 70, at 15.

[91] Charles Fried, *Constitutional Doctrine*, 107 HARV. L. REV. 1140 (1994).

[92] *Lochner v. New York*, 198 U. S. 45 (1905).

[93] *Plessy v. Ferguson*, 163 U. S. 537 (1896).

not indirectly,[94] as well as contemporary pronouncements in favor of applying strict scrutiny to classifications based on race[95] or against commandeering state government.[96] Precedent involves the use of previously decided cases to resolve later cases, and may be used by way of analogy or as binding authority. Most doctrine is identified with some precedent as the doctrine citations in the last sentence of the prior paragraph suggest.

Judicial decisions add gloss to the Constitution's text. The holdings and concepts embodied in judicial opinions often assume a life of their own and become the stuff of constitutional law.[97] Constitutional law includes judge-made rules which are developed in caselaw, especially the decisions of the Supreme Court that affect the distribution or the exercise of governmental authority.

Doctrine and precedent both recall a common law approach to constitutional law. They assign high status to judicial decisions and the principles they articulate. To be sure, as Justice Oliver Wendell Holmes observed, "[g]eneral propositions do not decide concrete cases";[98] although this admonition most clearly states a limitation on doctrine, precedent, too, does not always cover precisely the situations presented by new cases.

Use of precedent has some clear advantages. It preserves judicial resources, adds some certainty and stability to constitutional law, links current decisions to those of the past, and limits judicial discretion.[99]

Some question why doctrine and precedent should receive such deference. As Professor Fried posed the problem, "our allegiance and that of the judges is ultimately owed to the Constitution itself. Because only the Constitution has the authority of a founding document, the question arises: is it not wrong to substitute the course of judgments in the Supreme Court for that authority authentically discerned?"[100] The legal realists pointed out that judges have policy preferences and accordingly their decisions may mask as law their political predispositions. Why should later generations honor and perpetuate the work of earlier jurists? Critics complain that constitutional meaning turns on the text and original intent, not on subsequent interpretations.[101] As Justice William O. Douglas put it,

"A judge looking at a constitutional decision may have compulsions to revere past history and accept what was once written. But he remembers above all else that it is the Constitution which he swore to support and

---

[94] *United States v. E. C. Knight*, 156 U. S. 1 (1895).

[95] *Grutter v. Bollinger*, 539 U.S. 306, 123 S.Ct. 2325 (2003).

[96] *New York v. United States*, 505 U.S. 144 (1992).

[97] *See, e.g.*, STRAUSS, *supra* note 53, at 899–900.

[98] *Lochner v. New York*, 198 U.S. 45, 75 (1905) (Holmes, J. dissenting).

[99] *See generally* Geoffrey R. Stone, *Precedent, the Amendment Process, and Evolution in Constitutional Doctrine*, 11 HARV. J. L. & PUB. POL'Y 67, 70 (1988).

[100] FRIED, *supra* note 91, at 1140.

[101] *See, e.g.*, Gary Lawson, *An Interpretivist Agenda*, 15 HARV. J. L. & PUB. POL'Y 157, 161 (1992).

defend, not the gloss which his predecessors may have put on it. So he comes to formulate his own views, rejecting some earlier ones as false and embracing others. He cannot do otherwise unless he lets men long dead and unaware of the problems of the age in which he lives do his thinking for him."[102]

Moreover, doctrine often takes on a life of its own quite independent of text and original intent. Terms like "separate but equal," "clear and present danger," "direct or indirect effects", and "strict scrutiny" become vehicles to resolve cases even though they do not appear in the text itself.

Stare decisis, the practice of following precedent, is practiced in constitutional adjudication although not with the same rigor as in statutory cases. Justice Louis Brandeis explained:

> *Stare decisis* is usually the wise policy, because in most matters it is more important that the applicable rule of law be settled than that it be settled right. . . . But in cases involving the Federal Constitution, where corrections through legislative action is practically impossible, this Court has often overruled its earlier decisions. The Court bows to the lessons of experience and the force of better reasoning, recognizing that the process of trial and error, so fruitful in the physical sciences, is appropriate also in the judicial function.[103]

Thus, at times the Court abandons or overrules pernicious or anachronistic precedents or doctrine, as it did in *Brown* when it rejected the notion from *Plessy v. Ferguson*[104] that "separate but equal" was consistent with the Fourteenth Amendment; or as it did when it stopped using "freedom of contract" from *Lochner* to proscribe governmental regulations.

Yet the Court has also applied doctrine or precedent even though some justices with votes critical to establishing a majority indicated that they thought the earlier decision may have been wrong. Thus, in *Planned Parenthood v. Casey*[105] the Court affirmed the central holding of *Roe v. Wade*,[106] which recognized a woman's constitutional right to terminate a pregnancy, even though three justices repeatedly suggested that they may have had misgivings about *Roe* as an original matter. In *Casey*, Justices O'Connor, Kennedy and Souter suggested whether *stare decisis* should apply should turn upon several criteria: Was the earlier rule workable? Had it engendered substantial reliance? Had "related principles of law . . . so far developed as to have left the old rule no more than a remnant of abandoned doctrine?" Had facts changed so much "to have robbed the old rule of significant application or justification?"[107] Similarly, the Court applied judicial doctrine in an interesting manner in deciding that the warnings

---

[102] William O. Douglas, *Stare Decisis* in 1 BENJAMIN N. CARDOZO MEMORIAL LECTURES 285.

[103] *Burnet v. Coronado Oil & Gas Co.*, 285 U.S. 393, 406–08 (1932) (Brandeis, J., dissenting).

[104] 163 U.S. 537 (1896).

[105] 505 U.S. 833 (1992).

[106] 410 U.S. 113 (1973).

[107] *Casey*, 505 U.S. at 855.

to criminal suspects it required in *Miranda v. Arizona*[108] were constitutionally required. In *Dickerson v. United States*,[109] the Court considered the constitutionality of 18 U.S.C. § 3501 which conflicted with *Miranda*. Although several members of the Court's majority apparently had misgivings about "*Miranda*'s reasoning and its resulting rule"[110] that the warnings *Miranda* prescribed were constitutionally compelled, it declined to overrule *Miranda* on *stare decisis* grounds. The Court that decided *Miranda* and subsequent Courts had treated *Miranda* as stating a constitutional rule. Its "doctrinal underpinnings" had not suffered sufficient deterioration to overrule the decision even though several members of the Court's seven-justice majority would have interpreted the Constitution differently as an original matter.

In dissent, Justice Scalia, joined by Justice Thomas, pointed out that Chief Justice Rehnquist and Justices O'Connor and Kennedy were "on record as believing that a violation of *Miranda* is *not* a violation of the Constitution."[111] He accused the majority of adopting "a significant *new*, if not entirely comprehensible, principle of constitutional law" that the Court could strike down a congressional statute "not only when what they prescribe violates the Constitution, but when what they prescribe contradicts a decision of [the] Court that 'announced a constitutional rule?'"[112]

Yet the Court has not always applied these tests since *Casey* in determining whether to apply or abandon an earlier doctrine. Thus, in *Lawrence v. Texas*,[113] for instance, the Court overruled *Bowers v. Hardwick*[114] without assessing the earlier case against the *Casey* principles.

[5] Structural Arguments

In addition to historical arguments, constitutional interpretation often relies on structural argument, inferences from the structures and relationships of the Constitution.[115] Such arguments identify concepts implicit in the Constitution's architecture to interpret the document. Thus, notions of federalism, separation of powers, checks and balances, rule of law, and so forth emerge from constitutional structures although those terms do not themselves appear in the Constitution. Structural reasoning is linked to the text because it involves drawing general conclusions based upon the document. It differs from textual argument because its focus is not on one particular clause but on the relationship between, and the principles that

---

[108] 384 U.S. 436 (1966).

[109] 530 U.S. 428 (2000).

[110] *Id.* at 443.

[111] *Id.* at 445.

[112] *Id.*

[113] 123 S.Ct. 2472 (2003).

[114] 475 U.S. 186 (1986).

[115] *See generally* CHARLES L. BLACK, JR. STRUCTURE AND RELATIONSHIP IN CONSTITUTIONAL LAW (1969).

emerge from, various clauses. Structural reasoning features prominently in some of Chief Justice John Marshall's seminal opinions, such as *Marbury v. Madison*[116] and *McCulloch v. Maryland*.[117] Thus, in *Marbury* he concluded that the Constitution is paramount law, that Congress' powers are limited, and that citizens with rights must have remedies from basic concepts relating to constitutionalism and rule of law. In *McCulloch*, he cited the structural idea that constitutions are created to succeed and accordingly Congress can exercise means necessary to accomplish its enumerated ends. Moreover, he used the structural independence of the federal government and its democratic character as a basis to preclude a state from taxing its agencies. Structural reasoning is by no means a relic of earlier times. Professors Brannon P. Denning and Glenn Reynolds point out its prevalence in many recent decisions of the Rehnquist Court.[118] Proponents, like Charles Black, Jr., argued that "the method of reasoning from structure and relation" is more likely "to make sense — current, practical sense" than some other forms of legal reasoning.[119]

Critics find structural argument elusive and malleable. Thus, structural reasoning may not restrain judges but rather give them license to reach results they wish to reach. Moreover, structural argument seems better suited for questions involving the relationship of different institutions of government; they are less useful "to the task of protecting human rights."[120]

[6] Consequential Arguments

Prudential or consequentialist arguments proceed from the assumption that constitutional interpretation should take account of outcomes. This approach seeks to lend rationality to constitutional interpretation. It often balances competing constitutional principles. Thus, in *McCulloch v. Maryland*, Chief Justice Marshall justified the Court's conclusion that Congress had power to create a national bank by considering the difficulties that would exist if Congress lacked such a power. The Constitution was to succeed, not fail, and accordingly it needed to be interpreted in a fashion which "the exigencies of the nation may require."[121] Prudential arguments may, at times, lead the Court to duck deciding a case to avoid institutional harm.[122] It may lead a Court to hold that the federal government cannot operate segregated schools, as the Court held in *Bolling v. Sharpe*,[123] the

---

[116] 5 U.S. (1 Cranch) 137 (1803).

[117] 17 U. S. (4 Wheat.) 316 (1819).

[118] *See* Brannon P. Denning and Glenn Harlan Reynolds, *Comfortably Penumbral*, 77 B. U. L. Rev. 1089 (1997).

[119] Black, *supra* note 115 at 22.

[120] BOBBITT, *supra* note 61 at 89.

[121] *McCulloch*, 17 U.S. at 408–09.

[122] *See, e.g.*, ALEXANDER BICKEL, THE LEAST DANGEROUS BRANCH (1962).

[123] 347 U. S. 497 (1954).

companion case to *Brown v. Board of Education*. In *Bolling*, Chief Justice Warren wrote that "[i]n view of our decision that the Constitution prohibits the states from maintaining racially segregated public schools, it would be unthinkable that the same Constitution would impose a lesser duty on the Federal Government."[124] Consequential arguments may lead the Court to uphold a presidential foreign policy initiative to avoid adverse international impact.[125]

Consequential arguments, however, may involve the Court in speculation regarding political reactions. Considering outcomes strikes some as policy-oriented, not law-oriented, and involving courts in legislating, not adjudicating. Is this an appropriate role for judges? Such judicial activity might also lead to "intellectual laziness" if it becomes a substitute for engaging other legal materials.[126]

[7] Ethical Argument

At times, courts and lawyers invoke ethical or value arguments. These assertions seek to vindicate what is deemed moral, just, or desirable. Sometimes those arguments seem invited by the open-ended language of the Constitution i.e., due process, equal protection, and so forth. On other occasions, they are invoked when other arguments seem inconclusive. As Professor Ronald Dworkin writes, "[t]he moral reading proposes that we all — judges, lawyers, citizens — interpret and apply these abstract clauses on the understanding that they invoke moral principles about political decency and justice."[127] Moral argument has its critics, however.

It is sometimes criticized as contestable. Moral argument is unlikely to be conclusive since different people will reach different results. As such, some view moral argument as representing an effort to incorporate personal sentiments into constitutional law. Moreover, introducing moral argument into constitutional interpretation may diminish the role of elected decision-makers. Some argue that elected officials, not unelected judges, can best reflect the people's moral convictions.[128]

[8] Sociological Evidence

Two other forms of constitutional argument also merit mention. Courts sometimes use social facts as a basis for deciding constitutional cases.[129]

---

[124] *Id.* at 500

[125] *See, e.g., Dames & Moore v. Regan*, 453 U.S. 654 (1981).

[126] Richard Posner, *Pragmatic Adjudication*, 18 CARDOZO L. REV. 1, 16 (1996).

[127] RONALD DWORKIN, FREEDOM'S LAW: THE MORAL READING OF THE AMERICAN CONSTITUTION 2 (1996).

[128] *See generally* Michael W. McConnell, *The Importance of Humility in Judicial Review: A Comment on Ronald Dworkin's "Moral Readings" of the Constitution*, 65 FORD. L. REV. 1269 (1997).

[129] *See generally* Miller, *supra* note 70 at 17–20.

The Brandeis brief, offered in *Muller v. Oregon*[130] pioneered this approach.[131] Attorneys challenging school desegregation in the 1950s employed extensive psychological and sociological evidence to support their ultimately successful claim that separate but equal violated equal protection because of its impact on African-American children.[132] More recently, in a Michigan affirmative action case, the Court relied on evidence regarding the beneficial effects of affirmative action programs in college admissions.[133]

Such argument is subject to some qualifications. When presented in briefs, rather than offered in evidence, there may not be effective opportunity to impeach the evidence and offer rebuttal.[134] Moreover, it may make legal principles turn on sociological data and accordingly vulnerable to a change in circumstance. Would racial segregation be constitutional if findings showed it to be beneficial?[135]

[9] Comparative Constitutional Argument

Finally, some justices have recently argued that the practices and experiences of other countries furnish a basis for reaching decisions in American constitutional law. In cases dealing with assisted suicide,[136] homosexuality[137] and affirmative action[138] the Court has cited the way other countries handle these issues in resolving American constitutional principles. Although this cosmopolitan type of argument appears most often in cases involving constitutional rights, it has also appeared in structure cases, too.[139] Not all embrace the use of comparative constitutional law in interpreting our Constitution. Thus, Justice Scalia has suggested that the American Constitution should be interpreted without reference to the experience abroad.

§ 1.06 Conclusion

Some of the previous discussion has implicitly assumed that courts and lawyers have a special role in constitutional argument. Indeed, much constitutional argument is addressed to, or used by, the judiciary. The following chapter will introduce and explore the institution of judicial review, which recognizes the important judicial role in interpreting the

[130] 208 U. S. 412 (1908).

[131] ALPHEUS T. MASON, BRANDEIS: A FREE MAN'S LIFE (1946).

[132] *See generally* RICHARD KLUGER, SIMPLE JUSTICE (1977).

[133] *See Grutter v. Bollinger*, 539 U.S. 306 (2003).

[134] PAUL A. FREUND, THE SUPREME COURT OF THE UNITED STATES 151 (1961).

[135] *See Miller, supra* note 70 at 19.

[136] *See Washington v. Guicksberg*, 521 U.S. 702, 718 n.16 (1997).

[137] *See Lawrence v. Texas*, 123 S.Ct. 2472, 2481 (2003).

[138] *See Grutter*, 123 S.Ct. at 2347 (Ginsburg, J., concurring).

[139] *See, e.g., Printz v. United States*, 521 U. S. 898, 976–78 (1997) (Breyer, J. dissenting).

Constitution. The judiciary is the primary source of constitutional law, but it is by no means the only institution that shapes constitutional meaning. The President[140] and members of the executive and legislative branches[141] also take oaths to enforce the Constitution, an obligation which arguably allows them to interpret it. Indeed, Presidents Thomas Jefferson,[142] Andrew Jackson,[143] Abraham Lincoln[144] and Franklin D. Roosevelt[145] among others at times suggested that they had some independent authority to interpret the Constitution. Officials in the executive and legislative branches interpret the Constitution in the regular course of their duties.[146] When, for instance, the House of Representatives considered impeaching Presidents Richard M. Nixon and William Jefferson Clinton it had to interpret the Impeachment Clause to determine whether the acts alleged constituted "other high crimes and misdemeanor."[147] Congress sometimes considers constitutional arguments in legislating. For instance, Senator Thomas F. Eagleton argued and voted against the War Powers Resolution in 1973 because he concluded that the measure unconstitutionally gave the Presidents some of Congress' power to declare war.[148] When the bill passed nonetheless, President Nixon vetoed it because he thought it unconstitutionally encroached on the President's power.[149] In each case, their interpretation was based on their reading of the Constitution and their assessment of other constitutional materials. Neither Senator Eagleton's nor President Nixon's actions were unprecedented. On the contrary, members of the executive and legislative branches often consider constitutional arguments for or against proposed actions. At times the judiciary recognizes that one of the political branches has a superior right or competence to interpret a particular part of the Constitution. On other occasions, the Court adopts, or is influenced by, the constitutional views of the executive or legislative branches.

CON LAW

---

[140] U.S. CONST., art. II, § 1, cl. 8.

[141] U.S. CONST., art VI, cl. 3.

[142] THE WRITINGS OF THOMAS JEFFERSON 311 (Paul L. Ford ed., 1898) (Letter to John B. Colvin, Sept. 20, 1810).

[143] 3 MESSAGES AND PAPERS OF THE PRESIDENTS 1145 (James Richardson, ed., 1897).

[144] Abraham Lincoln, Special Session Message, *in* 7 MESSAGES AND PAPERS OF THE PRESIDENTS 3210) (James Richardson, ed., 1897).

[145] GERALD GUNTHER, CASES AND MATERIALS ON CONSTITUTIONAL LAW 24 (12th ed. 1991)

[146] *See generally* LOUIS FISHER, CONSTITUTIONAL DIALOGUES: INTERPRETATION AS POLITICAL PROCESS (1988).

[147] U.S. CONST. art. II, § 4.

[148] THOMAS F. EAGLETON, WAR AND PRESIDENTIAL POWER 163 (1974).

[149] Richard M. Nixon, Veto of the War Powers Resolution (Oct. 24, 1973) *in* PUBLIC PAPERS OF THE PRESIDENTS: RICHARD NIXON 1973, at 311 (1975).

CHAPTER 6
UNDERSTANDING CRIMINAL LAW

By

Joshua Dressler

Frank R. Strong Chair in Law
Ohio State University College of Law

Chapter 6

CRIMINAL LAW: AN OVERVIEW

§ 1.01 Nature of "Criminal Law"[1]

The study of the criminal law is the study of crimes and the moral principles of criminal responsibility.

[A] Crimes

[1] Comparison to Civil Wrongs

What is a crime? If we are to believe many judicial opinions and treatises, the answer is simple, circular, and useless: a "crime" is anything that lawmakers say is a crime. We need to look deeper for an answer to this question and, thus, to understand how a crime differs from a civil wrong, such as a tort or a breach of contract.[2]

First, unlike torts and contracts, the criminal law involves *public* law. That is, although the direct and immediate victim of a crime typically is a private party (e.g., a person who is robbed, assaulted, or kidnapped), and other individuals may indirectly be injured (e.g., a spouse of the direct victim), a crime involves more than a private injury: a crime causes "social harm,"[3] in that the injury suffered involves "a breach and violation of the public rights and duties, due to the whole community, considered as a community, in its social aggregate capacity."[4] For this reason, crimes are prosecuted by public attorneys representing the community at large, and not by privately retained counsel.

---

[1] See generally John C. Coffee, Jr., *Paradigms Lost: The Blurring of the Criminal and Civil Law Models—And What Can Be Done About It*, 101 Yale L.J. 1875 (1992); Claire Finkelstein, *Positivism and the Notion of an Offense*, 88 Calif. L. Rev. 335 (2000), Henry M. Hart, Jr., *The Aims of the Criminal Law*, 23 Law & Contemp. Probs. 401 (1958); Sanford H. Kadish, *Why Substantive Criminal Law—A Dialogue*, 29 Clev. St. L. Rev. 1 (1980); Susan R. Klein, *Redrawing the Criminal-Civil Boundary*, 2 Buffalo Crim. L. Rev. 679 (1999); John Q. LaFond, *Can Therapeutic Jurisprudence Be Normatively Neutral? Sexual Predator Laws: Their Impact on Participants and Policy*, 41 Ariz. L. Rev. 375 (1999); Stephen J. Morse, *Fear of Danger, Flight from Culpability*, 4 Psych., Pub. Policy, and Law 250 (1998); Stephen J. Schulhofer, *Two Systems of Social Protection: Comments on the Civil-Criminal Distinction, With Particular Reference to Sexually Violent Predator Laws*, 7 J. Contemp. Legal Issues 69 (1996); Carol S. Steiker, *Punishment and Procedure: Punishment Theory and the Criminal-Civil Procedural Divide*, 85 Geo. L.J. 775 (1997); William J. Stuntz, *Substance, Process, and the Civil-Criminal Line*, 7 J. Contemp. Legal Issues 1 (1996).

[2] For an effort to look deeper, see Finkelstein, Note 1, *supra*.

[3] For a definition of this term, see § 9.10[B], *infra*.

[4] 4 Blackstone at *5.

But, there is more that should distinguish a criminal wrong from its civil counterpart. A person convicted of a crime is punished. The technical definition of "punishment" awaits consideration in the next chapter,[5] but what is significant at this point is that "the essence of punishment . . . lies in the criminal conviction itself,"[6] rather than in the specific hardship imposed by a judge as a result of the conviction. The hardship suffered as a result of the criminal conviction may be no greater (or even less) than that which results from a civil judgment. For example, a person who lacks substantial financial resources might prefer to spend a few days in jail, rather than pay a civil judgment of $10,000. And, it is *not* the case that a civil proceeding can *never* result in loss of liberty: a mentally ill person may be involuntarily committed to a mental institution,[7] and so-called "sexual predators" may be confined, supposedly civilly, due to their perceived dangerousness to the community.[8] What, then, distinguishes the criminal law from its civil counterpart is, or at least should be, *the societal condemnation and stigma that accompanies the conviction.*[9]

When the factfinder (ordinarily, a jury) determines that a person is guilty of an offense, the resulting conviction is an expression of the community's moral outrage, directed at the criminal actor for her act. It follows, therefore, that a crime *should* be defined as "an act or omission and its accompanying state of mind which, if duly shown to have taken place, will incur a formal and solemn pronouncement of the moral condemnation of the community."[10] To the extent that conduct that does *not* justify condemnation is treated as criminal, as is sometimes the case,[11] the line between the civil and the criminal processes is unfortunately blurred.[12]

---

[5] See § 2.02, *infra.*

[6] George K. Gardner, *Bailey v. Richardson and the Constitution of the United States, 33 B.U. L. Rev. 176, 193 (1953).*

[7] See § 25.05[A], *infra.*

[8] E.g., Kan. Stat. Ann. § 59-29a01 et seq. (1994) (defining a sexual predator as "any person who has been convicted of or charged with a sexually violent offense and who suffers from a mental abnormality or personality disorder which makes the person likely to engage in the predatory acts of sexual violence"; and making such a person eligible for civil commitment). These laws are exceptionally controversial because they blur the line, perhaps to the point of extinction, between civil and criminal commitment. See also § 2.02[B], *infra.*

[9] Hart, Note 1, *supra,* at 404; see also Katz at 28 ("[P]unishment condemns, the [civil] penalty does not").

[10] Hart, Note 1, *supra,* at 405.

[11] See Chapter 11, *infra.*

[12] Do not assume that *all* morally wrongful conduct is criminal. In a society that values individual liberty, the criminal law serves a *minimalist* role: it only seeks to identify and regulate wrongful conduct that results in significant social harm; the criminal law does not seek "to purify thoughts and perfect character." *United States v. Hollingsworth,* 27 F.3d 1196, 1203 (7th Cir. 1994). The latter is the responsibility of religion, family, and other private institutions. For example, telling a lie may be a character flaw, but the criminal law punishes only the most harmful lies, e.g., material misstatements made under oath in judicial proceedings (perjury).

[2]　Classification of Crimes

The English common law[13] divided crimes into two general categories: felonies and misdemeanors.[14] A felony "comprise[d] every species of crime which occasioned at common law the forfeiture of lands and goods."[15] All common law felonies were punishable by death. The list of felonies was short: felonious homicide (later divided by statute into murder and manslaughter), arson, mayhem, rape, robbery, larceny, burglary, prison escape, and (perhaps) sodomy.[16] All other criminal offenses were misdemeanors.

In modern penal codes, the line distinguishing felonies from misdemeanors is drawn differently than it was in the past. Generally speaking, an offense punishable by death or imprisonment in a state prison is a felony; an offense for which the maximum punishment is a monetary fine, incarceration in a local jail, or both, is a misdemeanor. For sentencing purposes, the Model Penal Code,[17] and the statutory schemes of various jurisdictions,[18] divide felonies into degrees.[19] Some states, as well, have added an additional classification of crime, e.g., "violations"[20] or "infractions." These offenses encompass misconduct so minor that incarceration is prohibited.[21]

[B]　Principles of Criminal Responsibility

As one scholar has observed, "[i]t is deeply rooted in our moral sense of fitness that punishment entails blame and that, therefore, punishment may not justly be imposed where the person is not blameworthy."[22]

The study of the criminal law is, therefore, much more than the study of crimes. It is also the investigation of the doctrines that have developed over the centuries for determining when a person may justly be held criminally responsible for harm that she has caused. Put another way, the principles of criminal responsibility, which are at the core of the criminal law, identify the point at which it is believed fair to go from the factual

---

[13] The "common law" is judge-made law. See § 3.01[A], *infra*.

[14] Because of its special heinousness, treason was categorized separately, but strictly speaking it was a felony. 4 Blackstone at *95.

[15] *Id.* at *94.

[16] Perkins & Boyce at 14. The authors state that sodomy originally was punished as an ecclesiastical offense, and was made a felony by statute, but it is "old enough to be recognized as common law in this country." *Id.* at 15.

[17] For an explanation of the Model Penal Code, see § 3.03, *infra*.

[18] E.g. N.Y. Penal Law § 55.05 (McKinney 1998).

[19] E.g., Model Penal Code § 6.01(1) (dividing felonies into three degrees); §§ 6.03 and 6.06 (setting out the fines and terms of imprisonment, by degree of felony).

[20] Model Penal Code § 1.04(5).

[21] Usually, a violation or infraction involves conduct, e.g., breach of a traffic ordinance, that does not justify moral condemnation. To the extent that such an offense is characterized as "criminal," it runs counter to the definition of "crime" set out in subsection [1], *supra*. To avoid this apparent conflict, some scholars state that violations are not "true crimes." Perkins & Boyce at 18.

[22] Kadish, Note 1, *supra*, at 10.

CRIM LAW

premise, "*D* caused or assisted in causing X (a social harm) to occur," to the normative judgment, "*D should* be punished for having caused or assisted in causing X to occur." The rules of criminal responsibility are considered in Chapters 9–30, *infra*.

§ 1.02 Proving Guilt at the Trial

[A] Right to Trial by Jury

[1] In General

The Sixth Amendment to the United States Constitution provides that "in all criminal prosecutions, the accused shall enjoy the right to a speedy and public trial, by an impartial jury." The right to trial by jury is "fundamental to the American scheme of justice," and therefore applies in all criminal proceedings, both state and federal.[23] The Supreme Court has stated that the constitutional guarantee reflects a "profound judgment about the way in which law should be enforced and justice administered." The right is granted "in order to prevent oppression by the Government. . . . If the defendant prefer[s] the common-sense judgment of a jury to the more tutored but perhaps less sympathetic reaction of the single judge, he [is] to have it."[24]

Despite the Sixth Amendment phrase, "in all criminal prosecutions," the jury-trial right only applies to "non-petty" offenses. According to the Supreme Court, "no offense can be deemed 'petty' for purposes of the right to trial by jury where imprisonment for more than six months is authorized."[25] An offense is also non-petty, even if the maximum authorized period of confinement is six months or less, if any additional statutory penalties (including fines) "are so severe that they clearly reflect a legislative determination that the offense in question is a 'serious' one."[26] As a practical matter, this means that a criminal defendant has a constitutional right to trial by jury in all felony and many misdemeanor prosecutions.

[2] Scope of the Right

In the federal courts[27] and in most states, a jury in a criminal trial is composed of twelve persons who must reach a unanimous verdict to convict or acquit. Juries as small as six, however, are constitutional.[28] State laws

---

[23] *Duncan v. Louisiana,* 391 U.S. 145, 149 (1968).

[24] *Id.* at 155–56.

[25] *Baldwin v. New York,* 399 U.S. 66, 69 (1970).

[26] *Blanton v. City of North Las Vegas,* 489 U.S. 538, 543 (1989).

[27] Fed. R. Crim. P. 23(a) (setting the size of the jury at 12); 31(a) (unanimity requirement).

[28] *Williams v. Florida,* 399 U.S. 78 (1970) (a jury of six is permissible); *Ballew v. Georgia,* 435 U.S. 223 (1978) (a jury of five is too small).

permitting non-unanimous verdicts are also allowed, as long as the vote to convict represents a "substantial majority" of the jurors.[29]

Because the purpose of the jury system is to protect an accused from governmental oppression and to provide her with the common-sense judgment of the community, a defendant is entitled to a jury drawn from a pool of persons constituting a fair cross-section of the community.[30] This Sixth Amendment right is violated if large, distinctive groups of persons, such as women, racial minorities, or adherents of a specific major religion, are systematically and unjustifiably excluded from the jury pool.

[B] Burden of Proof

The due process clauses of the United States Constitution[31] require the prosecutor in a criminal trial to persuade the factfinder "beyond a reasonable doubt of every fact necessary to constitute the crime . . . charged."[32] The meaning of this language, and the effect of failing to meet this burden of proof, are matters considered in detail in Chapter 7.

[C] Jury Nullification[33]

[1] The Issue: In General

Are there circumstances in which a jury should acquit an individual, even if the prosecutor proves beyond a reasonable doubt that the accused committed the offense charged? For example, should jurors acquit a defendant if they believe that the criminal law she violated is immoral or unwise, because they feel that she has been "punished enough" already, or because they believe that the police or prosecutors misbehaved in some manner in bringing her to trial?

Juries ordinarily return general verdicts in criminal proceedings. That is, a jury does not explain its verdict; it simply finds the defendant "guilty" or "not guilty."[34] Moreover, the Fifth Amendment of the United States Constitution provides that "[n]o person shall . . . be subject for the same offense to be twice put in jeopardy." Therefore, the Government may not

---

[29] *Johnson v. Louisiana,* 406 U.S. 356 (1972) (a 9-3 guilty verdict is constitutional).

[30] *Taylor v. Louisiana,* 419 U.S. 522 (1975).

[31] The Fifth and Fourteenth Amendments each contain a due process clause. The Fifth Amendment applies in the federal system, whereas the Fourteenth Amendment pertains to the states.

[32] *In re Winship,* 397 U.S. 358, 364 (1970).

[33] See generally Thomas Andrew Green, Verdict According to Conscience (1985); Erick J. Haynie, Comment, *Populism, Free Speech, and the Rule of Law: The "Fully Informed" Jury Movement and Its Implications*, 88 J. Crim. L. & Criminology 343 (1997); Alan Scheflin & Jon Van Dyke, *Jury Nullification: The Contours of a Controversy*, 43 Law & Contemp. Probs. 51 (1980); Phillip B. Scott, *Jury Nullification: An Historical Perspective on a Modern Debate*, 91 W. Va. L. Rev. 389 (1989).

[34] One common exception exists: in many states a jury that acquits a defendant on the basis of insanity may return a verdict of "not guilty by reason of insanity." See § 25.02[C], *infra.*

prosecute a defendant again, for the same crime, after a "not guilty" verdict. Consequently, a jury *can* acquit a defendant without stating its reason and, no matter what its justification may have been, its verdict is non-reversible. In short, jurors have the raw power to acquit a person whom they believe, beyond a reasonable doubt, is legally guilty of an offense. But, *should* juries use this power to "nullify" the law? "Jury nullification" has been the subject of rich and eloquent debate over the centuries.

[2] The Debate

Advocates of jury nullification point out that the trial-by-jury right is recognized in order to protect against governmental oppression, and to provide the accused with the common sense judgment of lay people. [35] As Judge Learned Hand put it, the institution of the jury "introduces a slack into the enforcement of the law, tempering its rigor by the mollifying influence of current ethical conventions." [36] A finding of guilt is not simply a determination that the accused did the acts charged; it also represents a judgment by the jury—the "conscience of the community" [37] and "the oracle of the citizenry" [38] —that the defendant *should* be subjected to the condemnation and formal punishment that results from a conviction. The jury-nullification power, therefore, serves as the community's safeguard against morally unjust or socially undesirable (albeit legally proper) criminal convictions that less flexible judges might impose. [39] For example, in 1735, a colonial jury acquitted Peter Zenger, the confessed printer of a journal that published articles critical of British authorities, of seditious libel. And, in the nineteenth century, Northern juries acquitted individuals who assisted slaves to escape their "owners," who were prosecuted under then-existing federal fugitive slave laws.

Critics respond that although a jury has the raw power to nullify the law, it should not exercise it. They suggest that for every benevolent example of jury nullification to which its advocates point, there are "numerous and notorious examples" of malignant nullification, such as when Southern juries in the 1950s refused to convict white men for lynchings and other murders of civil rights workers, despite overwhelming evidence of guilt. [40] Moreover, to the extent that a jury acts on the basis of its conclusion that a particular law is unjust, the jury-nullification power "[c]ast[s] aside . . .

---

[35] See § 1.02[A][1], *supra*.

[36] *United States ex rel. McCann v. Adams,* 126 F.2d 774, 776 (2d Cir. 1942).

[37] *Witherspoon v. Illinois,* 391 U.S. 510, 519 & n.15 (1968).

[38] *United States v. Gilliam,* 994 F.2d 97, 101 (2d Cir. 1993).

[39] There is very little discussion in the literature of *judicial* nullification, although it doubtlessly occurs on occasion. The Model Penal Code provides for judicial authority to dismiss a prosecution in specified circumstances, notwithstanding the defendant's possible factual guilt. The Code does not characterize this as judicial nullification, but rather as the implementation of a "de minimis" defense. Model Penal Code § 2.12. See generally Stanislaw Pomorski, *On Multiculturalism, Concepts of Crime, and the "De Minimis" Defense,* 1997 B.Y.U. L. Rev. 51.

[40] See *United States v. Thomas,* 116 F.3d 606, 616 (2d Cir. 1997).

our basic belief that only our elected representatives may determine what is a crime and what is not, and only they may revise that law if it is found to be unfair."[41] Jurors take an oath before they are empaneled to obey the judge's instructions on the law. If jurors understand and yet ignore the law out of sympathy for the defendant, lack of compassion for the victim, or dislike for the governing law, the jurors have violated their oath. To require such an oath and yet recognize jury nullification "would confuse any conscientious citizen serving on a jury."[42]

[3] The Law

The issue of jury nullification may arise in various legal contexts. First, the judge might instruct the jury that, if it finds beyond a reasonable doubt that the defendant committed the crime charged, it "must" find her guilty. Or, the judge might expressly inform the jury that it has a duty to follow her instructions, even if it disagrees with them. The general rule is that such instructions are permissible because, "while the *power* to nullify exists, . . . there is no concomitant *right* to nullify."[43]

Second, the defense may be bold enough to request the judge to instruct the jury that it is entitled to act upon its conscientious feelings to acquit the defendant, or the issue may arise in the context of a defense counsel's call to the jury during closing arguments to exercise its power to nullify the law and acquit. Although a very few courts have allowed jury-nullification arguments to the jury,[44] the overwhelming rule is that such arguments and jury instructions in this regard are impermissible.[45] And, at least one court has stated that a judge may even refuse to inform a jury of its nullification power when it asks if it has such authority.[46]

Third, a prosecutor may seek to have a juror discharged during deliberations if there is evidence that she intends to nullify the law and vote to acquit. Trial courts are exceedingly hesitant to grant such motions. Jury deliberations are supposed to occur in secret, so that jurors may talk freely amongst themselves; a discharge motion cannot realistically be granted without intruding into the deliberative process. Moreover, it will often be very difficult to distinguish between a juror who has made a statement

---

[41] *State v. Ragland,* 519 A.2d 1361, 1369 (N.J. 1986).

[42] *Id.* at 1371.

[43] *People v. Engelman,* 92 Cal. Rptr. 2d 416, 418 (App.), *cert. granted,* 997 P.2d 1043 (Cal. 2000) (approving an anti-nullification instruction); see also *Watts v. United States,* 362 A.2d 706 (D.C. 1976) (*en banc*) (approving use of "must" in instruction); *State v. Ragland,* 519 A.2d 1361 (N.J. 1986) (*id.*).

[44] E.g., *United States v. Datcher,* 830 F. Supp. 411 (M.D. Tenn. 1993) (permitting the defense to argue to the jury that it should acquit because of a "draconian sentence" hanging over the defendant; but stating in dictum that it would not have permitted an instruction on jury nullification if it had been requested).

[45] E.g., *United States v. Dougherty,* 473 F.2d 1113 (D.C. Cir. 1972); *State v. Hatori,* 990 P.2d 115 (Hawaii App. 1999); *State v. Ragland,* 519 A.2d 1361 (N.J. 1986); *State v. Bjerkaas,* 472 N.W.2d 615 (Wis. Ct. App. 1991).

[46] *People v. Nichols,* 54 Cal. App. 4th 21, 62 Cal. Rptr. 2d 433 (1997).

indicating that she plans to nullify the law and one who simply believes that the Government has failed to satisfy its burden of proof. Although there is little case law on point, the better rule seems to be that judges "may not delve too deeply into a juror's motivations," and that "if the record evidence discloses any possibility that the request to discharge stems from the juror's view of the sufficiency of the government's evidence, the court must deny the request."[47]

[4] Race-Based Nullification[48]

Professor Paul Butler, a former prosecutor, recently wrote: "[F]or pragmatic and policy reasons, the black community is better off when some nonviolent lawbreakers remain in the community rather than go to prison."[49] Therefore, he has called on African-American jurors to acquit African-American defendants charged with victimless and nonviolent offenses, even if they are guilty, except in unusual circumstances. For example, he suggests, a jury should acquit a black thief who stole from an expensive department store, but perhaps should not acquit if the victim was a neighbor.

Butler states that his "goal is the subversion of American criminal justice, at least as it now exists."[50] He advocates "black self-help" outside the courtroom (through community-building activities, such as mentoring, tutoring, providing medical and legal care for the poor) and inside the courtroom (though jury nullification).[51] He defends his proposal on the ground that African-Americans are imprisoned disproportionately as a result of malignant factors (e.g., racial discrimination in the criminal justice system and society as a whole) and on the ground that imprisonment of nonviolent offenders causes more harm than good in the African-American community. Butler states that black jurors should send a message of their disapproval of, and lack of faith in, the justice system by acquitting nonviolent and victimless offenders.

Professor Andrew Leipold, while sympathetic to many of Butler's criticisms of the justice system, has argued forcefully against race-based jury nullification. First, he provides a narrow, technical argument: given ordinary rules of evidence, the typical jury will not have the information it needs (for example, information relating to the defendant's degree of dangerousness) to make an informed decision whether to nullify the law. Second, he

---

[47] *United States v. Brown*, 823 F.2d 591, 596 (D.C. Cir. 1987).

[48] See generally Paul D. Butler, *Race-Based Jury Nullification: Case-In-Chief*, 30 J. Marshall L. Rev. 911 (1997); Paul Butler, *Racially Based Jury Nullification: Black Power in the Criminal Justice System*, 105 Yale L.J. 677 (1995); Andrew D. Leipold, *Race-Based Jury Nullification: Rebuttal (Part A)*, 30 J. Marshall L. Rev. 923 (1997); Andrew D. Leipold, *The Dangers of Race-Based Jury Nullification: A Response to Professor Butler*, 44 UCLA L. Rev. 109 (1996).

[49] Butler, Yale Law Journal, Note 48, *supra*, at 679.

[50] *Id*. at 680.

[51] Butler, John Marshall Law Review, Note 48, *supra*, at 912–13.

fears that "[o]nce we have agreed that jurors can legitimately decide the outcome of cases by a cost-benefit analysis rather than by applying the law as written to the evidence presented, we have started down a dangerous road."[52] If blacks begin nullifying the law, other groups will do the same, and the result could be legal anarchy. For example, a jury might acquit a guilty wife beater because the victim nagged him: "We might be repelled by this reasoning, but we [would] not have any standing to complain about the process by which the outcome was reached."[53] Finally, Leipold rejects the Butler proposal because "whether you go to jail or get set free should not depend on the color of your skin."[54] He argues that race-based judgments are bad on principle, and bad because they encourage precisely the type of stereotyping that has unfairly led to the evils that inspired Butler's plan.

---

[52] Leipold, John Marshall Law Review, Note 48, *supra*, at 925.

[53] *Id*. at 926.

[54] *Id*.

CHAPTER 7
UNDERSTANDING EVIDENCE

By

Paul C. Giannelli

*Albert J. Weatherhead, III and Richard W. Weatherhead Professor
of Law
Case Western Reserve University School of Law*

Chapter 7
OVERVIEW OF EVIDENCE LAW

§ 1.01 Introduction

Lee Harvey Oswald either shot President Kennedy or he did not. This is an important question, but for trial lawyers, the question is whether a party — here, the prosecution — could have proved Oswald's guilt at a trial. This is where the rules of evidence come into play. They govern how we go about the task of attempting to determine what occurred in the past, often under circumstances of uncertainty. What if there were no eyewitnesses to a crime? What if there were two eyewitnesses, but they disagreed?

This chapter introduces the subject of "proof" at trial and then examines one way to classify the rules of evidence. Next, the Federal Rules of Evidence — their enactment and interpretation — are considered. Finally, some basic themes in evidence law are briefly explored.

§ 1.02 Proof at Trial

There are some basic issues that any system of proof would need to confront. We, of course, will focus on the adversarial system used in this country.[1]

Burdens of proof. A fundamental issue involves the allocation of burdens of proof: the burden of persuasion and the burden of production.[2] What if the evidence adduced at trial is insufficiently persuasive under some defined standard? Who should lose the case? Moreover, in defining the burden of persuasion do we want to favor one party over another by placing a thumb on the scales of justice, so to speak? There are two types of errors that can be made in a criminal case: (1) false positives — convicting the innocent, and (2) false negatives — acquitting the guilty. As a policy matter, we want to avoid the former more than the latter, and thus, we use a higher standard in criminal cases, *i.e.,* proof beyond a reasonable doubt. The same policy issue is absent in civil litigation. Thus, a preponderance of evidence standard is used because the system is expensive and we do not want a tie at the end of a one week, one month, or one year trial. Special procedural rules, called presumptions, assist parties in meeting their burdens of proof.[3]

EVIDENCE

---

[1] Our system of proof is very different from the system used in civil law countries in Europe and elsewhere. *See* Damaska, *Presentation of Evidence and Factfinding Precision*, 123 U. Pa. L. Rev. 1083 (1975); Langbein, *The German Advantage in Civil Procedure*, 52 U. Chi. L. Rev. 823 (1985); Van Kessel, *Adversary Excesses in the American Criminal Trial*, 67 Notre Dame L. Rev. 403 (1992).

[2] *See infra* chapter 4 (burdens of proof).

[3] Fed. R. Evid. 301. *See infra* chapter 5 (presumptions & inferences).

"Housekeeping" rules. We also need some "housekeeping" rules. In offering evidence, who should go first? Who goes second and does the first party have a right to rebut? The order of trial is: (1) plaintiff (prosecution) case-in-chief, (2) defense case-in-chief, (3) plaintiff rebuttal, and (4) defense surrebuttal.[4] The party with the burden of production goes first because if that party fails to meet that burden, the trial can end with a directed verdict right then. In examining witnesses, the same issues arise: who examines first, second, and should there be any further examination? The answer: (1) direct examination, (2) cross-examination, (3) redirect examination, and (4) recross examination.[5]

Testimonial proof. In the common law system, proof typically comes in the form of witness testimony. The first issue is who should be considered a *competent* witness.[6] Another issue is the *credibility* of witnesses, *i.e.,* their worthiness of belief.[7] Some witnesses lie, but more often witnesses are inaccurate for other reasons, such as poor eyesight, unconscious bias, or a poor opportunity to observe. Efforts to diminish a witness's credibility fall under the rubric of "impeachment."

Lay witnesses. Evidence law makes a distinction between ordinary witnesses (called "lay" or "fact" witnesses) and experts.[8] As for lay witnesses, the primary rule is that they testify based on their personal observations — the "firsthand knowledge" rule.[9] For example, persons who were not physically present at a bank robbery should not testify about how the bank was robbed based merely on their speculation. We want an eyewitness.

Hearsay. If the eyewitness from the bank robbery tells another person about the robbery, should that other person be allowed to testify about the robbery as a mere conduit? The hearsay rule says "no." We need to be able to cross-examine the eyewitness about what that person saw. For present purposes, hearsay may be defined as an out-of-court statement offered for the truth of its assertion. Oh, yes, there really are 29 exceptions, but you need to know only about a dozen major exceptions.[10]

Documentary evidence. In addition to testimony, proof may consist of documentary evidence. The use of writings at trial produced several rules. The first deals with *authentication*, which requires the offering party to establish that a document is what that party says it is.[11] Assume the accused has signed a written confession in a criminal case. Evidence law typically rejects *self-authentication*, *i.e.,* letting the document speak for itself. Thus, the prosecution would need to put a witness on the stand to

---

[4] *See infra* chapter 3 (stages of trial).

[5] *See infra* chapter 20 (examination of witnesses).

[6] *See infra* chapter 18 (witness competency).

[7] *See infra* chapter 22 (credibility of witnesses).

[8] *See infra* chapter 23 (lay witnesses); chapter 24 (expert testimony).

[9] Fed. R. Evid. 602.

[10] *See infra* chapters 31–35 (hearsay rule & a bunch of exceptions).

[11] Fed. R. Evid. 901. *See infra* chapter 28 (authentication of writings).

authenticate the confession — here, the detective who obtained the confession could testify that the accused signed the confession in the detective's presence.[12] In addition, a person sufficiently familiar with the accused's signature could identify that signature. Other methods of authentication include the "ancient document" rule[13] and the "reply rule."[14] We also permit an expert or the jury to compare a document with known exemplars. In contrast, certain types of documents such as public records are self-authenticating, and the Federal Rules has expanded this category to include newspapers, trademarks, commercial paper, and so forth.[15]

A second rule, known as the *rule of completeness*, allows a party to introduce a part of writing (or recording) immediately in order to place the writing in context if the other side has introduced a different part of the writing.[16] A third rule comes into play when a party tries to prove the contents of a writing, which might be important in a contract dispute or will contest. Although the phrase original document rule is the more apt description, this rule is typically called the *"best evidence"* rule.[17] In short, sometimes we want the original produced.

Real evidence. Another type of proof is referred to as "real" evidence.[18] An example would be a murder weapon, such as a gun, knife, or baseball bat. Perhaps the prosecution wants to trace the murder weapon back to the accused. If so, the prosecutor would have to show that the gun seized at the murder scene was the same weapon the prosecutor was attempting to admit at trial, at which time a witness could identify it as the defendant's gun. One way to do this is to establish the *chain of custody* for the gun.[19]

Photographs. Typically, photographs are taken at a murder scene, and courts have long admitted them into evidence, provided a witness to the crime scene can testify that the photographs are an "accurate and fair representation" of the scene.[20] The witness, who has firsthand knowledge of the scene, in effect, adopts the photograph as her testimony. This is known as the *pictorial communication* theory of admissibility. If this method is not possible (*e.g.,* surveillance camera in an empty store), the pictures can be admitted through the testimony of a person familiar with

[12] The prosecution could not call the accused to authenticate the confession because of the Fifth Amendment privilege against compulsory self-incrimination. *See infra* § 43.05 (accused's privilege at trial).

[13] "Ancient" here means 20 years. *See* Fed. R. 803(16); Fed. R. 901(b)(8). *See infra* § 28.07 (ancient documents).

[14] For example, I send you a letter and you reply. That's it. *See infra* § 28.5[A] (reply rule).

[15] Fed. R. Evid. 902.

[16] Fed. R. Evid. 106. *See infra* chapter 29.

[17] Fed. R. Evid. 1002. *See infra* chapter 30.

[18] *See infra* chapter 26.

[19] Fed. R. Evid. 901 covers real evidence as well as documentary evidence. Moreover, a chain of custody is not the only way to identify real evidence. For example, if the police officer who recovered the gun at the crime scene placed her initials on the weapon, the gun would be "readily identifiable" and thus admissible under most circumstances.

[20] *See infra* chapter 27 (photographs, videos, computer simulations).

the operation of the surveillance system (the *"silent witness"* theory). Comparable rules were developed for movies and later applied to videotapes.

Demonstrations, models, etc. Models, blackboards, and charts may be used to illustrate testimony.[21] In some cases, a witness may exhibit a scar or amputated arm to show the jury the result of an accident (*in-court exhibition*), or, perhaps demonstrate how she can no longer walk without a limp (*in-court demonstration*). Computer animations are now used for such illustrative purposes, although they can also be used for other purposes.

Judge & jury functions. In this system, we also need to allocate responsibility between the judge and jury.[22] The jury decides the "facts," which includes the credibility of witnesses. The judge decides the admissibility of evidence (once an objection is raised) and generally runs the trial.[23]

§ 1.03 Law of Evidence

When first approached, evidence law can appear to be just a "bunch of rules" — and it is that. But there are several ways to classify the rules of evidence that may be of assistance.[24] One way is by type of proof — testimonial, documentary, real, and so forth, as was done in the preceding section. Another way is to divide the subject into three major categories: (1) rules governing the substantive content of evidence, (2) rules governing witnesses, and (3) substitutes for evidence.

[A] Rules Governing the Content of Evidence

There are two main categories of evidentiary rules concerning the substantive content of evidence: *relevance rules* and *competence rules*.

[1] Relevance Rules

All evidence must be relevant. Irrelevant evidence is always inadmissible.[25] Stated another way — relevancy is the threshold issue in deciding the admissibility of all evidence. There are an almost infinite variety of relevancy problems. Some situations have come before the courts so often that "rules of thumb" on admissibility have developed — *e.g.*, "similar happenings," "adverse inferences," and "out-of-court experiments."[26] In other situations, categorical rules have resulted. For instance, character

---

[21] *See infra* chapter 26 (real & demonstrative evidence).

[22] *See infra* chapter 2 (roles of judge & jury).

[23] *See infra* chapter 6 (objections & offers of proof); chapter 7 (preliminary questions of admissibility).

[24] The organization of the Federal Rules of Evidence is set forth *infra* § 1.04[D].

[25] Fed. R. Evid. 402.

[26] *See infra* chapter 9 (relevancy & its counterparts).

evidence is generally prohibited, although there are exceptions.[27] Other relevance rules govern habit[28] and insurance evidence.[29]

[2] Competence Rules

Relevancy, however, is not enough. Relevant evidence may be excluded for various reasons. These reasons are found in competency rules, which can be divided into two subcategories.

[a] Rules Based on Reliability Concerns

Sometimes we exclude evidence because it is believed to be unreliable. The hearsay[30] and "best evidence" rules are examples.[31] Here, relevant evidence is inadmissible due to another evidentiary rule.

[b] Rules Based on External Policies

Competency rules may also be based on some policy extrinsic to the trial process — *i.e.*, rules of privilege. We exclude communications between client and lawyer because we want to encourage such communications. Other common privileges include communications between spouses, doctors-patients, psychotherapists-patients, and clergy-communicants.[32] Here, we exclude evidence that may be both relevant and reliable.

[B] Rules Governing Witnesses

Rules relating to witnesses can be divided into several categories: (1) competency of witnesses, (2) examination of witnesses, (3) types of witnesses (lay and expert), and (4) credibility of witnesses. These were briefly touched upon in the previous section.

[1] Competency of Witnesses

The competency of a witness (as opposed to the competence of the evidence discussed above) refers to the mental capacity of the witness to observe, recall, and relate what that witness has seen and the moral capacity to recognize the obligation to testify truthfully. At common law, competency rules excluded any person with an interest in the case (including the parties), children, the insane, and so forth. For the most part, these

---

[27] Rules 404, 405, and 412–15 deal explicitly with character. *See infra* chapters 10–11.

[28] Fed. R. Evid. 406. *See infra* chapter 12 (habit & routine practice).

[29] Fed. R. Evid. 411. *See infra* chapter 17 (insurance). Another set of relevance rules are based on ancillary policies. Rules 407– 410 all involve the exclusion of relevant evidence based on policy reasons external to the truth-seeking function of the trial. For example, subsequent remedial measures (Rule 407) are excluded in order to encourage people to make repairs after accidents. *See infra* chapters 13–16. The federal drafters placed these rules in Article IV, which is the relevancy article. However, these rules function as competence rules.

[30] *See infra* chapters 31–35 (hearsay rule & exceptions).

[31] *See infra* chapter 30 (best evidence rule).

[32] *See infra* chapters 37–43 on privileges.

EVIDENCE

rules have been transformed into credibility rules. Indeed, Federal Rule 601 states that everyone is competent to testify. Nevertheless, a few problems remain.[33] Will a two-year old child be permitted to testify?

[2] Examination of Witnesses

As noted in the previous section, there are housekeeping rules governing the order of evidence presentation at trial and the order of witness examination (direct, cross, redirect, and recross).[34] There, are additional rules. For example, "leading questions" are generally prohibited on direct examination but are allowed on cross-examination.[35] Moreover, witnesses forget stuff, so we let them refresh their recollections with documents.[36]

[3] Types of Witnesses

Evidence law divides witnesses into two categories — experts and lay witnesses; the latter are often called fact witnesses.

[a] Lay Witnesses

There are two principal rules relating to lay witnesses. First, lay witness testimony must be based on personal observations — *i.e.,* "firsthand knowledge" rule.[37] Second, we prefer witnesses to testify in terms of their primary sensory impressions rather than to opinions, inferences, or conclusions drawn from those perceptions. If possible, we prefer the witness to testify that the defendant drew a pistol, aimed it at the bank teller, and then fired the pistol, rather than: "The teller was killed in cold blood." This is the much misunderstood "opinion rule."[38]

[b] Expert Witnesses

Some topics are beyond the common understanding of most lay jurors, and in such situations, we use expert witnesses to educate the jurors.[39] For example, had the victim already died from a heart attack before the defendant negligently ran over the victim who was lying in the middle of the street? Here, a physician could provide the jury with helpful information. The use of experts requires a standard for defining the proper *subject matter* of expert testimony[40] and a rule on who *qualifies* as an expert in

---

[33] *See infra* chapter 18 (witness competency). There is still an oath requirement (Rule 603) and we don't want the judge or jurors testifying in the case. Rules 605 and 606(a).

[34] *See infra* chapter 3 (stages of trial) & chapter 20 (examination of witnesses).

[35] Fed. R. Evid. 611(c).

[36] Fed. R. Evid. 612. *See infra* chapter 21 (refreshing recollection).

[37] Fed. R. Evid. 602. *See infra* § 23.02 (firsthand knowledge rule).

[38] Fed. R. Evid. 701. *See infra* § 23.03 (opinion rule).

[39] *See infra* chapter 24 (expert testimony).

[40] The subject matter of expert testimony raises two issue. Some types of evidence, such as the polygraph, may be considered too unreliable for courtroom use. The second issue involves testimony that is so common that a lay juror can handle the issue without the assistance of

that subject matter.[41] In order to take advantage of the witness's expertise, the common law permitted an expert to testify in the form of an opinion, *e.g.*, "In my opinion, the victim died of a heart attack."

In addition, a rule on the *bases* of expert testimony is required.[42] Clearly, an expert with firsthand knowledge should be allowed to testify, *i.e.*, the physician who performed the autopsy. But what about a physician who was not present at the autopsy? Here, the common law dispensed with the firsthand knowledge requirement and provided the expert with the facts through the use of a *hypothetical question*, provided all the facts were established by other witnesses (facts in the record). The federal drafters went beyond the common law, permitting an expert to testify based on facts provided outside of court (nonrecord facts) if these facts are the type reasonably relied upon by experts in the field.[43]

[4] Credibility

Credibility is simply a witness's worthiness of belief.[44] Credibility may be viewed in three stages: (1) bolstering, (2) impeachment, and (3) rehabilitation. Credibility issues most often involve *impeachment, i.e.,* attempts to diminish or attack a witness's credibility.

There are five main lines of attack: bias, untruthful character,[45] sensory or mental defect, prior inconsistent statements (self-contradiction),[46] and specific contradiction.[47] There are no specific Federal Rules on bias or sensory-mental defect impeachment, but they are recognized in the cases.[48] In addition, the common law had a special impeachment rule for experts — the "learned treatise" rule.[49]

Bolstering and rehabilitation refer to attempts to support a witness's credibility; the difference is one of timing — bolstering comes before, impeachment and rehabilitation after.

---

an expert. For instance, we do not need expert testimony on the laws of gravity in a homicide case in which the accused is charged with throwing a large rock from a highway overpass, killing the occupants of a car traveling on the highway below.

[41] Fed. R. Evid. 702.

[42] *See infra* chapter 25 (bases of expert testimony).

[43] Fed. R. Evid. 703.

[44] *See infra* chapter 22 (credibility).

[45] There are several different ways to prove untruthful character: (1) reputation or opinion evidence, Rule 608(a), (2) prior conviction, Rule 609, and (3) specific instances reflecting untruthful character that have not resulted in a conviction, Rule 608(b).

[46] Fed. R. Evid. 613.

[47] A prior inconsistent statement involves self-contradiction by one witness — *i.e.*, the prior statement is inconsistent with the witness's trial testimony. Specific contradiction involves two different witnesses, *e.g.*, Smith testifies that the accused shot the victim, while Jones testifies that somebody else shot the victim.

[48] There are other rules on impeachment. Rule 610 prohibits the impeachment use of a witness's religious beliefs.

[49] Fed. R. Evid. 803(18). *See infra* § 33.16 (learned treatise hearsay exception).

[C] Substitutes for Evidence

The party with the burden of production is obligated to introduce evidence to satisfy that burden. This obligation is excused in two circumstances: (1) where the judge takes judicial notice of a fact[50] and (2) where the parties stipulate (agree) to a fact.[51]

§ 1.04 Federal Rules of Evidence

Before the Federal Rules were enacted in 1975, evidence law was basically a common law subject. There were, of course, a few exceptions; the law of privilege was mostly statutory, and most jurisdictions had codified hearsay exceptions for business and official records.

Several efforts at codification had been attempted. In 1942, the American Law Institute promulgated the Model Code of Evidence.[52] The Model Code, however, was considered so radical by the practicing bar that it was never adopted by any state. In 1953, the Commissioners on Uniform State Laws threw their hat into the ring, promulgating the Uniform Rules of Evidence.[53] Although not as radical as the Model Rules, the Uniform Rules were adopted by only a few jurisdictions. In 1967, California ventured out on its own and enacted an Evidence Code, which continues to this day.

[A] Drafting the Rules

In 1961, a committee appointed by Chief Justice Earl Warren recommended the adoption of uniform Federal Rules of Evidence.[54] Following the recommendation of this committee, the Chief Justice appointed an Advisory Committee to draft the Federal Rules in 1965.[55] The Advisory Committee published a preliminary draft in 1969[56] and a revised draft in 1971.[57] The

---

[50] *See infra* chapter 44 (judicial notice).

[51] *See infra* chapter 45 (stipulations).

[52] Model Code of Evidence (1942). When the ALI undertook the task of clarifying the common law through its Restatement of Law project, the law of evidence was considered. The ALI abandoned this project because "however much that law needs clarification in order to produce reasonable certainty in its application, the Rules themselves in numerous and important instances are so defective that instead of being the means of developing truth, they operate to suppress it." *Id.* at viii.

[53] *See* Uniform Rules of Evidence (1953). After the Federal Rules of Evidence were drafted, a new version, promulgated in 1974, was adopted; this version was patterned on the Federal Rules. The present version, which continues to follow the Federal Rules, was promulgated in 1999.

[54] *See A Preliminary Report on the Advisability and Feasibility of Developing Uniform Rules of Evidence for the United States District Courts*, 30 F.R.D. 73 (1962).

[55] *See* 36 F.R.D. 128 (1965).

[56] *See Preliminary Draft of Proposed Rules of Evidence for the United States District Courts and Magistrates*, 46 F.R.D. 161 (1969).

[57] *See Revised Draft of Proposed Rules of Evidence for the United States Courts and Magistrates*, 51 F.R.D. 315 (1971).

Federal Rules were promulgated by the Supreme Court in November 1972 and transmitted to Congress in February 1973.[58]

[B] Congressional Intervention

Congress reacted by enacting legislation that deferred the effective date of the Federal Rules,[59] and extensive hearings on the rules were held by both the House and Senate Judiciary Committees.[60] In 1975, the Federal Rules emerged from Congress in statutory form.[61] Congress had amended the Court-promulgated rules in a number of significant respects.[62] The legislative history of these amendments is found in the various committee reports[63] and in the Congressional Record.[64]

[C] Amendment of the Rules

The Federal Rules have been amended numerous times since their adoption. There are two ways in which the Rules may be amended: (1) an act of Congress, and (2) promulgation by the Supreme Court through its statutory rulemaking authority, which is subject to congressional supervision. Both vehicles have been used to make amendments.[65]

[D] Structure of Federal Rules

The Federal Rules are organized by Article:

Article I	General Provisions (objections, offers of proof, etc.)
Article II	Judicial Notice
Article III	Presumptions
Article IV	Relevancy (character, habit, remedial measures, etc.)
Article V	Privileges
Article VI	Witnesses (competency, impeachment, examination)
Article VII	Opinions (lay opinions, expert testimony)
Article VIII	Hearsay

---

[58] *See Rules of Evidence for United States Courts and Magistrates*, 56 F.R.D. 183 (1973).

[59] Act of March 30, 1973, Pub. L. No. 93-12, 87 Stat. 9. *See also* H.R. Rep. No. 93-52, 93d Cong., 1st Sess. (1973).

[60] *See Proposed Rules of Evidence: Hearings Before the Special Subcommittee on Reform of Federal Criminal Laws of the Committee on the Judiciary, House of Representatives*, 93d Cong., 1st Sess. (1973); *Federal Rules of Evidence: Hearings Before the Committee on the Judiciary*, U.S. Senate, 93d Cong., 2d Sess. (1974).

[61] Act of January 2, 1975, Pub. L. No. 93-595, 88 Stat. 1926.

[62] The single most important example was the rejection of Article V, which contained thirteen rules of privilege. *See infra* § 37.02 (Federal Rule 501).

[63] *See* H.R. Rep. No. 650, 93d Cong., 1st Sess. (1973), reprinted in 1974 U.S.C.C.A.N. 7075; S. Rep. No. 1277, 93d Cong., 2d Sess. (1974), reprinted in 1974 U.S.C.C.A.N. 7051; H.R. Rep. No. 1597, 93d Cong., 2d Sess, (1974), reprinted in 1974 U.S.C.C.A.N. 7098 (conference report).

[64] For a detailed history of the adoption of the Federal Rules, *see* 21 Wright & Graham, Federal Practice and Procedure § 5006 (1977).

[65] *See* Capra, *A Recipe for Confusion: Congress and the Federal Rules of Evidence*, 55 U. Miami L. Rev. 691 (2001).

Article IX   Authentication (documents, real evidence, etc.)

Article X   Original Document Rule ("best evidence rule")

Article XI   Miscellaneous Rules (excepting certain proceedings such as grand juries from the Rules of Evidence)[66]

§ 1.05 State Adoptions of the Federal Rules

Even before the Federal Rules of Evidence were adopted, some states enacted or promulgated evidence rules based on the preliminary and revised drafts of the Federal Rules. After the Federal Rules were proposed, a new version of the Uniform Rules of Evidence was promulgated (1974); this version was patterned on the Federal Rules and has been revised (1999). As of today, over forty jurisdictions, including the military, have rules patterned after the Federal Rules. Most states have made changes in the Federal Rules when adopting them; sometimes the changes have been extensive.

Even jurisdictions that have not adopted the Federal Rules in toto have sometimes accepted a single rule as part of that state's common law.[67] For example, in *Daye v. Commonwealth*,[68] the Massachusetts Supreme Judicial Court adopted Federal Rule 801(d)(1)(A) on prior inconsistent statements as a matter of state common law.

As a federal statute not intended to preempt state law, the Federal Rules are not binding on the states. Thus, a state court is not required to interpret a state evidence rule, even one identical to its federal counterpart, in the same way that the federal rule is construed. For example, the Arizona Supreme Court declined to follow the Supreme Court's decision in *Daubert v. Merrell Dow Pharm., Inc.*[69] That case involved an interpretation of Rule 702, which governs the admissibility of expert testimony. The state court noted that it was "not bound by the United States Supreme Court's non-constitutional construction of the Federal Rules of Evidence when we construe the Arizona Rules of Evidence."[70] The court also remarked: "Our rules . . . are court-enacted. While the United States Supreme Court considers congressional purpose, this court when construing a rule we have adopted must rely on text and our own intent in adopting or amending the rule in the first instance."[71]

---

[66] The numbering of each rule corresponds to this framework. Because Article VIII governs hearsay, all the hearsay rules begin with the number 8 — for example, Rule 801 defines hearsay and Rules 803, 804, and 807 contain the hearsay exceptions.

[67] The following states have not adopted the Federal Rules: Connecticut, Georgia, Illinois, Kansas, Massachusetts, Missouri, New York, and Virginia. California has its own code.

[68] 469 N.E.2d 483 (Mass. 1984).

[69] 509 U.S. 579 (1993).

[70] *State v. Bible,* 858 P.2d 1152, 1183 (Ariz. 1993).

[71] *Id.*

§ 1.06 Interpreting the Federal Rules: The "Plain Meaning" Debate

Federal Rule 102, the "purpose and construction" provision, provides: "These rules shall be construed to secure fairness in administration, elimination of unjustifiable expense and delay, and promotion of growth and development of the law of evidence to the end that the truth may be ascertained and proceedings justly determined." The goals set out in this rule (there are 5 or 6) often serve cross-purposes. Consequently, the rule is not particularly helpful.[72]

The principal problem concerns the relationship between the Rules and the common law. This raises two distinct issues. The first concerns "gaps" in the Rules, *i.e.,* evidence issues not addressed by any rule. The second issue concerns the use of the common law in interpreting specific rules.

The "gap" problem. The Federal Rules were not intended to be a complete codification of all evidentiary rules. Professor Cleary, the Reporter for the Rules, wrote that Rule 102 indicates "one thing of importance: the answers to all questions that may arise under the Rules may not be found in specific terms in the Rules."[73] For example, no provision in the Rules governs the use of bias as a method of impeachment. Nevertheless, when the issue came before the Supreme Court in *United States v. Abel,*[74] the Court held that impeachment of a witness for bias was proper. According to the Court, "the lesson to be drawn is that it is permissible to impeach a witness by showing his bias under the Federal Rules of Evidence just as it was permissible to do so before their adoption."[75]

The second issue concerns interpreting specific rules. There are numerous examples of the need to resort to the common law when interpreting the Rules of Evidence. For example, Rule 301 governs presumptions but does not define that term; the common law must be consulted.[76] Rule 406 governs habit evidence but does not define what habit is; again the common law must be consulted.[77] Rule 613 governs impeachment by prior inconsistent statements but provides no elaboration of the "inconsistency" requirement; there is a substantial body of evidence case law on this point.[78] As Judge Becker and Professor Orenstein have commented: "Unquestionably, the Federal Rules coexist with unstated common law assumptions that were

---

[72] (Nevertheless, it is good to have a Rule 102 to fill the gap between Rules 101 and 103.)

[73] Cleary, *Preliminary Notes on Reading the Rules of Evidence,* 57 Neb. L. Rev. 908, 908 (1978).

[74] 469 U.S. 45 (1984).

[75] *Id.* at 51. As one court noted, "It is clear that in enacting the Federal Rules of Evidence Congress did not intend to wipe out the years of common-law development in the field of evidence, indeed the contrary is true. The new rules contain many gaps or omissions and in order to answer these unresolved questions, courts certainly should rely on common-law precedent." *Werner v. Upjohn Co.,* 628 F.2d 848, 856 (4th Cir. 1980).

[76] *See infra* § 5.02 (presumptions defined).

[77] *See infra* § 12.02 (habit defined).

[78] *See infra* § 22.10[B] (inconsistency requirement).

never formally incorporated into the corpus of the Rules. The special relationship of the Federal Rules to the common law and the special expertise of the bench in evidentiary matters affect how the Rules should be interpreted."[79]

The Supreme Court, however, has not seen it that way. It has often, but not always, espoused an almost mechanical "plain meaning" approach in construing the Rules of Evidence, treating the Federal Rules as any other statute. In one case, the Court wrote: "We interpret the legislatively enacted Federal Rules of Evidence as we would any statute."[80] This approach has proved controversial. In a different case, Justice Blackmun criticized the Court for "espous[ing] an overly rigid interpretive approach; a more complete analysis casts significant and substantial doubt on the Court's 'plain meaning' easy solution."[81] Commentators' critiques are far stronger.[82]

The Supreme Court in 1995 indicated an intent to place greater reliance on the common law as a source of guidance in interpreting the Federal Rules. In *Tome v. United States*,[83] a case involving the admissibility of a prior consistent statement under Rule 801(d)(1)(B), the Court concluded that the Rule preserved the common-law requirement that the statement had to predate the motive to fabricate. In reaching its conclusion, the Court relied upon the intent of the Advisory Committee: "The [Advisory Committee's] Notes disclose a purpose to adhere to the common law in the

---

[79] Becker & Orenstein, *The Federal Rules of Evidence After Sixteen Years — The Effect of "Plain Meaning" Jurisprudence, the Need for an Advisory Committee on the Rules of Evidence, and Suggestions for Selective Revision of the Rules*, 60 Geo. Wash. L. Rev. 857, 868 (1992).

[80] *Daubert v. Merrell Dow Pharm.*, 509 U.S. 579, 587 (1993). To support its position, the Supreme Court has cited an article by Professor Cleary, the principal drafter. Cleary wrote: "In principle, under the Federal Rules of Evidence no common law of evidence remains. 'All relevant evidence is admissible, except as otherwise provided.' In reality, of course, the body of common law knowledge continues to exist, though in the somewhat altered form of a source of guidance in the exercise of delegated powers." Cleary, *supra* note 72, at 915. However, other parts of Cleary's article point in a different direction: "If what is meant is that meaning is to be ascertained by reading the statute with the aid only of a dictionary and such aphorisms of construction as noscitur a sociis and ejusdem generis as may be suitable, then it must be discarded as unrealistic." *Id.* at 911.

[81] *Bourjaily v. United States*, 483 U.S. 171, 187–88 (1987) (Blackmun, J., dissenting).

[82] *See* Jonakait, *Text, Texts, or Ad Hoc Determinations: Interpretation of the Federal Rules of Evidence*, 71 Ind. L.J. 551, 571 (1996) ("Sometimes we must look beyond the words of the Rules to understand evidentiary doctrine. We must do so when the Rules are not definitive or are ambiguous . . . but sometimes even when the text is clear."); Jonakait, *The Supreme Court, Plain Meaning, and the Changed Rules of Evidence*, 68 Tex. L. Rev. 745, 786 (1990) ("Inevitably, the plain-meaning standard will produce worse evidence law by freezing evidence into a literalistic mold, by eliminating its dynamism, and by mandating results without any attempt to satisfy the policy goals of evidence law."); Weissenberger, *The Supreme Court and the Interpretation of the Federal Rules of Evidence*, 53 Ohio St. L. J. 1307, 1338 (1992) (The Court's approach "has recast the method of interpreting evidentiary principles in a manner that ignores the wisdom of the common-law history of the Federal Rules of Evidence and the capability of enlightened growth."). *But see* Imwinkelried, *A Brief Defense of the Supreme Court's Approach to the Interpretation of the Federal Rules of Evidence*, 27 Ind. L. Rev. 267 (1993).

[83] 513 U.S. 150 (1995).

application of evidentiary principles, absent express provisions to the contrary. Where the Rules did depart from their common-law antecedents, in general the Committee said so."[84] The Court also acknowledged that the "common law of evidence was the background against which the Federal Rules were drafted."[85]

§ 1.07 Themes in the Federal Rules

One of the purposes listed in Federal Rule 102, the "purpose and construction" provision, is the ascertainment of truth.[86] Although the truth-seeking function of the trial can be considered its main goal, it is not the only one. The law of privileges, for example, precludes the admissibility of evidence that may be both relevant and reliable.[87] Practical considerations such as the consumption of time is also a counterweight.[88]

Admissibility favored. Even when the ascertainment of truth is the goal, how to achieve that goal is often a matter about which reasonable people may disagree. Here, the federal drafters adopted several guiding principles. First, the Federal Rules are biased in favor of admissibility. When the drafters came to a split in the common law cases, they typically adopted the approach that was more permissive, even if it was the minority view.[89] At other times, the drafters adopted both a majority and minority position.[90] This theme is most pronounced in the rules on hearsay and expert testimony. This position is based on a view that juries are capable of dealing

---

[84] *Id.* at 160-61.

[85] *Id.* at 157.

[86] *See also Portuondo v. Agard,* 529 U.S. 61, 80 (2000) (dissenting opinion) ("truth-finding function of trials"); *Tennessee v. Street,* 471 U.S. 409, 415 (1985) ("there were no alternatives that would have . . . assured the integrity of the trial's truth-seeking function"); *Funk v. United States,* 290 U.S. 371, 381 (1933) ("And, since experience is of all teachers the most dependable, and since experience also is a continuous process, it follows that a rule of evidence at one time thought necessary to the ascertainment of truth should yield to the experience of a succeeding generation whenever that experience has clearly demonstrated the fallacy or unwisdom of the old rule.").

[87] *See infra* § 37.03 (rationale for privileges).

[88] *See* Fed. R. Evid. 403 (relevant evidence may be excluded if its probative value is substantially outweighed by waste of time, undue delay, needless presentation of cumulative evidence); Fed. R. Evid. 611(a). Even Rule 102 recognizes other values: "These rules shall be construed to secure fairness in administration, elimination of unjustifiable expense and delay, and promotion of growth and development of the law of evidence to the end that the truth may be ascertained and proceedings justly determined."

[89] *See* Fed. R. Evid. 803(4) (hearsay exception for statements made for medical treatment or diagnosis); Fed. R. Evid. 804(b)(3) (declarations against penal interests).

[90] Several hearsay exceptions are illustrative. The drafters adopted both a present sense impression exception and excited utterance exception. Fed. R. Evid. 803(1) & (2). The Rules also contain a hearsay exemption for authorized admission and agent-servant admissions. Fed. R. Evid. 801(d)(2)(C) & (D).

with most types of evidence and would reach better decisions with more, rather than less, information. [91]

Trial judge discretion. Another theme is judicial discretion. Although many trial lawyers want fixed rules, which they argue make evidence law more predictable, the drafters believed that too many unforeseen contingencies can arise at trial, and therefore the judge must be given leeway to shape the rules of evidence to deal with them. Rule 807, which recognizes a residual hearsay exception, is perhaps the best example.

Another issue worth considering is the conventional wisdom that much of the law of evidence is designed to keep information from the jury. This position can be traced to Professor Thayer, who wrote his classic text at the turn of the 20th Century. [92] Professor Nance has challenged this view, arguing that many evidence rules are designed to force attorneys to introduce the "best evidence." In short, attorney-control, not jury-control, is the underlying principle. [93]

§ 1.08 Criminal & Civil Trials

Although the Rules of Evidence apply to both criminal and civil cases, a number of rules recognize a distinction between civil and criminal trials — explicitly or by implication. Several rules apply only to criminal proceedings. For example, Rule 104(c) requires an out-of-court hearing to determine the admissibility of a confession. Rule 404(a) recognizes three exceptions to the rule prohibiting the use of character evidence; two of the three exceptions apply only in criminal cases. [94] Similarly, Rule 609(a) requires a special balancing test when a prior felony conviction is offered to impeach a criminal defendant; in all civil cases and for witnesses other than an accused in criminal cases, a prior felony conviction is admissible subject to a different balancing analysis (Rule 403). In effect, there is a higher threshold requirement when evidence of prior convictions is offered to impeach the accused. Another example is found in Rule 803(8), which contains a special limitation on the use of public records in criminal prosecutions.

On the other hand, a number of rules, due to their subject matter, apply only in civil cases — for example, Rule 407 (subsequent remedial measures) and Rule 411 (liability insurance).

Constitutional issues. In criminal prosecutions, application of the Rules must be consistent with constitutional provisions that bear on evidentiary

---

[91] *See* Weinstein, *Rule 702 of the Federal Rules of Evidence is Sound; It Should Not Be Amended*, 138 F.R.D. 631, 631 (1991) ("The Rules were designed to depend primarily upon lawyer-adversaries and sensible triers of fact to evaluate conflicts."). Judge Weinstein was on the drafting committee of the Federal Rules.

[92] Thayer, A Preliminary Treatise on Evidence at the Common Law (1898).

[93] Nance, *The Best Evidence Principle*, 73 Iowa L. Rev. 227 (1988).

[94] Fed. R. Evid. P. 404(a)(1) (an accused may offer evidence of her own character); Fed. R. Evid. P. 404(a)(2) (an accused may offer evidence of the victim's character in some circumstances).

matters. For example, the Confrontation Clause may require the exclusion of hearsay statements even if a statement falls within a recognized hearsay exception.[95]

§ 1.09 Key Points

The Federal Rules of Evidence were enacted in 1975, and over forty jurisdictions, including the military, have rules patterned after the Federal Rules. As a federal statute not intended to preempt state law, the Federal Rules are not binding on the states. Thus, a state court is not required to interpret a state evidence rule, even one identical to its federal counterpart, in the same way that the federal rule is construed.

The paramount goal of a trial is truth-seeking, but that is not the only goal. The law of privileges, for example, precludes the admissibility of evidence that may be both relevant and reliable. Even when the ascertainment of truth is the goal, how to achieve that goal is often a matter about which reasonable people may disagree. Here, the federal drafters adopted several guiding principles. First, the Federal Rules are *biased in favor of admissibility*. Another theme is *judicial discretion*. Although many trial lawyers want fixed rules, which they argue are predictable, the drafters believed that too many contingencies can arise, and therefore the trial judge must be given leeway to shape the rules of evidence to deal with them.

Civil & criminal cases. Although the Rules of Evidence apply to both criminal and civil cases, a number of rules recognize a distinction between civil and criminal trials — explicitly or by implication. A number of rules, due to their subject matter, apply only in civil cases — for example, Rule 407 (subsequent remedial measures), and Rule 411 (liability insurance). Further differences in applicability in criminal and civil proceedings arise due to constitutional principles — *e.g.*, right of confrontation.

Classification of Evidence Law

Evidence law may be divided into three major categories: (1) rules governing the substantive content of evidence, (2) rules governing witnesses, and (3) substitutes for evidence.

 I. Rules Governing the Content of Evidence

  A. Relevance Rules

   1. Character evidence

   2. Other acts evidence

   3. Habit evidence

---

[95] *See infra* chapter 36 (right of confrontation). *See also Davis v. Alaska,* 415 U.S. 308 (1974) (Confrontation Clause requires cross-examination on prior juvenile adjudication notwithstanding state exclusionary rule); *Chambers v. Mississippi,* 410 U.S. 284 (1973) (due process requires admission of reliable hearsay evidence); *Bruton v. United States,* 391 U.S. 123 (1968) (Confrontation Clause requires exclusion of confession implicating codefendant in joint trial).

        4.   Insurance evidence

    B.   Competence Rules

        1.   Rules Based on Reliability Concerns

           a.   Hearsay rule

           b.   "Best evidence" rule

        2.   Rules Based on External Policies

           a.   Privileges (*e.g.,* attorney-client)

           b.   Quasi privileges

               (1)   Subsequent remedial measures

               (2)   Offers of compromise

               (3)   Payment of medical expenses

II.   Rules Governing Witnesses

    A.   Competency of Witnesses

    B.   Examination of Witnesses

        1.   Order of examination (direct, cross, redirect, recross)

        2.   Leading questions

        3.   Refreshing recollections

    C.   Types of Witnesses

        1.   Lay witnesses

           a.   Firsthand knowledge rule

           b.   Opinion rule

        2.   Expert witnesses

           a.   Subject matter requirement

           b.   Qualifications requirement

           c.   Bases of expert opinions

    D.   Credibility of witnesses

        1.   Bolstering

        2.   Impeachment

           a.   Bias

           b.   Untruthful character

           c.   Sensory or mental defect

           d.   Prior inconsistent statements

           e.   Specific contradiction

        3.   Rehabilitation

III.   Substitutes for evidence

    A.   Judicial notice of fact

B. Stipulations

CHAPTER 8
UNDERSTANDING CORPORATE LAW

By

Arthur R. Pinto

Professor of Law
Co-Director of the Center for the
Study of International Business Law
Brooklyn Law School

Douglas M. Branson

W. Edward Sell Chair in Business Law
University of Pittsburgh
School of Law

Chapter 8
INTRODUCTION AND FORMATION

§ 1.01 INTRODUCTION

The corporation is one of several ways to structure a business. Partnerships and sole proprietorships, as forms of business, far outnumber corporations. However, the economic impact of the corporate format is significant, since it is the form chosen by most large enterprises. Although there is no standard definition for the term "corporation," the United States Supreme Court in the *Dartmouth College* case described it as follows:

> A corporation is an artificial being, invisible, intangible, and existing only in contemplation of law. Being a mere creature of law, it possesses only those properties which the charter of its creation confers upon it, either expressly, or as incidental to its very existence.[1]

A corporation is a separate legal entity[2] which owes its existence to the state. Its owners, called shareholders (sometimes "stockholders" by some state statutes) because they own shares of stock, elect a distinct group, known as the board of directors, to oversee the management of the business and select officers to run it (the directors and officers are often called the "managers"). A significant aspect of the study of corporate law (which includes state corporate law and federal securities law) involves corporate governance and the means by which the relationships between shareholders and managers are governed.

---

[1] *The Trustees of Dartmouth College v. Woodward*, 17 U.S. (4 Wheat.) 518, 636 (1819). In theory, one could establish most of the attributes of a corporation by contract among all participants. For a discussion of the corporation as a nexus of contracts see § 5.07[C][3], *infra*.

[2] Issues have been raised to the extent that the corporation, as a separate legal entity, is protected under the Constitution. In *Santa Clara v. Southern Pacific Ry.*, 118 U.S. 394 (1886), the Supreme Court held that a corporation is entitled to equal protection under the Fourteenth Amendment. In *Minneapolis & St. Louis Ry. Co. v. Beckwith*, 129 U.S. 26 (1888), the Court held it was entitled to due process of law. But in *Hale v. Henkel*, 201 U.S. 43 (1906), a corporation was not entitled to the Fifth Amendment protection against self incrimination but was protected from unreasonable searches and seizures under the Fourth Amendment. The corporation's right to free speech under the First Amendment has also been raised. In *First Nat. Bank of Boston v. Bellotti*, 435 U.S. 765 (1978), the majority found that the state had not shown a compelling interest in regulating corporate expenditures in a referendum. There was no evidence of either a corrupting influence or need to protect the shareholders. But in *Austin v. Michigan St. Chamber of Commerce*, 494 U.S.652 (1990), the Court upheld a Michigan law that prohibited corporate expenditures in state elections. The majority focused on the state providing the means by which corporations can amass large amounts of money that can be used unfairly in political contests. These cases are not only interesting from a constitutional point of view but the different opinions express a variety of views on the nature of a corporation and its relationship to the state.

While the number of experiences varies widely in business formation, we will describe one that may help the reader relate to the material in this book. A business often starts with an idea or invention but requires money or other people to get started or expand (contribution of goods or services is also possible). The initial business can be formed as a corporation, partnership, limited partnership or limited liability company. The capital can be invested in the business in two general ways.[3] If capital is lent, then the relationship between the lenders and the business creates a debtor-creditor relationship where the creditor is looking for eventual repayment plus some current return in the form of interest on the loan. If the capital is provided for an ownership stake, then the investors are willing to forgo a promise to be paid interest or a set return on the investment for the potential for sharing in the success of the business as owners. Their investment provides equity for the business. The source of debt or equity can be friends, family, banks or groups of private investors who are willing to invest to start up or expand a new business with the hope of making a profit when the business is successful. Those private investors are often called venture capitalists.[4]

Many businesses continue to operate and expand with a small number of investors. These corporations are called closely-held corporations. But as businesses grow, they often require substantial capital. To attract capital, a business may have several options. It can attract capital by finding more private investors or having another established business invest in the business. Another alternative is for the business to sell its equity or debt more widely to the public in which case the corporate form is required.[5] The first going public process for selling equity is called an "IPO," initial public offering, and is regulated by federal securities laws.[6] The money raised in going public can be used either to fund expansion of the business or to pay back the initial investors or venture capitalists.[7] Once a corporation has a public offering, the shares are publicly traded in some stock market where investors can continually trade shares of the corporation.[8] Most of the well known large businesses in the United States are

---

[3] For a discussion of the financing of businesses in more detail, see Chapter 4.

[4] For example, in 2003, venture capitalists invested $18.2 billion in 2,715 deals. Some venture capital may also be used in restructuring of businesses and going private transactions. Ann Grimes, *Venture-Capital Investments Increased 6% in Fourth Quarter*, Wall St. J., January 27, 2004 at C5. The money supplied to venture capitalists can come from individuals or institutional investors. For a discussion of institutional investors and corporate governance, see § 5 *infra*.

[5] For a discussion of why the corporate form is used, see § 1.04[B] *infra*.

[6] For a discussion of federal securities laws and the process of going public, see § 7.03 *infra*.

[7] For example, in 2003, 84 companies went public, raising $14.86 billion. In 2002, 94 companies went public, raising $28.19 billion. Raymond Hennessey, *IPO Market Ended Year Better Than It Started*, Wall St. J., January 2, 2004 at R15. A corporation may also decide to go public to provide a market for its shares so that those shares could be used to acquire other corporations or to support the use of employee stock options.

[8] The Securities and Exchange Act of 1934 deals with the stock markets and corporations that have publicly traded shares. *See* Chapters 7, 13.

publicly held corporations, i.e., the shares are held by a large number of shareholders and the shares trade in a stock market.

As discussed in this book, there are different types of corporations which have different attributes, rules and legal issues depending upon the ownership structure. In closely held corporations, where there are few shareholders, the distinction between the shareholders and managers may be insignificant because they may substantially overlap. When there is a group of shareholders constituting the majority who control the business and another group in the minority, issues may arise as to their relationships.[9] In some publicly held corporations, a group of shareholders (maybe the founders or their family) or another corporation may retain control and thus the public shareholders are minority shareholders.[10] Again, in that context, issues will arise as to the relationship between the majority and minority shareholders.[11] In many publicly traded corporations, the original or controlling shareholders may have sold off most of their shares and no longer control the corporation. In that case, there may not be any large group of shareholders controlling the business. Instead there are numerous and widely dispersed shareholders where no group of shareholders holds enough shares to control the election of the directors and hence, the management of the corporation. The dispersion of ownership allows the managers to control the corporation even though they might own relatively few shares. In this context, issues arise as how these dispersed publicly traded shareholders monitor those managers.[12]

The fundamental problem shareholders face when owning shares where they do not control the corporation is that those who manage or control the business will either mismanage the business or unfairly self deal, i.e., steal. In both cases the shareholders are harmed. Much of the discussion of corporate law in this book seeks ways to minimize those problems.

§ 1.02 SOURCES OF CORPORATE LAW

Every state has a corporate law statute that provides the rules for corporations incorporated in that state (hereinafter "the statute"). The statutes indicate how to incorporate, deal with financing and legal capital rules, establish the basic structure of the board of directors, deal with shareholder power and rights, and disposes of a variety of other issues. Every state also has judicially created law or common law applicable to corporations. The courts not only interpret the statutes but create important legal principles. For example, a shareholder's right to sue on behalf of the corporation in a derivative suit was developed by the courts.[13]

---

[9] For a discussion of closely held corporations, see Chapter 11.

[10] For example, Microsoft is a large publicly held corporation but the original founders, Bill Gates and Paul Allen, are significant shareholders and have effective control.

[11] For a discussion of controlling shareholders, see Chapter 10.

[12] For a discussion of corporate governance in these publicly traded corporations, see Chapter 5.

[13] For a discussion of shareholder litigation, see Chapter 14.

CORP LAW

Federal securities law is also a source of corporate law and much of its regulation is disclosure-oriented and intended to affect the relationships within the corporation.[14] The stock markets where the shares of publicly traded corporations are traded have rules with which corporations must comply.[15]

Independent legal organizations also influence the legislative and judicial development of corporate law. The American Law Institute (the "A.L.I.") which is known for its restatements of law has produced the *"Principles of Corporate Governance: Analysis and Recommendations."*[16] The Project attempts to look at corporate law and suggest an approach to corporate governance issues. The Project is not intended to be a restatement of the law but rather as a suggestion of good corporate practice and rules. The Model Business Corporation Act (the "MBCA") is a product of the American Bar Association and has also been influential in the development of various states corporate law statutes. The approach has not been to seek uniformity among the states, but to suggest an approach to issues allowing for local differences. A number of states have adopted the MBCA as their corporate statute.

§ 1.03 HISTORICAL BACKGROUND

Since the formation of a corporation is facilitated by the state, understanding the historical development of state regulation is significant to understanding modern corporate law. The historical development of American corporate law provides an interesting study of political and economic forces which influenced the development of that law.[17]

In the early 19th century, American law restricted the use of corporations. In order to form a corporation in the United States, one had to petition one's state legislature for a charter granting the right to operate as a corporation. Articles of incorporation were not freely given due to suspicion of the private power of corporations. However, the state understood that corporations could serve a useful public purpose. Thus, early American corporations were often established to allow private resources to accomplish public functions. For example, corporations were used to run the railroads, or build roads and bridges.

Over time, business practices changed and the economy grew, resulting in a greater demand for articles of incorporation. This led to the enactment of general corporate statutes under which legislative chartering was no longer required and articles of incorporation were standardized. It also turned the corporate form into a generally available right, as opposed to the privilege of a few.

---

[14] *See* Marc Steinberg, UNDERSTANDING SECURITIES LAW (2001). *See also* Chapter 7.

[15] For an example of such rules see § 5.02[B][2], *infra*.

[16] Sections of the A.L.I. project will be cited in the book as *A.L.I. Corp. Gov. Proj.*

[17] *See generally* Lawrence M. Friedman, *A History of American Law* (2nd ed. 1986).

Economic reality also dictated the need to use corporations for broader purposes. Throughout the 19th century, America expanded its frontiers and experienced the industrial revolution. The expansion of industry transformed America from an agrarian to an industrial society, in which large amounts of capital were required for business. In addition, the public began to invest in private corporations. With public investment in corporations, there was also a rise in financial scandals. As a result, corporate law developed to try to protect investors. For example, shareholder suits developed to allow injured investors to recover for frauds or breaches of fiduciary duty by corporate managers.

In the late 19th century, a number of states lowered taxes on corporations and enacted corporate statutes removed many traditional limitations on the corporation and its managers. These statutes became more enabling and corporations were allowed broader powers. Some of the changes were viewed as more pro-management as opposed to pro-shareholders. It has been suggested that managers would chose a state in which to incorporate which had rules most favorable to management and least favorable to shareholders so states tried to attract incorporations by favoring the managers. New Jersey was the first state to liberalize its law. Delaware eventually took the lead and became the most attractive state for publicly held corporations.[18] Today, all state corporate statutes are generally enabling, although there are some differences among the states.

While state law became more "liberal," the federal government became more suspicious as the power of corporations grew. Thus, federal regulations were developed, including antitrust laws and regulation for certain industries, such as transportation. The stock market crash of 1929 and many of the frauds committed against public investors in the 1920s resulted in Congress enacting federal securities laws during the New Deal in the 1930s to protect these investors. However, Congress chose not to preempt most state law dealing with corporations.[19] In 2001 and 2002, there were corporate scandals associated with Enron, Worldcom and other publicly traded corporations what caused Congress to enact the Sarbanes-Oxley Act of 2002 to protect shareholders.[20]

§ 1.04 CHOICE OF FORM

In organizing and operating a business, the owners may choose a variety of forms. The major choices are corporations, partnerships, limited partnerships, sole proprietorships and limited liability companies. Factors that often influence the choice are the need for limited liability, free

CORP LAW

---

[18] For a discussion of Delaware's dominance among the states for incorporations see § 1.08[A], *infra*. For an in-depth analysis of Delaware corporate law, see David A. Drexler, et al., DELAWARE CORPORATION LAW AND PRACTICE (2003).

[19] *See generally* J. Willard Hurst, THE LEGITAMACY OF THE BUSINESS CORPORATION IN THE LAW OF THE UNITED STATES 1780-1970 (1970).

[20] For a discussion of Sarbanes-Oxley, see § 5.08, *infra*.

transferability of interests, continuity of existence, centralized management, costs, access to capital and taxation.

[A] Sole Proprietorship

The simplest form of business is the sole proprietorship, where an individual decides to go into business as the sole owner. There are no formal requirements for the formation or operation of a sole proprietorship and ownership and management can exist in the sole owner. The owner is the principal and can employ people as agents to represent and work for her business. As owner, she is personally liable for the obligations of the business. In addition, all profits and losses are personal and part of her individual tax return.

[B] Partnership v. Corporation

Once an individual decides to go into business with other people as owners, there are other choices she can make as to business form.[21]

The two primary choices for business format are partnership and corporation. To form and operate a corporation, one must comply with a list of requirements, one of which is the filing of articles of incorporation with the state.[22] The services of an attorney are often needed to help prepare the necessary documentation; retention of counsel, of course, increases the costs of doing business.

Another format in which to conduct business is the partnership. The partnership is defined as "an association of two or more persons to carry on as co-owners a business for profit."[23] The formation of a partnership requires no formal action or written agreement. Individuals acting together to run a business may result in a partnership being formed.[24] However, it is advisable to have an agreement among partners or among shareholders of a closely held corporation to protect the interests of the parties. In the

---

[21] Although a sole owner can incorporate to take advantage of certain corporate benefits such as limited liability, a partnership requires at least two owners. Uniform Partnership Act ("UPA") § 6(1) (1914); RUPA § 101(6) (1998).

[22] For a discussion of formation see § 1.07, *infra*

[23] UPA § 6(1) (1914) and Revised Uniform Partnership Act ("RUPA") § 101(6) (1996).

[24] A partnership results from contract, either expressed or implied. If a court finds that the parties have in fact acted as partners, it will find the existence of a partnership with all the legal consequences that flow from it. Courts look for two elements of co-ownership in determining the existence of a partnership: profit sharing and control. Under the definition of partnership, creditors who lend money and receive a share of profits and either contract for or act with extensive control, may be treated as partners with unlimited liability. In *Martin v. Peyton,* 246 N.Y. 213, 158 N.E. 77 (1927), a creditor escaped liability even though a contract gave the creditor considerable control and profit sharing; the court found that the control existed primarily through the use of negative covenants designed to protect the creditor's loan. Generally, the receipt of profits is prima facie evidence of partnership status, except that certain situations are excluded, such as interest on a loan or wages. *See* UPA § 7(4) (1914); RUPA § 202(3) (1998).

absence of an agreement, partnership law is generally more protective of all the owners than corporate law.[25]

The choice between the corporate form and partnership depends on comparing the different attributes of the two forms and then determining which attributes are significant to one's business. The key considerations are limited liability, free transferability of interests, continuity of existence, centralized management, costs, access to capital and taxation. While these differences are significant, practical considerations may make them irrelevant.[26] It is also important to note that each of these attributes may be modified by contract among the interested parties.[27]

The major differences between the partnership and corporation flow primarily from the fact that partnerships are generally viewed as an aggregate that is composed of its owners, while the corporation is viewed as a separate legal entity distinct from its owners.[28] For example, since the partnership is generally legally viewed as the aggregate of its owners, it follows that each owner is personally liable for the debts of the partnership. Since the corporation is a separate legal entity, it is able to incur its

---

[25] Partnership law originally developed under the common law, but in 1914 the Uniform Partnership Act (the "UPA") was promulgated and now provides many of the rules governing partnerships. The UPA allows partners to modify the rules by contract. In 1994, a Revised Uniform Partnership Act ("RUPA") was adopted with the intent of superseding the UPA. Partnership law has been described as supplementary in the sense that if there is no contract, the UPA provisions govern. The resulting rules tend to reflect what most parties in small businesses would have agreed to or expected in most cases. For example, most owners of a small business would assume that they would have a right to participate in management; this is provided under partnership law. See UPA § 18(e) (1914); RUPA § 401(f) (1998). Corporate law provides that to be involved in management, a shareholder needs to be elected to the board by a majority vote. Most corporate statutes are traditionally more regulatory and designed to deal with both closely held corporations and large publicly held corporations. Thus the rules may not be as protective of minority shareholders in closely held corporations. In order to protect minority interest in a closely held corporation, there usually needs to be a contract to adapt the law, while most partnership law without a contract is protective. Thus, minority shareholders should provide by contract to have a voice or a return on their investment. For a discussion of contracts in closely held corporations, see § 11.03, infra.

[26] For example, there is free transferability in the corporate form which allows the shareholders to freely sell their shares. However, while shareholders may have the legal right to sell, there may be no real market for the shares, especially if the shares represent a minority interest in a closely held corporation. For a discussion of the problems of the minority shareholders of a closely held corporation, see § 11.01, infra.

[27] For example, although the corporate form provides limited liability, creditors may insist on personal guarantees from the shareholders to induce it to loan to the business. Conversely, in a partnership, if the partners are in a strong bargaining situation, they could contract for limited liability with the creditors of the partnership, agreeing to only go after the assets of the partnership. Contracting in the context of a small business is very important in both the partnership and closely held corporate context.

[28] The aggregate concept has been modified by the UPA for particular situations. For example, under an aggregate approach, partnership property would have to be held in the name of each partner. However, the UPA allows it to be held in the partnership name. See UPA § 8 (1914). There is a now a Revised Uniform Partnership Act that among other things, uses an entity approach in most cases, but does not change the basic differences between a partnership and a corporation. See RUPA § 201 (1998).

own liabilities, shielding the shareholders as owners from personal liability.[29] This limited liability means that in most cases, the shareholders will only lose their investment in the corporation. This advantage is the primary reason why the corporate form is chosen for many businesses.

Partnership interests are not freely transferable, since any change in the identity of the partners will alter the aggregate. While new partners may be added, there must be a unanimous consent for changes in the makeup of the partnership[30] unless there has been a contractual modification of this rule. On the corporation side, since shareholders are separate from the corporation, they can freely transfer shares; different owners have no effect on the separate corporate entity.

If there is any change in the partnership, there is a dissolution of that partnership. This rule limits the continuity of the business.[31] Therefore, the death or bankruptcy of one partner causes a dissolution of the partnership because the aggregate changes when the original partner is replaced by another: death precipitates the appointment of an executor and bankruptcy heralds the designation of a trustee. Death or bankruptcy of a shareholder or desire of a shareholder to terminate ownership does not affect the corporation because it is a separate legal entity unaffected by changes in ownership. Thus, corporations provide for a perpetual existence.[32]

In addition, a partner may at any time cause the dissolution of the partnership by merely deciding to end the relationship.[33]

A dissolution of partnership does not necessarily mean an end to the business, particularly when there is a partnership agreement allowing for continuity. However, in the absence of such an agreement, there will be a winding up of the business.

Partners, as co-owners of the business, have the right to participate in the management of the partnership.[34] In addition, each partner has the power to bind the partnership as agent in the usual course of business.[35]

---

[29] Entity status need not have this or other attributes. For example, under early English law there were corporations with unlimited liability.

[30] See UPA § 18(g) (1914); RUPA § 401(i) (1998). However, UPA § 27(1914) permits partners to transfer their interest in profits of the partnership without dissolving the partnership or giving the assignee any other partnership rights. See RUPA § 502 (1998).

[31] UPA § 29 (1914). A dissolution only means a change in the partnership makeup and does not mean that there is a winding up or termination of the business. Compare RUPA §§ 601–603 (1998).

[32] One can, however, provide in the articles for termination or a shorter duration for a corporation. See, e.g., MBCA § 3.02

[33] UPA § 31(1)(b)(1914). Under RUPA § 601 (1998), dissolution is defined differently, reducing the events which will actually dissolve the partnership. Instead, a "dissociation" may occur which will sometimes result in an actual dissolution.

[34] UPA § 18(e) (1914); RUPA § 401(f) (1998). A majority vote will resolve differences on ordinary partnership matters. Unanimity is required for acts in contravention of any agreement between the partners. See UPA § 18(h) (1914); RUPA § 401(j) (1998).

[35] UPA § 9 (1914); RUPA § 301 (1998).

In the corporate context, the corporation, as a separate legal entity from its owners, has a board of directors that manages the business. The board is elected by the shareholders. The use of a board of directors allows for a group other than owners to manage and thus a centralization of management separate from the owners. Since a majority vote is usually required for election of the board, a minority shareholder must gain votes of other shareholders to participate in the management of the corporation. While in closely held corporations the shareholders may contract to place minority shareholders on the board, all shareholders (unlike partners) usually do not have the automatic right to manage or be on the board.

Businesses that need to raise large amounts of capital by attracting public investors as shareholders will choose the corporate form. Limited liability, free transferability, centralized management and continuity are all attributes that are necessary to attract public shareholders interested in passively investing and trading shares in the markets. [36] For example, it would be hard to imagine every shareholder of General Motors having a right to participate in management of the company. Limited liability is another important characteristic of the corporate format without which every investor would be personally liable for the obligations of the business. Without limited liability, each shareholder's joint liability would depend on the personal worth of the other owners. This would make it impossible to value and trade shares because share value would be dependent upon, among other things, the potential liability of different shareholders. [37]

§ 1.05　TAXATION

Another significant difference between the partnership and corporate formats is the respective tax treatment given each entity. One way in which the two are treated differently is that corporations, apart from its shareholders, pay taxes as a legal entity. By contrast, a partnership is considered an aggregate of individuals and usually not a legal entity; thus, the partnership is not subject to taxation. The partnership is required to file a tax return, known as an informational return. The purpose of an informational return is to determine how much tax the individual partners will pay on the income derived from the operation of the partnership business but not to tax the partnership.

[A]　Double Taxation

Corporations pay tax on the profits they receive and when that profit is distributed to shareholders in the form of dividends, it is again taxed in the hands of the individual shareholders This practice has been called "double taxation." [38] Since the partnership pays no tax, the income from

---

[36] For a discussion of shareholder passivity, see § 5.05[C][4], *infra*.

[37] For a discussion of limited liability and public ownership of shares, see § 3.01, *infra*.

[38] The top tax rate for corporations is 35% and dividends are paid out of after-taxed profits.

the business flows through to the partners and is only taxed individually (even if the partnership income is never distributed). Thus, there is no double taxation.

In the corporate context, when there is a loss from the business operations, the corporation can use the loss to offset other corporate profits from the past or in the future. However, in the partnership, the partners report the losses on their individual tax returns. These losses may be used to offset other personal income and thus reduce personal taxes.

When there are expected to be business profits, tax advisors seek means of avoiding double taxation. Often, this means the formation of the business as a partnership or some other business form that allows a flow through of profits (or losses) to the investor without being taxed twice. In a large business, it is usually impossible to operate as a partnership because of other limitations of the partnership form, such as lack of free transferability of interests and the need for limited liability and centralized management. However, in a small business, the partnership form can be advantageous from a tax point of view.

Alternatively, the tax advisor may form the business as a corporation but seek to structure it to minimize the effect of double taxation. For instance, since income is only taxed a second time once it is distributed to the shareholder, a corporation may retain the earnings in the business and not pay a dividend. Another way to avoid double taxation is to distribute the funds to the shareholders in a form other than a dividend so that the corporation may deduct the payment as a business expense and not pay taxes on that amount. For example, if the shareholder is an employee, the amount which would otherwise be paid to him as a dividend could be paid to him as a salary. Similarly, if one's investment in a corporation is in the form of a bond or a note, the interest paid may substitute for dividends. If one owns the corporation's plant or equipment, rent paid is deductible by the corporation. The payments of salary, interest on debt and rent are usually tax deductible. There are important caveats to these comments since unreasonable attempts to avoid double taxation may result in tax penalties.[39]

[1] Subchapter S Corporation

Another corporate format which plays a significant role in tax consequences is the S corporation. The S corporation is a corporation which has

---

Prior to 2003, dividends received by individual shareholders would be included in income and taxed again at as much as 38.6% and thus resulting in a high amount of double tax (total tax of 73.6% not including local taxes). The Tax Act enacted in 2003 lowered the tax rate paid by shareholders for dividends received to a maximum of 15% which lessens the impact of the double tax.

[39] Internal Revenue Code (hereinafter "IRC") § 162(a). For example, the Internal Revenue Service may attack the retention of earnings or the payment of salaries as unreasonable and may consider the payments an illegal attempt to avoid double taxation. In the event of such a finding, the IRS would likely impose penalties in addition to the payment of taxes on those amounts.

elected to be taxed under the provisions of Subchapter S of the Tax Code. This provision allows a corporation to pay no tax. Instead, all the corporate income is taxed to the shareholders, whether or not such income is actually distributed thereto. Subchapter S corporations are generally treated like partnerships for tax purposes. Certain restrictions may preclude election as a Subchapter S corporation, such as a the requirement that there be a maximum of 75 shareholders, or the preclusion of non-resident alien or corporate shareholders, or the use of only one class of shares.

[2] Limited Liability Companies

All states have enacted legislation that authorizes the use of a new kind of business entity, called the "limited liability company." The limited liability company for tax purposes is an unincorporated organization.[40] The intent is to provide additional business organizations with limited liability, but without the double taxation consequence of corporations or the restrictions of the Subchapter S Corporation.

The limited liability company is not restricted as to the number of shareholders who may be called members (although too large a number may deem it publicly traded and subject it to double taxation), type of shareholders and capital structure. Although the legislation differs among the states, limited liability companies generally enjoy limited liability and centralized management by an entity such as a board of directors. Under the "check the box" regulations, limited liability companies now qualify for partnership tax treatment even if they have other corporate attributes such as free transferability and perpetual existence. States usually require a contract among members called an operating agreement. The operating agreement establishes or modifies the characteristics of the organization.

In order to provide some certainty on tax treatment, the IRS has provided for "check-the-box" regulations which simplify the issue of how a business organization will be treated for tax purposes. The regulations provide that every business organization that is not a corporation is a "pass-through entity," which means it will be treated like a partnership for tax purposes. The regulations list eight organizations which are corporations per se, including the statutory corporation.[41] More significantly the list does not include other business organizations such as limited partnerships and limited liability corporations. If not listed, then the organization is an eligible entity, allowing for a pass through tax treatment and no double

---

[40] Limited liability partnerships ("LLP") and limited liability limited partnerships may also be formed in some states. These organizations require registration and partnership form but the partners are exempt from some of the partnership liabilities (e.g., tortious conduct of a partner may not create liability to other partners). The LLP has been used by some accounting and law firms.

[41] IRC § 7701 and regulations thereunder. Prior to 1997, the classification for tax purposes of different business entities depended on its characteristics which were: (1) associates, (2) an objective to carry on a business and divide the profits, (3) continuity of life, (4) centralized management, (5) limited liability, and (6) free transferability of interests.

taxation. Thus an eligible entity by default is treated like a partnership for tax purposes unless it elects to be treated like a corporation.

§ 1.06 LIMITED PARTNERSHIPS

A limited partnership is a business organization which provides partnership-style tax treatment and limited liability for some of the owners.[42] A limited partnership must have at least one general partner with unlimited liability;[43] the other owners may be limited partners with limited liability (like shareholders). Unlike corporate shareholders who can serve as officers and directors and still have limited liability, if a limited partner gets involved in the control of the limited partnership, she may lose limited liability.[44] Unlike the partnership, it is created by compliance with state law which includes the paying of fees and the filing of a certificate.[45] Much of the structure of the limited partnership is usually established by the provisions of the certificate or contract among the participants.

[42] There are some publicly traded limited partnerships which attempted to avoid the double taxation of the corporate form. Currently under IRC § 7704, a publicly traded limited partnership is usually taxed as a corporation.

[43] Under the Uniform Limited Partnership Act (the "ULPA") and the UPA, corporations can serve as general partners of a limited partnership. States which permit a corporation to be the sole partner in a limited partnership have created limited liability for the general partner. A problem arises when a corporation is a general partner of a limited partnership and an individual limited partner also controls the corporation (the general partner). Does the limited partner become liable as a result of that control? If the limited partner acts on behalf of the corporation in controlling the corporation as general partner, there is usually no individual liability. While § 303(b) of the Revised Uniform Limited Partnership Act (the "RULPA") precludes liability when one acts for the corporation, the result is not as clear under the "ULPA." *See Frigidaire Sales Corp. v. Union Properties, Inc.*, 562 P.2d. 244 (1977)(the limited partners acted solely as agents of the corporation and the third party did not rely on them as general partners).

[44] The original Uniform Limited Partnership Act § 7, created liability for a limited partner when she participates in the control of the business. The open ended concept of control resulted in litigation and uncertainty. RULPA § 303 attempted to clarify the situation by enumerating certain conduct that a limited partner may carry on without being deemed to have taken part in control of the business. Under RULPA § 303, a limited partner may, among other things, consult with and advise a general partner with respect to the business of the limited partnership; be a contractor agent, or employee of the limited partnership; act as surety or guarantor for the limited partnership; propose, approve or disapprove of a variety of actions involving the limited partnership.

[45] ULPA § 2 requires a certificate of limited partnership to be filed with the secretary of state (or some other state official). The certificate shall set forth the following information concerning the limited partnership: the name and address; the names and addresses of all agents for service of process; the names and business addresses of all general partners; the latest date upon which the limited partnership is to dissolve; and any matters the general partners determine to include. The limited partnership is formed at the time of the filing or any date specified in the certificate. In addition, RUPLA § 201 allows for substantial compliance in filing, which is similar to the de facto incorporation doctrine. For a discussion of the doctrine see § 2.03[B], *infra*.

§ 1.07 INCORPORATION AND ORGANIZATION

In forming a corporation, at least one person must act as the incorporator. She is responsible for filing the articles of incorporation (sometimes called a charter or certificate of incorporation). The articles of incorporation are usually filed with the secretary of state. The process is simple and relatively inexpensive. The articles of incorporation contain some basic information about the company and must comply with statutory requirements. [46] The name of the corporation must be different from the name of any other corporation to avoid confusion or deception. Corporations must also use a denomination after the name, such as the words "Inc.," "Corp.," "Ltd." to make clear that the company is a corporation. The articles may also contain other significant discretionary provisions authorized by the statute.

Upon acceptance of the articles of incorporation by the state official, corporate existence commences. Once the corporation exists, all further actions on the corporation's behalf must be taken by the incorporator. In order to complete the formation of the corporation, the incorporator must adopt a set of bylaws, hold the initial shareholders' and directors' meetings, arrange for the election of directors and officers, open a bank account for the corporation, issue the shares and conduct other significant initial acts. The bylaws contain the internal rules dealing with the governance of the corporation. [47] Unlike the articles of incorporation, the bylaws are not publicly filed. Once established, the corporation must comply with the requirements of the state statutory scheme such as holding annual meetings of both directors and shareholders. [48]

Attorneys are often involved in this process. Counsel may advise the client on the advantages of the different business forms and draft the necessary legal papers. Often, the incorporation process is pro forma, using standard forms for the articles of incorporation and the bylaws. As discussed in Chapter 11, the articles and the bylaws may be modified, particularly to protect minority shareholders of a closely held corporation from potential oppression by majority shareholders. Thus, the preparation of the documents may involve potential or actual conflicts of interests among the shareholders. If retained, an attorney must identify these conflicts and disclose them. While it is advisable that all shareholders retain their own counsel

---

[46] For example under MBCA § 2.02(a), the articles of incorporation must include: a corporate name; the number of shares which the corporation is authorized to issue; the street address of the corporation's initial registered office, the name of its initial authorized agent; and the name and address of each incorporator.

[47] Bylaws often contain rules regarding important aspects of running the corporation such as shareholders' meetings (for example, the location, notice, waiver of notice, rules for special meetings, voting rights, rules for proxies, quorum requirements etc.); the operation of the board of directors, (such as their number, compensation, method of filling vacancies, and removal of directors and officers); the rules concerning officers, agents and employees (duties, salaries, titles, etc.); the rules for issuing share certificates and the transfer of shares; and the method for conducting special corporate acts, such as signing checks and amending the bylaws.

[48] Failure to comply with the formalities may be a factor in deciding whether to hold individual shareholders liable on a piercing of the corporate veil theory. See § 3.03[C], infra.

CORP LAW

to represent their interests, clients sometimes regard the need for individual counsel as an unnecessary expense, particularly when the parties prefer not to use corporate funds for legal fees.

The Code of Professional Responsibility allows an attorney to represent the corporation[49] and set up the business. However, it is important that all the parties understand the potential for conflicts of interest, particularly if a contract is written among the shareholders which addresses their relationship to the corporation and each other.

§ 1.08 CHOICE OF LAW

In organizing the corporation, the incorporator must choose the state in which to file the articles of incorporation. State statutes indicate how to incorporate, deal with financing and legal capital rules, establish the basic structure of the board of directors, deal with shareholder power and rights, and a variety of other issues. Every state has a corporate statute that sets out the corporate rules. Although the state statutes are generally standard, a few statutory rules differ significantly from state to state. These differences may include treatment of shareholder voting rights, the ability to sue directors, and the extent of the directors' fiduciary duty.

Also, every state has a judicially created common law which governs various aspects of corporate life, such as the concept of fiduciary duty and its application to the managers of the corporation.[50] While fiduciary duty is often defined by statute, the courts ultimately decide how to apply the statute to a particular set of facts. Court decisions have resulted in differences among states concerning the extent of protection of shareholders by corporate law.

The law of the state of incorporation should govern most intra-corporate relationships, such as between the corporation and its officers, directors and shareholders.[51] This is known as the internal affairs doctrine. With the use of a single law, the doctrine attempts to avoid a corporation being faced with conflicting demands, while it also encourages convenience and predictability of legal application. This does not mean that the law of the state of incorporation governs other corporate dealings, such as commercial transactions, contracts or tort law. In addition, a given state may have a sufficient interest in a corporation incorporated elsewhere but doing business in the state, to subject it to local taxation, jurisdiction for litigation and filing as a foreign corporation.

While Congress could have enacted a federal scheme of incorporation,[52] it has chosen, by not acting, to allow the states to provide the mechanism

---

[49] Model Code of Professional Responsibility DR 5 (1980).

[50] For an introduction to fiduciary duty see Chapter 8.

[51] Restatement (Second) of the Conflict of Laws § 302 (1971).

[52] This theory would be premised on the Commerce Clause. Under the Commerce Clause, Congress has the power to regulate interstate activity, which would include most corporate activities.

and law that govern the internal affairs of the corporation. As we will see in subsequent chapters, there is an extensive federal presence through federal securities laws that affects the internal affairs of a corporation. However, defining and regulating the relationship between the shareholders and the managers of the corporation remains primarily an issue of state law.

[A] Delaware's Dominance

Local businesses usually incorporate in the state in which they maintain a principal place of business to avoid paying extra taxes or fees to a state in which the business has no real interest.[53] Larger corporations do not necessarily incorporate in the state in which they are headquartered. A large number of publicly held corporations have chosen to incorporate in Delaware. Over 50% of the largest companies in America, what is known as the "Fortune 500," are incorporated in Delaware while over 40% of the companies that were traded on the New York Stock Exchange were also incorporated in Delaware.[54] However, most of these companies have a small presence in Delaware. Why do corporations choose Delaware? Why do other states recognize Delaware law?

Most states have respected the internal affairs doctrine and do not attempt to impose their rules on corporations incorporated in other states. To some extent the "full faith and credit clause"[55] and the Commerce Clause[56] of the United States Constitution support the idea that states should respect the laws of other states. However, the application of one state's corporate law is arguably more a principle of conflict of laws than constitutional law and some states have provisions of their corporate law that apply to foreign corporations (that is, corporations incorporated in another state, but with a presence in that state). Some states have attempted to apply some of their internal affairs laws to corporations incorporated in other states.[57] This practice is infrequent and its validity remains unclear.[58]

Delaware's prominence as a state of incorporation has been criticized as causing a "race to the bottom."[59] Some claim that Delaware has laws which

---

[53] For example, if a local business operates primarily in New York but incorporates in Delaware it may be considered a foreign corporation in New York, i.e., incorporated in another state but doing business in New York. As a result, it would pay Delaware fees and still have to file as a foreign corporation in New York and pay fees pursuant to N.Y.B.C.L. Article 13.

[54] Forward to R. Franklin Balotti and Jesse A. Finkelstein DELAWARE LAW OF CORPORATIONS AND BUSINESS ORGANIZATIONS F1 (2nd ed. 1994). *See also* David A. Drexler, et al., DELAWARE CORPORATION LAW AND PRACTICE (1999).

[55] U.S. Const. art. 1, § 10.

[56] U.S. Const. Art. 1, § 8.

[57] *See e.g.* N.Y.B.C.L. §§ 1317–20.

[58] *See* Arthur R. Pinto, *The Constitution and the Market For Corporate Control: State Takeover Statutes After CTS. Corp.,* 29 Wm. & Mary L. Rev. 699, 754-774 (1988).

[59] "Lesser states, eager for the revenue derived from the traffic in articles of incorporation, had removed safeguards from their own incorporation laws. Companies were early formed to

favor corporate management over shareholders. Managers who decide where to incorporate will likely choose a state with favorable laws that protect their interests, such as Delaware.[60]

Why would Delaware provide this pro-management environment? In 1986, Delaware received 16 % of its revenues from corporate fees.[61] In addition, the corporate bar of Delaware is actively involved in representing corporations in litigation arising under Delaware law. Arguably, Delaware has a direct economic interest in encouraging incorporation within its borders.

Some commentators have argued contrary to the "race to the bottom" theory that incorporating in Delaware is beneficial to shareholders. They argue that corporate management would not choose to incorporate in a state with pro-management laws that hurt shareholders because to do so would depress the value of the shares, reflecting the potential opportunism of the managers. Lower priced shares would hurt the corporation and the managers. The lower priced shares could result in various market mechanisms being used to protect shareholders. For example, if shares are priced too low, the company could become a takeover target, where the purchasing company would likely replace the managers. Since managers fear replacement, they are more apt to try to keep the price of the shares high. According to this argument, managers can be expected to seek state laws that will benefit shareholders and enhance the market value of the shares to avoid the takeover.[62] Thus, states can be expected to compete in the market for corporate charters to attract incorporations with optimal law.[63] However, empirical studies concerning manager influence in choice of state of incorporation fail to resolve the dispute and the debate continues.[64]

Ultimately, Delaware dominates state corporate law in the United States. One of the major advantages of incorporating in Delaware is that with so many corporations incorporated there, its bar and judiciary have an excellent understanding of the complexities of corporate law. Its extensive case law also facilitates planning and research on corporate law issues.

---

provide articles of incorporation in states where the cost was lowest and the laws least restrictive. The states joined in advertising their wares. The race was not one of diligence but of laxity . . . ." *Liggett v. Lee*, 288 U.S. 517, 557-58 (1933)(Brandeis, J., dissenting).

[60] *See generally* William Cary, *Federalism and Corporate Law: Reflections on Delaware,* 83 Yale L.J. 663 (1974).

[61] *See* Barrett, *Delaware Moves Closer to Adopting Law to Deter Hostile Takeovers,* Wall St. J., Dec. 9, 1987, at 41.

[62] For a discussion of other market mechanisms that protect shareholders, see § 5.03[C][2], *infra.*

[63] *See,* Ralph K. Winter, *State Law, Shareholder Protection, and the Theory of the Corporation,* 6 J. Leg. St. 251 (1977).

[64] *See* Roberta Romano, *The State Competition Debate in Corporate Law,* 8 Cardozo L. Rev. 709, 710-12 (1987).

§ 1.09 ULTRA VIRES

Ultra vires results when a corporation has acted beyond its purpose (the object of the incorporation) or powers (the means by which the corporation carries out the object). For example, a corporation established for the purpose of washing windows would have the power to enter contracts to wash windows. However, a contract to replace windows might be ultra vires and beyond its purpose.

In the 19th century, incorporation was difficult because there were concerns about corporate influence and power. Legislatures would grant certificates of incorporation with limited purposes and powers. If a corporation was authorized to build a road and decided to contract to build an inn so that travelers could stop on their travels, the contract could be ultra vires. The corporation or the party with which the corporation contracted could thus attempt to avoid the contract. Courts attempted to avoid the harsh results of ultra vires. For example, a court could find the corporation had an implied power to build an inn; or could use an estoppel argument based upon the reliance of the third party; or a quasi contract theory. But even with judicial attempts to alleviate the unfairness of ultra vires, there was uncertainty.

Ultra vires is less significant now. Incorporation is much easier and there are no longer legislative restrictions so corporations can be formed with broad purposes and powers to act in any lawful means and purpose.[65] In addition, even if a corporate action is ultra vires, statutory provisions restrict the use of the ultra vires defense in order to protect third parties. For example, MBCA § 3.04 limits challenges based upon ultra vires to shareholders seeking to enjoin executory contracts; shareholders suing the directors for the violation; or a proceeding by the attorney general to dissolve the corporation. Even if the contract is executory and there is an attempt to enjoin it under the statute, that action must be equitable.[66]

Ultra vires may still be raised in some particular contexts.[67] Corporate guarantees of third party debts that do not benefit the corporation may be

---

[65] "Every corporation incorporated under this Act has the purpose of engaging in any lawful business unless a more limited purpose is set forth in the articles of incorporation." MBCA § 3.01(a).

[66] *See* MBCA § 3.04 (official comment). In *Goodman v. Ladd Estates Co.,* 427 P.2d. 102 (Or. 1967) shareholders were unable to challenge a corporate guaranty having no business purpose even though it was ultra vires because Oregon had a similar statute. Plaintiff-shareholder claimed the guaranty was inequitable because it was ultra vires. The fact that the guaranty may have been ultra vires did not make it inequitable under the statute because the statute now validates ultra vires transactions. To be inequitable would require something more. In addition, it was not inequitable because the plaintiffs bought the shares of the corporation from the previous owner who was involved in the ultra vires guaranty and they had knowledge of the guaranty.

[67] When corporations act as partners in a partnership, issues of ultra vires are raised. The other partners can make decisions which adversely affect the corporation and impinge on the role of the directors in managing the business. Most statutes now explicitly permit a corporation to enter into partnerships *See, e.g.,* MBCA § 3.02(9).

attacked.[68] In addition, nonprofit corporate activity such as excessive charitable contributions or unauthorized, unjustified payments to third parties may be wasteful and viewed as ultra vires.

§ 1.10 CORPORATE SOCIAL RESPONSIBILITY

Issues of corporate social responsibility involve issues of corporate philanthropy and corporate governance. The issue involves determining whether a corporation should be managed solely to benefit its shareholders.[69]

The advocates of shareholder-gain as the sole motive for corporations believe that corporations are formed to run a business for a profit and other activities should not be within their focus. Allowing managers to pick and choose philanthropic or socially beneficial activities permits use of corporate funds for management's personal charities and enables the managers to act as a sort of unelected civil servant. In addition, critics complain that profit is the yardstick used to measure the success of a business. Ultimately, profit maximization is the most socially responsible activity.[70]

Advocates for a broader view recognize that large publicly traded corporations have considerable power and play a significant role in the economy. Their view of corporate governance looks to include stakeholders other than shareholders and corporate managers in corporate decision making. These stakeholders might include employees, consumers, creditors[71] or members of the community. Thus philanthropy should be encouraged and the fiduciary duty of managers should be owed to the enterprise, not just to shareholders, and viewed in a larger context.[72]

[A] Philanthropy

Reasonable amounts of corporate philanthropy are not only specifically authorized by state statutes but are common and significant. Originally the issue of corporate philanthropy was raised in the context of the doctrine

---

[68] See Goodman, note 66, supra.

[69] Shareholder primacy underlies most theories of the firm in the United States although some commentators argue for a more expansive view. Margaret M. Blair and Lynn A. Stout, A Team Production Theory of Corporate Law, 85 Va. L. Rev. 247 (1999).

[70] See e.g., Milton Friedman, CAPITALISM AND FREEDOM (1962).

[71] When a corporation is insolvent, the fiduciary duty shifts to the creditors because insolvency means that there is no equity and the creditors become the owners. The Delaware courts have recognized that there may be some obligation to creditors even prior to actual insolvency but near it. Credit Lyonnais Bank Nederland, N.V. v. Pathe Communications Corp., 1991 WL 277613 (Del. Ch. 1991); 17 Del. J. Corp. L. 1099 (Dec. 30, 1991).

[72] A.L.I. Corp. Gov. Proj. § 2.01 takes a compromise position indicating that corporations should have as their objective business activities with a view to enhancing corporate profit and shareholder gain. Notwithstanding this objective, a corporation may take ethical considerations into account and devote reasonable amounts to public welfare, humanitarian, educational, and philanthropic purposes.

of ultra vires,[73] that is, whether the contribution was beyond the power and purpose of a corporation. Most state statutes now authorize reasonable philanthropic activities.[74] Even prior to statutory enactments, courts have found philanthropy to be beneficial and within a corporation's implied powers. In *A.P. Smith Mfg. Co. v. Barlow,*[75] the corporation was incorporated prior to a statutory enactment allowing philanthropic corporate payments. It was argued that the change in the statute allowing philanthropy violated the Constitution's Contract Clause because it was a change in the contract (reflected in the law and the articles of incorporation) between the State and the corporation. However, the state had in its corporate statute a reserved power clause which allowed it to change the law subsequently to alter the articles of incorporation.[76] The court also recognized the importance of such contributions to society and to the corporation as a good citizen.[77]

[B] Stakeholders

Issues have arisen as to the extent to which those who manage the corporation may look out for interests of other than shareholders who have a stake in the corporation. Those interests include labor, creditors, consumers and the community where the business operates.[78] Concern for these stakeholders may involve lower profits for the business. In a variety of contexts, courts have identified the primary purpose of the corporation as the making of profits. For example, in *Dodge v. Ford Motor Co.,*[79] ("*Ford*") Henry Ford, who controlled Ford Motor Co. (a closely held corporation), wanted to benefit society by lowering the price of cars and sharing the profits with consumers. He cut back the dividend paid to the shareholders. The court ordered the payment of a dividend to the shareholders, a rare outcome, because such decisions are normally protected by the business judgment rule which limits courts in second guessing business decisions.[80] The court would allow incidental expenditures to benefit society but a

---

[73] For a discussion of ultra vires, see § 1.09, *supra.*

[74] *See e.g.,* MBCA § 3.02(13)

[75] 98 A.2d 581 (N.J. 1953)

[76] *See, e.g.,* MBCA § 1.02

[77] The court found a contribution to Princeton University within the power of a corporation even though not specifically authorized in its articles of incorporation. The court noted that the contribution was not made to a "pet" charity or motivated by personal considerations and would benefit a part of the community in which it operates. *A.P. Smith Mfg. Co. v. Barlow,* 98 A.2d 581 (N.J. 1953). *See Theodora Holding v. Henderson* 257 A.2d 398 (Del. Ch. 1969) (the test is one of reasonableness and used the 5% federal tax deduction limitation as evidence). If the decision to contribute is made by independent directors in an informed manner and not wasteful, it would be protected by the business judgment rule. *Kahn v. Sullivan* 594 A.2d. 48 (Del. 1991). For a discussion of the business judgment rule, see § 8.03[C], *infra.*

[78] *See generally* Lawrence Mitchell, *A Theoretical Framework for Enforcing Corporate Constituency Statutes,* 70 Tex. L. Rev. 579 (1992).

[79] 170 N.W. 668 (Mich. 1919).

[80] For a discussion of the business judgment rule, see § 8.03[C], *infra.*

corporate general purpose to benefit society would be improper. The court emphasized that corporations should be run to generate profits for shareholders. Given the espoused view of Mr. Ford and the failure to argue that potential profits that could result because lowering prices would increase demand, the decision was predictable.[81]

In *Shlensky v. Wrigley*[82] a minority shareholder brought a derivative suit (an action on behalf of the corporation) claiming that the directors of the Chicago Cubs had breached their fiduciary duty because they had not installed stadium lights so that more profitable night baseball games could be played. Plaintiff tried to rely on the *Ford* case claiming that Wrigley, the controlling shareholder, was motivated by his beliefs on what was good for baseball and the neighboring community, not the interests of the shareholders in maximizing profits. Unlike *Ford,* in which the court emphasized the need to make profits and benefit the shareholders, the Illinois court saw the issue as matter of business policy which was untainted by fraud, illegality or self dealing. Further the concerns for the neighborhood could possibly benefit the baseball park and the corporation in the long term. The court recognized that while the decision may be wrong, there was no dereliction of duty (no self dealing or negligence in directors making the decision). It was not up to the courts to second guess directors because their decisions are presumed to be in good faith. The *Ford* case may be distinguished from *Shlensky* because in *Ford* the large amount of money was being withheld as dividends and the problems of the minority shareholders in a closely held corporation, needing a return on their investment. However, the tone of the *Shlensky* case gives directors broad discretion in making business decisions and in considering interests other than those of the shareholders.

Over the years, there have been attempts by groups to change the board of directors to include representatives of different constituencies or the public interest. Rarely have these attempts made any progress.[83] Attempts to change or modify corporate activities have been more successful when shareholders have submitted proposals on social issues through the federal proxy rules.[84] Even in that context, a proposal needs to be within the power of the corporation to effectuate.

---

[81] It is also possible to view Mr. Ford's activity as ultra vires because the purpose of a corporation was to make profits.

[82] 237 N.E.2d 776 (Ill. 1968).

[83] Labor has not generally sought representation on the board. A rare example is when Chrysler had a labor representative on its board as a result of its precarious financial situation in the 1970's. Eventually labor wanted to be off the board and preferred collective bargaining with management. When Daimler–Benz, a German company, merged with Chrysler, a representative of American labor was placed on their Supervisory Board where German labor under German law has one half the seats. Allowing labor on the board in Germany is called co-determination.

[84] For a discussion of shareholder proposals, see §5.05[C][3] and 7.05, *infra*.

When some publicly traded corporations have been subject to a hostile takeover (because directors oppose the takeover)[85] the directors have argued that in considering the takeover, there should be consideration of the impact of the takeover on other constituencies, such as creditors and employees who may be harmed by the reorganization or financing of the corporation after it is acquired. As a result, the managers should be given greater power to oppose the takeover. Others view these arguments as an attempt to protect the directors from losing their jobs rather then protecting constituencies. The Delaware Supreme Court had expressed concern for these other constituencies but also has indicated that while "concern for various corporate constituencies is proper when addressing a takeover threat, that principle is limited by the requirement that there be some rationally related benefit accruing to the shareholders."[86] Many states have gone further and enacted statutes which attempt to broaden the fiduciary duty of directors to consider other constituencies in exercising their power. The impact of these statutes remains uncertain because it is unclear whether they will be broadly or narrowly interpreted and used.[87]

It is interesting to note that other well developed capitalist systems have a different attitude toward constituencies other than shareholders. In Germany, employee participation in corporate decision making is the norm. German law requires labor representation on a corporation's supervisory board.[88] In Japan, lifetime employment for workers affects business decisions which may not be directly beneficial to the shareholders.[89]

---

[85] A hostile takeover may often start as a hostile tender offer where the bidder offers to buy the shares directly from the shareholders. For a discussion of hostile tender offers and fiduciary duty, see § 12.05, *infra*.

[86] *Revlon Inc. v. MacAndrews & Forbes Holdings, Inc.*, 506 A.2d 173, 176 (Del. 1985).

[87] Some of these enactments only apply when there is a change of control and the managers are allowed to consider these other interests in that context. Other statutes are applicable in broader contexts. *See generally* Roberta Karmel, *Implications of the Stakeholders Model*, 61 Geo. Wash. L. Rev. 1156 (1993). These statutes may be more about protecting management from a hostile takeover than about protecting shareholders. For a discussion of state statutes and hostile tender offers, see § 12.07, *infra*.

[88] In Germany there are two boards: a supervisory board and a management board. The former has few management functions but does select and supervise the management.

[89] *See generally* Mark J. Roe, STRONG MANAGERS WEAK OWNERS (1994).

CHAPTER 9
UNDERSTANDING CRIMINAL PROCEDURE

By

Joshua Dressler

Frank R. Strong Chair in Law
Ohio State University College of Law

Chapter 9
INTRODUCTION TO CRIMINAL PROCEDURE

§ 1.01 The Relationship of "Criminal Law" to "Criminal Procedure"

At one level, the relationship of criminal procedure to criminal law is straightforward. Criminal procedural law ("criminal procedure," for short) is composed of the rules that regulate the inquiry into whether a violation of a criminal law ("substantive" criminal law, to distinguish it from "procedural" criminal law) has occurred, and whether the person accused of the crime committed it.

Logically, substance is anterior to procedure.[1] The substantive criminal code defines the conduct that society wishes to deter and to punish. Procedural law functions as the means by which society implements its substantive goals. For example, assume the criminal law makes it a crime to possess cocaine. Criminal procedure sets the rules for discovering violations of this criminal statute—e.g., police may not entrap suspects, subject them to unreasonable searches and seizures, or coerce confessions. If the police violate these or other procedural rules, various procedural consequences may arise, such as exclusion of evidence at trial or dismissal of the charge.

Unfortunately, the relationship of procedure to substance is more complicated than the simple description in the preceding paragraph suggests. First, procedural rules can frustrate the implementation of a community's substantive goals. For example, if the rules unduly hinder the police and prosecutors in their pursuit of law violators, some persons who deserve to be punished are apt to avoid criminal sanction, and the deterrent value of the criminal law is likely to be undermined. On the other hand, if the rules are lax, the police may mistreat suspects, and prosecutors may be able to introduce unreliable evidence against the accused, enhancing the likelihood of unjust convictions and punishment.

Second, the existence of some procedural rules may motivate lawmakers not to enact proposed criminal statutes. For example, suppose that a legislature is debating whether to prohibit consensual homosexual conduct by adults in private places, i.e., their homes. Further assume that the lawmakers determine that the only realistic way to seriously combat such conduct is for police officers to entrap suspects in the investigation of this offense. If procedural rules provide that entrapment (however defined) is illegal, lawmakers might hesitate to prohibit the conduct in the first place, even though they wish to deter or condemn it.[2]

---

[1] Herbert L. Packer, *Two Models of the Criminal Process*, 113 U. Pa. L. Rev. 1, 3 (1964).

[2] *See id.* at 4.

Third, some legal doctrines involve a mixture of procedure and substance. Consider the constitutional rule that the government must prove beyond a reasonable doubt "every fact necessary to constitute the crime . . . charged."[3] This is a procedural rule, but it cannot properly be enforced unless the term "crime," a substantive criminal law concept, is defined. For example, does the "crime" of murder include as an ingredient the "absence of a legitimate claim of self-defense"—that is, is "murder" a killing that occurs in the absence of self-defense—or is self-defense an affirmative defense to the "crime" of murder? In short, the answer to the procedural question—who has the burden of proof regarding the matter of self-defense?—depends on the definition of murder, a substantive criminal law concept.

§ 1.02   Sources of Procedural Law

[A]   Formal Sources

Various layers of laws and regulations govern the conduct of the partici- pants in the criminal justice system. First, starting at the highest level, various provisions of the United States Constitution, in particular those found in amendments 4, 5, 6, 8, and 14 thereto, restrict the power of law enforcement officers in their relations to persons suspected of criminal ac- tivity, and also govern the way in which pre-trial and criminal trials and appeals are conducted. The United States Supreme Court and lower federal and state courts frequently are called upon to interpret the federal constitu- tional provisions. As a result of substantial constitutional litigation, the study of some aspects of criminal procedure—in particular, police prac- tices—is principally a study of constitutional law.

Second, at the state level, state constitutions are an increasingly impor- tant source of procedural law. In the past few decades, as the United States Supreme Court and lower federal courts have become less sympathetic to the *federal* constitutional claims of individual petitioners, a body of *state* constitutional jurisprudence has developed, in which some state courts, interpreting their own constitutions, have granted relief to their residents that would be unavailable under the federal Constitution.[4] This trend is

---

[3] *In re Winship*, 397 U.S. 358, 364 (1970).

[4] *See* Barry Latzer, *The Hidden Conservatism of the State Court "Revolution,"* 74 Judicature 190 (1991) (providing a list, by state, of the number of cases in which each state's highest court has rejected or adopted United States Supreme Court's criminal procedure decisions, from the late 1960s through 1989); Ronald K.L. Collins & David M. Skover, *The Future of Liberal Legal Scholarship*, 87 Mich. L. Rev. 189, 217 (1988) (reporting that, in their research, state courts in at least 450 cases recognized rights not available under the federal constitution). This treatise provides non-exhaustive citations to state constitutional law decisions.

Not all state courts have the authority to interpret their constitution differently than the United States Constitution. *E.g.,* Calif. Const. art. I, § 24 (in which the state constitution was amended by the initiative process to provide that in criminal cases various enumerated constitutional rights of the defendant "shall be construed by the courts of this state in a manner consistent with the Constitution of the United States"); Fla. Const. art. I, § 12 (in which the state charter was amended by initiative to provide that it "shall be construed in conformity

significant because a state supreme court is the final arbiter of the meaning of its own constitution.[5]

Third, legislatures have enacted statutes and courts have adopted written rules of criminal procedure governing many aspects of the state and federal criminal justice systems. For example, at the federal level, Congress has enacted laws governing such matters as electronic surveillance of private conversations,[6] pretrial detention of dangerous persons,[7] and the qualifications for jury service.[8] Also, Congress has granted authority to the Supreme Court to promulgate written rules to govern proceedings in the federal courts, which the Court has done in the form of the Federal Rules of Criminal Procedure. In turn, Federal Rule 57 authorizes District Courts (trial courts) to make rules governing local practice.

Fourth, some law enforcement agencies promulgate written regulations that their employees are required to follow. For example, police departments frequently have rules governing, among other matters, the use of deadly force to effectuate arrests, the techniques to be followed in conducting lineups, and the procedures to be used in inspecting the contents of automobiles taken into police custody. Although these regulations do not have the force of law, their violation may result in internal sanctions.

Fifth, on occasion the Supreme Court invokes its so-called "supervisory authority" over the administration of criminal justice in the federal courts

---

with the 4th amendment to the United States Constitution, as interpreted by the United States Supreme Court").

It should be noted that a state court may interpret its own constitutional charter *less* protectively than its federal constitutional counterpoint, but if it does so, then the state court "must go on to decide the claim under federal law, assuming it has been raised." Hans A. Linde, *E Pluribus—Constitutional Theory and State Courts*, 18 Ga. L. Rev. 165, 179 (1984). If a state court interprets the state law *more* protectively to the individual, however, it need not turn to federal law—the state petitioner wins her claim.

[5] The importance of state constitutional law cannot easily be overstated, in terms of its potential impact on litigation in the early decades of the twenty-first century. For thoughtful discussion of so-called "judicial federalism" generally, or of its application in criminal cases, *see generally* Barry Latzer, State Constitutional Criminal Law (1995); Barry Latzer, State Constitutions and Criminal Justice (1991); Shirley S. Abrahamson, *Criminal Law and State Constitutions: The Emergence of State Constitutional Law*, 63 Tex. L. Rev. 1141 (1985); Catherine Greene Burnett & Neil Colman McCabe, *A Compass in the Swamp: A Guide to Tactics in State Constitutional Law Challenges*, 25 Tex. Tech. L. Rev. 75 (1993); William J. Brennan, Jr., *State Constitutions and the Protection of Individual Rights*, 90 Harv. L. Rev. 489 (1977); Paul G. Cassell, *The Mysterious Creation of Search and Seizure Exclusionary Rules Under State Constitutions: The Utah Example*, 1993 Utah L. Rev. 751 (1993); George E. Dix, *Judicial Independence in Defining Criminal Defendants' Texas Constitutional Rights*, 68 Tex. L. Rev. 1369 (1990); James A. Gardner, *The Failed Discourse of State Constitutionalism*, 90 Mich. L. Rev. 761 (1992); Paul Marcus, *State Constitutional Protection for Defendants in Criminal Prosecutions*, 20 Ariz. St. L.J. 151 (1988); Stanley Mosk, *State Constitutionalism: Both Liberal and Conservative*, 63 Tex. L. Rev. 1081 (1985); Special Project, *State Constitutions and Criminal Procedure: A Primer for the 21st Century*, 67 Ore. L. Rev. 689 (1988).

[6] 18 U.S.C. §§ 2510–2521 (1997).

[7] 18 U.S.C. §§ 3141–3150 (1997).

[8] 28 U.S.C. § 1865 (1997).

to announce rules that apply throughout the federal judicial system. Similarly, some federal circuit courts have developed rules that apply to the district courts within their jurisdiction. Federal supervisory authority rules do not apply in the state courts and are subject to revision by Congress.[9]

[B] Informal Sources: A Taste of Reality

Although criminal procedural rules are primarily promulgated "from on high"—by the United States Supreme Court, state supreme courts, and federal and state legislatures—the law that is enforced daily on the streets often looks considerably different. As Professor Anthony Amsterdam once observed about United States Supreme Court case law: "[o]nce uttered, these pronouncements will be interpreted by arrays of lower appellate courts, trial judges, magistrates, commissioners and police officials. *Their* interpretation . . ., for all practical purposes, will become the word of god."[10] Put more bluntly, the law at the end of a billy club or police firearm may look very different than the law handed down by nine Justices of the United States Supreme Court or by a legislative body.[11]

This dichotomy between formal and informal law is inevitable. The United States Supreme Court, and each state's highest court, lack daily supervisory control over the actions of the police. Judicial authority is limited to litigated cases, and most of what occurs on the street between police officers and the citizenry is legally invisible. Even if a police officer breaches a constitutional or statutory rule, the victim of the breach may not bring the matter to the attention of a judicial body. Even if she does, state supreme courts and the United States Supreme Court can only hear a tiny fraction of the cases affecting criminal suspects.

§ 1.03 Stages of a Criminal Prosecution

[A] In General

Analytically and in law school curricula, "criminal procedure" is often divided into two parts, the investigatory and the adjudicatory stages. In the investigatory phase, the primary actors in the "drama" are police officers and those whom they suspect of criminal activity. This is the "cops and (alleged) robbers" stage of the process.

The adjudicatory phase begins when the government commits itself to bringing a suspect to trial for her alleged criminal conduct. In this stage,

---

[9] The concept of "supervisory authority" is discussed more fully at § 4.04, *infra*.

[10] Anthony G. Amsterdam, *The Supreme Court and the Rights of Suspects in Criminal Cases*, 45 N.Y.U. L. Rev. 785, 786 (1970).

[11] Gregory Howard Williams, *Police Discretion: The Institutional Dilemma—Who Is In Charge?*, 68 Iowa L. Rev. 431, 437 (1983) ("There is little assurance that policy established by the Supreme Court will be implemented by patrol officers").

the focus of attention turns to the legal profession—the prosecutors, defense lawyers, and judges—who participate in the adversarial judicial system. This is the "bail-to-maybe-jail" phase of the process.

In studying criminal procedure, it is important to understand the procedural context in which the legal rules apply. What follows, therefore, is a brief overview of the stages of a typical criminal prosecution. Because adjudicatory procedures differ by state and depend on whether the defendant is charged with a felony or a misdemeanor, primary emphasis is on *felony* prosecutions in the *federal* system.

[B] Investigatory Stage

A criminal investigation commonly begins when a police officer, on the basis of her own observations and/or those of an informant, comes to believe that criminal activity may be afoot or has already occurred. Because there are no formal stages of a criminal investigation, most Criminal Procedure courses survey the constitutional law pertaining to the most common police investigative practices.

Police officers usually search and seize persons and property during the investigatory stage. Searches and seizures occur in an almost infinite variety of ways: for example, by stopping ("seizing") a suspect on the street and frisking her ("searching") for weapons or evidence; by entering a house in order to look for a suspect or evidence of a crime; by opening containers found in an automobile stopped on the highway; and by wiretapping in order to monitor the conversations of suspects.

The Fourth Amendment to the United States Constitution prohibits unreasonable searches and seizures. At one time, most especially in the late 1950s through the early-to-mid 1970s, this proscription was interpreted to mean that, except in limited circumstances, police officers were not allowed to search or seize property without a search warrant, supported by probable cause, issued by a judge (or "magistrate"). This warrant requirement (or, at least, warrant presumption) came to be honored primarily in the breach, and is of limited value today in determining the lawfulness of police conduct. Not only do police officers today rarely seek a warrant, but many searches and seizures can be conducted on less than probable cause.[12]

The police also interrogate suspects and witnesses during criminal investigations. Some interrogations occur in a police-dominated atmosphere, such as in a police station. In other circumstances, questioning occurs in a less coercive environment, such as in a person's home, automobile, or on the street, sometimes in the presence of family or friends. An interrogation may trigger various constitutional questions, including: (1) is the suspect entitled to be represented by counsel during the questioning?; and (2) was any ensuing confession obtained voluntarily? In particular, the Fifth Amendment privilege against compulsory self-incrimination, the due process clauses of the Fifth and Fourteenth Amendments, and the Sixth

---

[12] *See generally* chapters 18–19, *infra.*

Amendment guarantee of assistance of counsel during criminal prosecutions, are potentially implicated during police interrogations.[13]

The police also conduct lineups, show witnesses photographs of potential suspects, take handwriting and voice exemplars, and conduct other identification procedures. The police may conduct many of these activities without prior judicial approval, and without intervention by defense counsel. Nonetheless, in some cases the Sixth Amendment right-to-counsel provision applies and, in all cases, the procedures must be conducted in a constitutionally reliable manner.[14]

Assuming that a criminal investigation results in a police determination that there is probable cause to believe that the suspect committed a crime, she may be arrested. When a routine arrest occurs in a private home, the police must ordinarily be armed with a warrant to take the suspect into custody. Arrests in public places usually can be made without an arrest warrant.[15]

Upon arrest, the suspect is usually searched and taken to the police station or to a jail, where she is "booked" (i.e., her name is logged in an arrest book or on a computer), photographed, fingerprinted, and more fully searched. Typically, any personal belongings found in her possession at the station or jail are inventoried and placed in custody for safekeeping.

[C] Adjudicatory Stage

[1] Issuance of a Complaint

After a suspect is arrested and booked, a complaint is prepared by the police or a prosecutor and is filed with the court. A "complaint" is "a written statement of the essential facts constituting the offense charged."[16] It serves as the official charging document until either an "information" or an "indictment," each of which is discussed below,[17] is issued.

[2] Probable Cause (Gerstein) Hearing

The police may not constitutionally arrest a person unless they have probable cause to believe that a crime has occurred and that the suspect committed it. In order to implement the Fourth Amendment bar on unreasonable seizures of persons, the Supreme Court has held that, whenever practicable, a probable cause determination should be made by a neutral and detached magistrate, rather than by a police officer.[18]

---

[13] See generally chapters 22–25, infra.

[14] See generally chapter 27, infra.

[15] See generally chapter 10, infra.

[16] Fed. R. Crim. P. 3.

[17] See §§ 1.03[C][4]–[5], infra.

[18] See Johnson v. United States, 333 U.S. 10 (1948).

If the police apply for an arrest warrant, the requisite judicial oversight occurs. However, when the police arrest a suspect without an arrest warrant—the vast majority of cases—a prior judicial determination of probable cause is lacking. Therefore, the Supreme Court ruled in *Gerstein v. Pugh*[19] that, following a *warrantless* arrest, the Fourth Amendment requires that a prompt judicial determination of probable cause be made as a precondition to any extended restraint of the arrestee's liberty.

Because a so-called *"Gerstein* hearing" serves as a post-arrest equivalent of a pre-arrest warrant-application hearing,[20] the proceeding may be conducted in the same manner as a warrant hearing—in the defendant's absence, and the probable cause determination may be based on hearsay testimony. If the arrestee is permitted to be present during the hearing, she is not constitutionally entitled to representation by counsel or to the full panoply of adversarial safeguards available at trial. In many jurisdictions, the probable cause hearing is conducted in the suspect's presence at her first appearance before a judicial officer, a proceeding which is discussed immediately below.[21]

[3]　First Appearance Before the Magistrate

An arrested person must be taken "without unnecessary delay,"[22] usually within 24 hours except on weekends, before a judicial officer, for a hearing variously called the "initial arraignment," "arraignment on a warrant," "arraignment on a complaint," or, simply the "first" or "initial" "appearance."

At the hearing, the arrestee receives formal notice of the charges against her, her constitutional rights in the impending prosecution are explained to her, and a date is set for a preliminary hearing. If the suspect is indigent and not presently represented by counsel, a lawyer is appointed for her at this time. If the suspect was arrested without a warrant, a probable cause determination (a *Gerstein* hearing) is usually made at the first appearance. Finally, and perhaps most significantly, the magistrate determines at this time whether the arrestee should be set free on her own recognizance, released on bail, or detained pending further proceedings.[23]

---

[19] 420 U.S. 103 (1975).

[20] *See* § 11.02, *infra.*

[21] How promptly must the *Gerstein* hearing be held? *In County of Riverside v. McLaughlin,* 500 U.S. 44 (1991), the Supreme Court stated that the Constitution "permits a reasonable postponement of a probable cause determination while the police cope with the everyday problems of processing suspects through an overly burdened criminal justice system." Therefore, if a state wishes to combine the probable cause hearing with other pretrial proceedings, such as the first appearance before the magistrate, it may do so as long as the hearing occurs, as a general matter, within 48 hours from the time of arrest. However, a delay "for delay's sake," out of ill-will toward the suspect, or in order to secure evidence that will justify the arrest, is constitutionally unreasonable, even if it falls within the presumptive 48-hour period.

[22] Fed. R. Crim. P. 5(a).

[23] *See generally* chapter 30, *infra.*

[4] Preliminary Hearing

In most jurisdictions, a preliminary hearing (or "preliminary examination") is held within two weeks after the arrestee's initial appearance before the magistrate, unless the defendant waives the hearing.[24] The primary purpose of a preliminary hearing is to determine whether there is probable cause to believe that a criminal offense has occurred and that the arrestee committed it.[25]

A preliminary hearing is adversarial in nature, and runs somewhat like a trial. Because it is considered a critical stage of the prosecution, the defendant is constitutionally entitled to representation by counsel.[26] At the hearing, the prosecutor and the defendant may call witnesses on their behalf and cross-examine adverse witnesses. However, many jurisdictions permit the introduction of hearsay and of evidence obtained in an unconstitutional manner, although such evidence usually is inadmissible at trial.[27]

The significance of the preliminary hearing in the criminal process depends on whether the state is an "indictment jurisdiction" (i.e., a state in which the defendant ordinarily cannot be brought to trial unless she is indicted by a grand jury) or an "information jurisdiction" (i.e., a state in which an indictment by a grand jury is not required). In *information* jurisdictions, once the magistrate determines that there is sufficient evidence to "bind over" the defendant for trial, the prosecutor files an "information" with the trial court. The "information" is a document stating the charges against the defendant and the essential facts relating to them. The information replaces the complaint as the formal charging document.

In the alternative, if the magistrate in an information jurisdiction does *not* find sufficient evidence to bind over the defendant, the complaint is dismissed and the defendant is discharged. If the prosecutor wishes to proceed with the dismissed case, various options are available: (1) she may file a new complaint, in which case the prosecution begins anew;[28] (2) in some states, she may appeal the magistrate's dismissal to the trial court; and/or (3) in some circumstances, she is permitted to seek an indictment from a grand jury.

In indictment jurisdictions, by contrast, the preliminary hearing functions as little more than an adversarial *Gerstein*-type hearing.[29] Indeed, the magistrate's probable cause determination may be superseded by the actions of the grand jury, i.e., if the grand jury does not indict the defendant, she must be released, even if the preliminary hearing magistrate previously

---

[24] In the federal system, the hearing must be held no later than 10 days following the initial appearance, if the arrestee is in custody, or within 20 days if she is not. Fed. R. Crim. P. 5(c).

[25] Fed. R. Crim. P. 5.1(a).

[26] *Coleman v. Alabama,* 399 U.S. 1 (1970).

[27] Fed. R. Crim. P. 5.1(a).

[28] This is not a violation of the double jeopardy clause of the United States Constitution. *See* § 32.01[A][2], *infra.*

[29] *See* § 1.03[C][2], *supra.*

determined that there was probable cause to believe that the arrestee committed an offense. In the federal system, which is an indictment jurisdiction, the preliminary examination is not held if the defendant is indicted before the date set for the preliminary hearing.[30]

[5] Grand Jury Proceeding

In indictment jurisdictions, a person may not be brought to trial for a serious offense unless she is indicted by a grand jury or waives her right to a grand jury hearing. The purpose of a grand jury is to stand "between the accuser and the accused . . . [in order] to determine whether a charge is founded upon reason or was dictated by an intimidating power or by malice and personal ill will."[31] Because of the grand jury's historical role as the guardian of the rights of the innocent, the Fifth Amendment to the United States Constitution provides that in federal prosecutions, "[n]o person shall be held to answer for a capital, or otherwise infamous crime, unless on a[n] . . . indictment of a Grand Jury . . . ." The constitutional term "infamous crime" encompasses all felony prosecutions.

Today, for various reasons, a grand jury proceeding may not in fact shield an innocent person as well as a preliminary hearing. First, the putative defendant, *i.e.*, the person targeted for indictment, is not permitted to be present during the grand jury proceedings, except if and when she is called as a witness. Only the grand jurors, the prosecutor, the witness, and a transcriber of the proceedings, is present in the jury room during the hearing.

Second, witnesses, including the putative defendant, do not have a constitutional right to have counsel present while they testify before the grand jury.[32] Third, because no judge is present during the proceedings, rules of evidence do not apply. An indictment is not invalid even if it is based solely on inadmissible hearsay evidence[33] or unconstitutionally obtained information.[34] Fourth, the prosecutor is not required to disclose to the grand jurors evidence in her custody that might exculpate the putative defendant.[35]

Upon conclusion of the prosecutor's presentation of her case, the grand jurors deliberate privately. If a majority of them determine that sufficient evidence was introduced by the prosecutor,[36] the jury (through the

---

[30] Fed. R. Crim. P. 5(c).

[31] *Wood v. Georgia*, 370 U.S. 375, 390 (1962).

[32] *In re Groban*, 352 U.S. 330 (1957) (dictum); *United States v. Mandujano*, 425 U.S. 564 (1976) (dictum) (plurality opinion).

[33] *Costello v. United States*, 350 U.S. 359 (1956).

[34] *See United States v. Calandra*, 414 U.S. 338 (1974).

[35] *United States v. Williams*, 504 U.S. 36 (1992).

[36] Most jurisdictions, including the federal courts (*see United States v. Calandra*, 414 U.S. at 343), apply a probable cause standard, similar to that employed in preliminary hearings. Some states use a higher, "directed verdict," standard, *i.e.*, whether there is evidence which, if unexplained, would warrant a conviction at trial.

prosecutor) issues an "indictment," a document that states the charges and the relevant facts relating to them. If the jury does not vote to indict the defendant (a "no-bill"), the complaint issued against the defendant is dismissed and she is discharged.

[6] Arraignment

If an indictment or information is filed, the defendant is arraigned in open court. At the arraignment, at which time defense counsel is permitted to be present, the accused is provided with a copy of the indictment or information, after which she enters a plea to the offenses charged in it. She may plead "not guilty," "guilty," "*nolo contendere*,"[37] or (in some states) "not guilty by reason of insanity."

[7] Pretrial Motions

After arraignment, the defendant may make various pretrial motions. Among the defenses, objections, and requests that often are raised prior to trial are: (1) that the indictment or information is defective, in that it fails to allege an essential element of the crime charged, or that it fails to give the defendant sufficient notice of the facts relating to the charge against her;[38] (2) that the venue of the prosecution is improper or inconvenient;[39] (3) that the indictment or information joins offenses or parties in an improper or prejudicial manner;[40] (4) that evidence in the possession of one of the parties should be disclosed to the opposing party;[41] (5) that evidence should be suppressed because it was obtained in an unconstitutional manner; and (6) that the prosecution is constitutionally barred, such as by the double jeopardy and/or speedy trial clauses of the Constitution.[42]

In some circumstances, if a defendant's pretrial motions are successful, the judge will dismiss the charges on her own or on the prosecutor's motion.[43] For example, if the prosecution is barred by the double jeopardy clause, dismissal is obligatory. Or, if the judge grants the defendant's motion to suppress key evidence, the prosecutor might determine that continuation of the proceedings would be futile and, therefore, request dismissal of the charges.

---

[37] Literally, the plea means "I will not contest it [the charge]." For most purposes in a criminal proceeding, the plea is treated the same as a guilty plea.

[38] *See, e.g.,* Fed. R. Crim. P. 12(b)(2).

[39] *See, e.g.,* Fed. R. Crim. P. 18, 21(a).

[40] *See, e.g.,* Fed. R. Crim. P. 8, 14.

[41] *See, e.g.,* Fed. R. Crim. P. 16.

[42] U.S. Const. amend. V (". . . nor shall any person be subject for the same offence to be twice put in jeopardy of life or limb . . ."); U.S. Const. amend. VI ("In all criminal prosecutions, the accused shall enjoy the right to a speedy . . . trial. . . .").

[43] *See, e.g.,* Fed. R. Crim. P. 48.

[8] Trial

[a] Right to Trial by Jury

If a defendant does not plead guilty and the charges are not dismissed, a trial is held. The Sixth Amendment entitles a defendant to trial by jury in the prosecution of any serious, *i.e.,* non-petty, offense. Although the boundaries of the term "non-petty" have not been fully laid out, the right to a jury trial applies, at a minimum, to any offense for which the maximum potential punishment is incarceration in excess of six months.[44]

Trial juries usually consist of twelve persons.[45] However, a jury as small as six in number is constitutionally permitted.[46] In most jurisdictions, the jury verdict to acquit or to convict must be unanimous.[47] However, state laws permitting non-unanimous verdicts have been upheld as constitutional.[48]

[b] Composition of the Jury

The Sixth Amendment guarantees a defendant trial "by an impartial jury." An individual juror is not impartial if her state of mind as to any individual involved in the trial, or as to the issues involved in the case, would substantially impair her performance as a juror in accordance with the law and the court's instructions.[49]

Moreover, although the accused is not entitled to a jury that mirrors the community as a whole, she is entitled to one drawn from a pool of persons constituting a fair cross-section of the community. This right is violated if large, distinctive groups of persons, such as women or members of a racial group, are systematically excluded from the jury pool.[50]

[c] Selection of Jurors

In order to discover possible bias, the trial judge and (in some jurisdictions) the attorneys examine the prospective jurors ("venirepersons") regarding their attitudes and beliefs relating to the case (*i.e.,* conduct a *"voir dire"*). If either side believes that a venireperson is partial, that side may

---

[44] *Blanton v. City of North Las Vegas,* 489 U.S. 538 (1989). A defendant who is prosecuted in a single proceeding for multiple petty offenses does not have a Sixth Amendment right to a jury trial, even if the aggregate prison terms authorized for the offenses exceeds six months. *Lewis v. United States,* 518 U.S. 322 (1996).

[45] *See, e.g.,* Fed. R. Crim. P. 23(b).

[46] *Williams v. Florida,* 399 U.S. 78 (1970) (jury of six is allowed); *Ballew v. Georgia,* 435 U.S. 223 (1978) (jury of five is not allowed).

[47] *See, e.g.,* Fed. R. Crim. P. 31(a).

[48] *Johnson v. Louisiana,* 406 U.S. 356 (1972) (upholding a 9-3 guilty verdict because the vote constituted a "substantial majority" of the jurors); *but see Burch v. Louisiana,* 441 U.S. 130 (1979) (striking down a statute permitting 5-1 guilty verdicts by six-person juries).

[49] *See Adams v. Texas,* 448 U.S. 38 (1980).

[50] *Taylor v. Louisiana,* 419 U.S. 522 (1975).

CRIM PRO

challenge the juror "for cause." If the judge grants the challenge, the prospective juror is excused.

The law also recognizes "peremptory" challenges, *i.e.*, challenges not based on cause. The primary purpose of a peremptory challenge is to allow a party to exclude a person from the jury if it believes, as a matter of intuition or as the result of the *voir dire*, that the individual is biased, but whose partiality has not been proved to the satisfaction of the judge. Both the defense and prosecution are entitled to exercise a specified number of peremptories.[51]

Peremptory challenges may not be exercised in an unfettered manner. Under the equal protection clause of the Fourteenth Amendment, neither the prosecution,[52] nor the defense,[53] may exercise challenges to remove persons from the venire *solely* on the basis of the prospective juror's race or gender,[54] *i.e.*, on the assumption or intuitive judgment that the person will be biased in the case solely because of the defendant's and juror's shared (or different) race or sex.

[d] Other Constitutional Trial Rights

The defendant is constitutionally entitled to employ counsel at trial. An indigent is entitled to the appointment of counsel in all felony prosecutions, as well as at any misdemeanor trial in which she will be incarcerated if convicted.[55] The defendant may also call witnesses on her own behalf, and confront and cross-examine the witnesses who testify against her.[56] The defendant is not required to testify in her own behalf, and she "must pay no court-imposed price for the exercise of [her Fifth Amendment] constitutional privilege not to testify."[57]

[9] Appeal

If the defendant is acquitted by the jury or by the judge in a bench trial, the government is barred by the double jeopardy clause to appeal the acquittal.[58]

---

[51] *E.g.,* Fed. R. Crim. P. 24(b) (in non-capital felony trials, the government is entitled to 6, and the defense to 10, peremptory challenges; in capital trials, each side is entitled to 20 peremptories).

[52] *Batson v. Kentucky,* 476 U.S. 79 (1986).

[53] *Georgia v. McCollum,* 505 U.S. 42 (1992).

[54] *Batson v. Kentucky,* 476 U.S. 79 (1986) (race); *J.E.B. v. Alabama ex rel. T.B.,* 511 U.S. 127 (1994) (gender).

[55] *Gideon v. Wainwright,* 372 U.S. 335 (1963) (felony cases); *Argersinger v. Hamlin,* 407 U.S. 25 (1972) (misdemeanor cases). *See generally* chapter 29, *infra.*

[56] U.S. Const. amend. VI ("In all criminal prosecutions, the accused shall the enjoy the right . . . to be confronted with the witnesses against him; [and] to have compulsory process for obtaining witnesses in his favor. . . .").

[57] *Carter v. Kentucky,* 450 U.S. 288, 301 (1981); *see also Griffin v. California,* 380 U.S. 609 (1965).

[58] *See* § 32.03[A][1], *infra.*

If the defendant is convicted, she has no constitutional right to appeal her conviction. [59] However, all jurisdictions statutorily permit a convicted defendant (now the "appellant") to appeal. In state court systems, she may appeal to an appellate court below the state supreme court or, if there is none, directly to the state supreme court. In the federal courts, a defendant may appeal her conviction to the United States Court of Appeals for the circuit with jurisdiction over the case.

If the appellant is unsuccessful in her statutory appeal of right, she may be entitled to discretionary appeals to a higher court. For example, in a state in which an appeal of right is brought to an intermediate appellate court, the state supreme court is permitted, but usually is not required except in capital cases, to hear the appellant's second appeal. She may also petition the United States Supreme Court to consider her case. If her appeal is ultimately successful, she ordinarily may be reprosecuted. [60]

[10] Collateral Attack of a Conviction: Habeas Corpus[61]

After a defendant's appeals are exhausted—*i.e.*, once her conviction is final—she may file a petition for a writ of habeas corpus in a federal district court, if she believes that her continued incarceration is in violation of the United States Constitution or of a federal law. [62] A post-conviction habeas corpus proceeding is not part of the criminal appeal process itself. It is a civil action designed to overturn a presumptively valid criminal judgment. As such, it is considered a collateral attack on a criminal conviction, as distinguished from a direct criminal appeal. The purpose of a habeas petition is to convince the district (trial) court that it should compel the warden of the jail or prison holding the petitioner to bring her before the court so that it can determine whether she is being held in custody against the law.

Federal habeas corpus jurisprudence involves exceedingly intricate rules, and recent legislation has made it more difficult than in the past for petitioners to obtain a hearing on the merits of their federal claims.

---

[59] *See McKane v. Durston*, 153 U.S. 684 (1894) (dictum); *Jones v. Barnes*, 463 U.S. 745 (1983) (dictum).

[60] *See* § 32.05[A], *infra*.

[61] *See generally* Graham Hughes, The Decline of Habeas Corpus (Occasional Papers from the Center for Research in Crime and Justice, N.Y.U. School of Law, No. VIII, 1990); Joseph L. Hoffmann, *The Supreme Court's New Vision of Federal Habeas Corpus for State Prisoners*, 1989 Sup. Ct. Rev.165; Kathleen Patchel, *The New Habeas*, 42 Hastings L.J. 939 (1991); Yale L. Rosenberg, *Kaddish for Federal Habeas Corpus*, 59 Geo. Wash. L. Rev. 362 (1991); Robert Weisberg, *A Great Writ While It Lasted*, 81 J. Crim. L. & Criminology 9 (1990); Larry W. Yackle, *A Primer on the New Habeas Corpus Statute*, 44 Buffalo L. Rev. 381 (1996); Note, *The Avoidance of Constitutional Questions and the Preservation of Judicial Review: Federal Court Treatment of the New Habeas Provisions*, 111 Harv. L. Rev. 1578 (1998).

[62] 28 U.S.C. §§ 2241–2244, 2253–2255, 2261–2266 (1997). Some states have their own habeas corpus procedures, which must be exhausted before a convicted person seeks *federal* habeas relief.

However, if the proper allegations are made, the district court may grant the petition and conduct an evidentiary hearing into the federal claim.

Because a habeas corpus petition constitutes a collateral attack on a judgment that is already final, and because federal courts are hesitant to intrude on state proceedings, the standards that a petitioner must satisfy to obtain ultimate relief in habeas are often stricter than those that apply on direct appeals. However, if the district court determines that the petitioner is being held in custody in violation of federal law or the Constitution, it may vacate the conviction. The ruling of the district court— whether to grant or deny the petition—is subject to appeal by the losing party.

§ 1.04 Studying Constitutional Law Cases

The study of many aspects of criminal procedure, particularly the law relating to police practices, is largely the study of constitutional law, especially the decisions of the United States Supreme Court. Consequently, the following suggestions are offered to students inexperienced in analysis of constitutional cases.

[A] Read Concurring and Dissenting Opinions

To the extent that your casebook permits, pay attention to concurring and dissenting opinions, if any, in the assigned cases. Various reasons support this recommendation. First, the ideas expressed in the concurring or dissenting opinions of today sometimes become the majority views of tomorrow.

Second, sometimes a concurring or dissenting opinion explains the views of the majority better than the latter's own opinion, calls attention to unresolved issues, or suggests where the logic of the majority opinion may lead. Indeed, on occasion a concurring opinion takes on a life of its own, and is cited or applied in subsequent opinions in preference to the majority opinion.[63]

Third, as discussed in subsection [C], it is often necessary to analyze these opinions in order to determine the long-term significance of a constitutional holding.

[B] Learn Case Names

Pay attention to the names of Supreme Court cases. Unlike cases applying common law doctrine, which often are fungible, a United States Supreme Court constitutional decision represents the final official[64] word on the issue in question.[65] These opinions have the "power to shake the

---

[63] *E.g.,* Justice Harlan's concurring opinion in *Katz v. United States,* 389 U.S. 487 (1967). *See generally* § 7.03[C], *infra.*

[64] *But see* § 1.02[B], *supra,* for a "taste of reality."

[65] Of course, the Supreme Court can overrule itself, or the Constitution can be amended to override an unpopular decision.

assembled faithful with awful tremors of exultation and loathing."[66] Consequently, lawyers tend to talk about constitutional issues in a shorthand (*e.g.,* "Was the suspect Mirandized[67] ?"). It is helpful to understand and speak this language.

[C] Count Votes

If the casebook permits, take note of the vote breakdown in important cases. For various reasons, vote counting can prove insightful, and sometimes is essential. First, the long-term importance of a decision may depend on the size of the majority. A 5-4 decision is not equivalent to a 9-0 ruling. A unanimous opinion often carries greater moral suasion with the public and within the legal community than one decided by the slimmest of margins. Moreover, a 5-4 precedent is a prime target for overruling (or, at least, narrowing) when a Justice in the majority leaves the Court.

Second, vote counting is essential in ascertaining the precedential value of some cases. For example, suppose that *D* appeals her conviction on two independent grounds: (1) that police officers conducted an unconstitutional search of her house (issue A); and (2) that the officers coerced a confession from her (issue B). Assume that if either of these claims is successful *D*'s conviction must be overturned.

Assume the following scenario: four judges agree with *D* on issue A, but express no opinion regarding issue B. One judge concurs in the judgment; she rules against *D* on issue A, but in *D*'s favor on issue B. Four dissenters reject both of *D*'s claims. Thus, *D* gets what she wants: she wins her appeal, as five judges believe that she is entitled to a new trial, albeit for different reasons.

However, a good lawyer with a client who wishes to raise issue A on similar facts would observe that her chances of success with the same court are not good: four members of the court are likely to favor her client's claim regarding issue A, while five (the dissenters and the concurring judge) will probably oppose her. Likewise, another attorney, but one who seeks to raise issue B, can expect that at least four judges will oppose, and only one will favor, her client. The case would depend on the views of the four court members who expressed no opinion on issue B.

---

[66] Amsterdam, Note 10, *supra*, at 786.

[67] *Miranda v. Arizona,* 384 U.S. 436 (1966).

[D] Learn the Views of Individual Justices[68]

Suppose that a lawyer is considering the wisdom of appealing a criminal conviction in a case in which the law is fuzzy, *i.e.*, there is no rule or precedent on point. In order to determine whether to recommend an appeal and, if so, what arguments are most apt to be persuasive, the attorney needs to "get into the head" of the judges on the court that will hear the case. One aspect of this is to identify each judge's judicial and legal philosophy, as well as her overall belief-system.[69]

It is usually too simplistic (although not always[70]) to treat a judge as a "liberal" or a "conservative" (or as an "activist" or a "non-activist"), whatever these terms may mean to the user. Some judges are "liberal," for example, in matters relating to freedom of speech but are "conservative" on question of criminal justice. Even in the latter area, a particular judge might believe that the police should not generally be required to obtain warrants before they conduct searches (a pro-police position), but that they should usually be required to have probable cause before they conduct the searches (a pro-defense position).

In the field of Criminal Procedure, where the focus is primarily on the Supreme Court, lawyers and law students need to pay attention to the voting patterns of individual members of the Supreme Court. Over time, an observer can develop a sense of a Justice's philosophy and can more accurately predict her vote on specific issues.

---

[68] For discussion of the jurisprudence of various currently sitting Justices, *see generally* Richard A. Cordray & James T. Vradelis, Comment, *The Emerging Jurisprudence of Justice O'Connor*, 52 U. Chi. L. Rev. 389 (1985); M. David Gelfand & Keith Werham, *Federalism and Separation of Powers on a "Conservative" Court: Currents and Cross-Currents from Justices O'Connor and Scalia*, 64 Tul. L. Rev. 1443 (1990); George Kannar, *The Constitutional Catechism of Antonin Scalia*, 99 Yale L.J. 1297 (1990); Christopher E. Smith, *Justice Antonin Scalia and Criminal Justice Cases*, 81 Ky. L.J. 187 (1992); Christopher E. Smith, *Supreme Court Surprise: Justice Anthony Kennedy's Move Toward Moderation*, 45 Okla. L. Rev. 459 (1992). For one analysis of a recently retired Justice, see Kit Kinports, *Justice Blackmun's Mark on Criminal Law and Procedure*, 26 Hastings Const. L.Q. 219 (1998).

[69] The focus here is on the appellate court level, but lawyers must especially be sensitive to the belief-system of *trial* judges, where the vast majority of cases are ultimately resolved. In regard to the backgrounds and voting patterns of President Bill Clinton's appointments to the federal court of appeals, *see* Rorie L. Spill & Kathleen A. Bratton, *Clinton and Diversification of the Federal Judiciary*, 84 Judicature 256 (2001) and Susan B. Haire, Martha Anne Humphries, & Donald R. Songer, *The Voting Behavior of Clinton's Court of Appeals Appointees*, 84 Judicature 274 (2001).

[70] As an example, Justice William Douglas took the "civil libertarian" position in 90 percent of the cases in which he cast a vote between 1953 and 1975. In contrast, Justice William Rehnquist took a civil libertarian position in only 19.6% of the cases decided between 1972, when he joined the Court, and 1985. Jeffrey A Segal & Harold J. Spaeth, *Decisional Trends on the Warren and Burger Courts: Results from the Supreme Court Data Base Project*, 73 Judicature 103, 105–06 (1989).

[E] Be Sensitive to Supreme Court History[71]

Just as individual Justices have specific philosophical perspectives, the Supreme Court as a body—or, more correctly, a majority of it—possesses, at any given time, an institutional philosophy or attitude regarding constitutional adjudication or, in the case of criminal procedure, criminal law jurisprudence. Moreover, certain small-group dynamics develop among the sitting Justices, which affect interpersonal relations, and ultimately, shape the work product. It is worthwhile, therefore, to be sensitive to the place of a Supreme Court opinion in the larger historical constitutional and institutional picture.

Lawyers tend to talk in general terms about the philosophical views of the "Warren Court," the "Burger Court," and the "Rehnquist Court," the shorthand titles for the Supreme Court, and the opinions decided by it, under the three most recent Chief Justices, Earl Warren (1953-1969), Warren Burger (1969-1986), and William Rehnquist (1986-Present).

As the footnote at the beginning of this subsection may suggest, countless book and articles have been written about the philosophies of the Warren, Burger, and Rehnquist Courts. As a generalization, the Warren Court was an activist Court that used its judicial power to develop rules favorable to individuals *vis a vis* the government. In the context of criminal procedure,

---

[71] For discussion of the so-called Warren Court, *see generally* Francis A. Allen, *The Judicial Quest for Penal Justice: The Warren Court and the Criminal Cases*, 1975 U. Ill. L.F. 518; A. Kenneth Pye, *The Warren Court and Criminal Procedure*, 67 Mich. L. Rev. 249 (1968); Yale Kamisar, *The Warren Court and Criminal Justice: A Quarter-Century Retrospective*, 31 Tulsa L.J. 1 (1995).

Regarding the Burger Court and a comparison of it to the Warren Court, *see generally* The Burger Years (H. Schwartz ed. 1987); Albert W. Alschuler, *Failed Pragmatism: Reflections on the Burger Court*, 100 Harv. L. Rev. 1436 (1987); Peter Arenella, *Rethinking the Functions of Criminal Procedure: The Warren and Burger Courts' Competing Ideologies*, 72 Geo. L.J. 185 (1983); Jerold H. Israel, *Criminal Procedure, the Burger Court, and the Legacy of the Warren Court*, 75 Mich. L. Rev. 1319 (1977); Stephen A. Saltzburg, *The Flow and Ebb of Constitutional Criminal Procedure in the Warren and Burger Courts*, 69 Geo. L.J. 151 (1980); Stephen J. Schulhofer, *The Constitution and the Police: Individual Rights and Law Enforcement*, 66 Wash. U. L.Q. 11 (1988); Louis Michael Seidman, *Factual Guilt and the Burger Court: An Examination of Continuity and Change in Criminal Procedure*, 80 Colum. L. Rev. 436 (1980); Robert Weisberg, *Criminal Procedure Doctrine: Some Versions of the Skeptical*, 76 J. Crim. L. & Criminology 832 (1985).

Regarding the Rehnquist Court, *see generally* Tinsley E. Yarbrough, The Rehnquist Court and the Constitution (2000); Craig M. Bradley, *Criminal Procedure in the Rehnquist Court: Has the Rehnquisition Begun?*, 62 Ind. L.J. 273 (1987); Brian K. Landsberg, *Race and the Rehnquist Court*, 66 Tul. L. Rev. 1267 (1992); Robert H. Smith, *Uncoupling the "Centrist Bloc"—An Empirical Analysis of the Thesis of a Dominant, Moderate Bloc on the United States Supreme Court*, 62 Tenn. L. Rev. 1 (1994); Carol S. Steiker, *Counter-Revolution in Constitutional Criminal Procedure? Two Audiences, Two Answers*, 94 Mich. L. Rev. 2466 (1996).

For a political history of the appointments to the Supreme Court, see Henry J. Abraham, Justices and Presidents (1974). For a perspective on various twentieth century Justices, see The Supreme Court and Its Justices (Jesse Choper, ed. 1987). For a valuable statistical analysis of each Supreme Court term, including figures on voting alignments, see the annual study of the Supreme Court term, published in the first issue of each volume of the Harvard Law Review.

the Warren Court was responsible for most of the constitutional decisions that expanded the rights of persons accused of crime. Indeed, the "criminal justice revolution"—as it has often been called—was largely led by the Warren Court (or, more accurately, a majority of its members).[72]

In contrast, the current-day Rehnquist Court (and, somewhat less so, the Burger Court) has favored the "crime control" model of criminal procedure,[73] in that it has granted legislatures and prosecutorial agencies considerable discretion in defining, investigating, and prosecuting crime. The Rehnquist Court has usually placed greater emphasis than did the Warren Court on the matter of obtaining (or, at least, its critics would claim, more rhetoric of obtaining) a factually reliable outcome at trial, and less emphasis than the earlier Court on the methods employed by the government to obtain the evidence used to convict defendants.

Some criminal procedure casebooks include a chart showing the dates on which individual Justices joined the Court. If your book has such a chart, look at it often to see where specific cases fit in. If your book does not have such a chart, the following brief review may be helpful.

In theory, the Warren Court began in 1953 when President Dwight Eisenhower appointed Earl Warren as Chief Justice. However, the civil libertarian thrust of the Court did not develop immediately, but rather took effect gradually as new appointments were made. Already on the Court in 1953, and sympathetic to the Chief Justice's views as they developed, was William Douglas, who was appointed in 1939 by President Franklin D. Roosevelt. After the Chief Justice was appointed, William Brennan (1956) and Potter Stewart (1958) joined the Court. Brennan was a major participant in the Warren Court decisions, and Stewart sometimes provided a crucial fifth vote.

The Warren Court reached its civil libertarian peak in the mid-1960s, after Presidents John F. Kennedy and Lyndon B. Johnson replaced outgoing members of the Court with: Arthur Goldberg (1962, by J.F.K.), who was himself replaced by Abe Fortas (1965, by L.B.J.); Byron White (1962, by J.F.K.); and Thurgood Marshall (1967, by L.B.J.). Of the replacements, only Justice White was often critical of Warren Court values.

The shift away from the Warren Court philosophy was as gradual as its ascendancy. It began in 1969 with the election of Richard Nixon, who campaigned for office in part on the promise to nominate "law and order" justices.[74] President Nixon almost immediately filled two Court vacancies: Warren Burger (1969) and Harry Blackmun (1970), who replaced Chief Justice Warren and Justice Fortas respectively. He subsequently appointed two more Justices: William Rehnquist (1972) and Lewis Powell (1972), who replaced centrist Justices John Harlan and Hugo Black, respectively.

---

[72] For a summary of the "revolution" (or, failed revolution, according to the author) see Craig M. Bradley, The Failure of the Criminal Procedure Revolution 6–36 (1993).

[73] See § 2.02[B], infra.

[74] Liva Baker, Miranda: Crime, Law and Politics 221–324 (1983).

President Gerald Ford appointed John Stevens (1975) to replace Justice Douglas. In the context of criminal procedure, each of these changes in personnel resulted in a high court somewhat more disposed to crime control outcomes. (However, over time, Stevens has become the Court's most consistent advocate of the displaced Warren Court values.)

It was not until the 1980s that the shift away from Warren Court values became clearly evident. During this decade, Sandra Day O'Connor (1981), Antonin Scalia (1985), and Anthony Kennedy (1988) were appointed by President Ronald Reagan, replacing Justice Stewart, Chief Justice Burger,[75] and Justice Powell, respectively. With the appointment of Justice Kennedy, the balance of power definitively tipped in favor of the crime control model of criminal justice, and the Court increasingly cut back on the holdings of the Warren Court era.

The 1990s saw the departure of the remaining members of the Warren Court. Justices Brennan (1990) and Marshall (1991), strong believers in Warren Court values, retired. President George Bush replaced them with David Souter and Clarence Thomas, respectively. In 1993, the last member of the Warren Court, Byron White, retired. President William Clinton appointed Ruth Bader Ginsburg as his replacement. The year 1994 saw the first departure of a Burger Court Justice, Harry Blackmun, with Stephen Breyer taking his place on the Court. The criminal justice opinions of Justices Souter, Ginsburg, and Breyer have frequently run counter to the now prevailing pro-government position of the Rehnquist Court;[76] in contrast, Justice Thomas is a consistent advocate for crime control values.

---

[75] Technically, Chief Justice Burger was replaced by Justice Rehnquist, who was elevated to Chief Justice. Justice Scalia filled Justice Rehnquist's old spot.

[76] See generally Karen O'Connor & Barbara Palmer, The Clinton Clones: Ginsburg, Breyer, and the Clinton Legacy, 84 Judicature 262 (2001).

CHAPTER 10
UNDERSTANDING LAWYERS' ETHICS

By

Monroe H. Freedman

Professor of Law
Hofstra University
School of Law

Abbe Smith

Professor of Law & Co-Director
Criminal Justice Clinic and E. Barrett Prettyman Fellowship
Program
Georgetown University Law Center

Chapter 10

UNDERSTANDING THE RULES OF LAWYERS' ETHICS

ETHICS

§ 1.01 INTRODUCTION

Understanding the rules of lawyers' ethics is essential because so much turns on them. Wherever you practice in the United States, ethical rules will determine whether you can be a member of the bar and how you conduct your practice. Disciplinary sanctions against lawyers include private reprimands, public censure, suspension of the right to practice, and disbarment.

In addition, although rules of ethics are drafted principally with a view to professional discipline, courts are increasingly turning to ethical rules as sources of law in litigation. One area of major importance is malpractice actions, in which lawyers can lose substantial fees or suffer compensatory and even punitive damages for conduct that falls short of professional standards. Also, motions to disqualify counsel from representing adverse parties are increasingly common. As a result, lawyers are being ordered to stop representing valued clients, sometimes in circumstances in which disqualification could have been avoided by taking appropriate precautions in accordance with the rules.

The rules governing lawyers' conduct also have a profound effect upon the rights of our clients. In some cases these rights run against us, the lawyers. If a client has the power to discharge a lawyer without cause, for example, the lawyer has lesser contract rights than, say, a construction worker who has been hired for the duration of a building project. Other obligations that we owe to our clients may have considerable effect on the interests of others. For example, a rule of lawyer-client confidentiality might prevent the lawyer from informing the victim of a client's fraud when the lawyer has learned of the fraud from the client. Of course, if that rule were changed to permit the lawyer to help the victim to remedy the fraud, the client's rights would be diminished and some clients might be less willing to confide in their lawyers.

A further reason for studying the ethical codes is to learn how to draft and analyze statutes. Some of the ethical rules deal with specific, narrow issues, like forbidding a lawyer to commingle her funds with a client's or to talk with a judge about a case when the other party's lawyer isn't present. Others are the loosest of canons, forbidding conduct that "adversely reflects on [the lawyer's] fitness to practice law" or that is "prejudicial to the administration of justice." All the rules present questions of policy, drafting, and interpretation.

195

§ 1.02 SELF-GOVERNANCE

Because of the far-reaching effects of lawyers' ethical rules — extending as broadly as the administration of justice itself — we might wonder why the Congress and state legislatures have, for the most part, delegated this important public function to lawyers. With the exception of occasional statutes that deal with specific issues, the rules that govern lawyers' professional conduct have been drafted into comprehensive codes by a private organization, the American Bar Association, and these codifications ordinarily have been adopted by state courts rather than by legislatures.[1] Whatever merit it may have, this procedure is contrary to democratic ideals.

One justification might be that law practice is too esoteric and complex for nonlawyers to regulate. When we consider, however, that legislatures regularly draft laws governing criminal law and procedure, taxation, nuclear policy, and defense procurement, it becomes obvious that legislators are not ordinarily discouraged by the fact that they do not fully understand everything they are legislating about.

The suggestion is sometimes made that self-regulation is essential to maintaining the independence of the bar.[2] On one reading, the proposition is tautological: to be independent means simply to be free of regulation from others. It is true that *legislative* regulation of lawyers' ethics would impose restraints on lawyers, but any ethical regulation imposes restraints on lawyers. Another reading might be that the independence of lawyers to represent their clients zealously and without conflicting obligations to others would be in jeopardy if legislatures were to write rules of professional ethics. There is no evidence that supports that notion, however, and the established bar has not been constant in its dedication to zealous representation free of conflicting obligations to others. In fact, as we will see, the principal concerns of the established bar often have been elsewhere.

Another reason for delegating such vast public responsibility to a private organization might be that the ABA has done the job so disinterestedly and so well. That proposition does not hold up either. Three times in the past century the ABA has attempted to draft a comprehensive, coherent, and enforceable code of professional conduct for lawyers, and each time it has failed to do an adequate job.

---

[1] Before a code or rule of ethical conduct can be enforced against a lawyer, it must be adopted by the jurisdiction in which the lawyer is practicing. A private bar association can criticize a lawyer who acts contrary to its rules, and can expel the lawyer from membership in the organization, but it cannot affect the lawyer's status as a member of the bar.

One lawyer, upon being expelled from the American Bar Association for "advertising" himself in an autobiographical book, commented that it was a little like being told that you can no longer belong to the Book of the Month Club.

[2] *See, e.g.*, Model Rules of Professional Conduct, Preamble (1983).

§ 1.03 THE ABA'S ETHICAL CODES

The ABA's first codification of ethical rules was the Canons of Professional Ethics in 1908. The Canons consisted of about forty numbered paragraphs, each expressing a norm and, in some instances, a brief explanatory comment or explanation.

The Canons were not inspired purely by disinterested concerns with improving the ethical conduct of lawyers. Rather, they were largely motivated by the influx of Catholic immigrants from Italy and Ireland and Jews from Eastern Europe in the latter part of the nineteenth century. Just as labor unions of the time joined in demanding restrictive immigration laws to restrain competition for jobs, the established bar adopted educational requirements, standards of admission, and "canons of ethics" designed to maintain a predominantly native-born, white, Anglo-Saxon, Protestant monopoly of the legal profession. It is not coincidental that immigration into the United States reached an all-time peak in 1908, the year the Canons were promulgated by the ABA.

As Jerold Auerbach has shown in his excellent book, *Unequal Justice*, leaders of the bar left no doubt about why the new Canons of Professional Ethics were necessary. "What concerns us," said a member of a bar admissions committee, "is not keeping straight those who are already members of the Bar, but keeping out of the profession those whom we do not want."[3] In other public statements, establishment lawyers identified the ethical threat as second-generation Americans who, they said, "are almost as divorced from American life and American traditions as though they and their parents had never departed from their native lands."[4] Because of the "historical derivation" of these new citizens, "it will be impossible that they should appreciate what we understand as professional spirit."[5] As if these failings were not enough, the pained observation was made of these aspiring lawyers that even their "gestures are unwholesome and over-commercialized."[6]

One of those who spoke out about the threat posed by new citizens to the bar's ethical standards was Henry S. Drinker, a chairman of the ABA's Committee on Professional Ethics and Grievances, and long regarded as the bar's leading authority on lawyers' ethics. Drinker complained publicly of lawyers who had come "up out of the gutter," and who were "merely following the methods their fathers had been using in selling shoe-strings and other merchandise."[7] His particular concern was those he referred to as "Russian Jew boys."[8] Drinker's own ethical sensitivity is illustrated further by his analysis of the meaning of "conduct involving moral

---

[3] JEROLD AUERBACH, UNEQUAL JUSTICE 125 (1976).

[4] *Id.* at 123.

[5] *Id.*

[6] *Id.*

[7] *Id.* at 127.

[8] *Id.*

turpitude" as a ground for professional discipline.[9] A case that Drinker considered "difficult" to judge in terms of moral turpitude was that of a lawyer who had participated in the lynching of an African-American.[10]

Women, African-Americans, and lawyers of Asian and Latin descent were not a principal focus of the bar's new "ethical" rules because they were being excluded from the profession by rules and practices that denied them admission to law schools and membership in the bar. In addition, those few who finally did get into law schools faced widespread discrimination. Until 1954 the ABA denied membership to African-Americans.[11] When A. Leon Higginbotham, Jr. graduated from Yale Law School in 1952 with an outstanding record and a high recommendation from the Dean, he was told by a Yale alumnus in Philadelphia that his only chance of a job was with "two colored lawyers" who practiced in the city. Years later, Higginbotham became the Chief Judge of the U.S. Court of Appeals for the Third Circuit.

Few law schools admitted women until the middle of the twentieth century, and then only in small numbers. When women were belatedly admitted to Harvard Law School, they were welcomed by the Dean with the announcement that he had opposed their admission because each of them was "taking the place of a good man." In 1952, Sandra Day O'Connor graduated near the top of her class at Stanford Law School. The future Supreme Court Justice was then offered a position at a good law firm as a secretary. Five years later, Justice Ruth Bader Ginsburg graduated first in her class at Columbia Law School, but was rejected by law firms in New York City. As recently as 1964, Roberta Cooper Ramo (who became the first woman president of the American Bar Association in 1995), could not find a law firm position in the Raleigh-Durham-Chapel Hill area because of her gender.

Because the 1908 Canons of Professional Ethics were vague and self-contradictory, they were effective weapons for discriminatory enforcement. Predominant attention in enforcement was given to the canons proscribing advertising and solicitation — rules that were designed to make competition from nonestablished lawyers more difficult. As is shown in Chapter Twelve, *infra*, some of the early solicitation rules that overtly discriminated on socioeconomic grounds have been carried over in ABA codes and in state and federal ethical rules that are still being enforced.

The 1908 Canons governed lawyers' conduct for about sixty years. They were finally repudiated by the ABA, with the explanation that the Canons failed to give adequate guidance, lacked coherence, omitted reference to

---

[9] *See, e.g.*, Model Code of Professional Responsibility, DR 1-101(A)(3) (1969).

[10] HENRY DRINKER, LEGAL ETHICS 43 (1953). Another close case of "moral turpitude" in Drinker's view was that of a bona fide conscientious objector who had refused to further the war effort. *Id.*

[11] The National Lawyers' Guild, an organization committed to pursuing social justice, was founded in 1936 as an alternative to the ABA. Black lawyers were welcomed into the Guild. *See* ANN FAGAN GINGER & EUGENE TOBIN, THE NATIONAL LAWYERS GUILD: FROM ROOSEVELT THROUGH REAGAN (1988).

important areas of practice, and did not lend themselves to meaningful disciplinary enforcement.[12] That is, of course, a devastating indictment of the rules under which the established bar had been governing the profession for over half a century.

The next comprehensive body of ethical rules was the ABA's Model Code of Professional Responsibility in 1969.[13] The Model Code was quickly adopted, with some variations of substance, by virtually all jurisdictions, and remains in force in a small number of states, notably New York.

In 1977, only eight years after promulgating the Model Code, the ABA appointed a commission to reconsider it. The commission was chaired by Robert J. Kutak, and became known as the Kutak Commission. Kutak characterized the Model Code as incoherent, inconsistent, and unconstitutional, and noted that its ambiguous and contradictory language could be used unfairly against lawyers in malpractice actions. The Model Code was also attacked by Robert W. Meserve and Geoffrey C. Hazard, Jr. Meserve was a former president of the ABA and succeeded Kutak as Commission Chairman; Hazard was Reporter for the Commission. Meserve and Hazard condemned the Model Code as internally inconsistent, ambiguous, unrealistic, and harmful to effective service to clients.[14] Anyone who thinks the ABA's Model Code is working well, they concluded, is "living in a dream world."[15]

Once again, therefore, the failure of the ABA to produce a serviceable codification of ethical rules for lawyers was acknowledged in the strongest terms by the ABA's own leadership.

The work of the Kutak Commission culminated in the ABA's adoption of the Model Rules of Professional Conduct in 1983.[16] Almost all jurisdictions have adopted the Model Rules, California[17] and New York being the major exceptions.[18] The Model Rules improve upon the Model Code in some respects. However, we believe that the Model Rules are, in many respects, less satisfactory overall than the Model Code. Our reasons are given throughout this book.

The way the ethics codes are interpreted and redrafted will be influenced by the American Law Institute's Restatement of the Law Governing

---

[12] Model Code, Preface.

[13] The word "Model" was actually a later addition to the title, in order to persuade the Department of Justice that the codification was merely an academic model and not a scheme among bar members to lessen competition in fees and advertising in violation of the antitrust laws.

[14] Robert Meserve & Goeffrey Hazard, *We Should Adopt the Model Rules of Professional Conduct*, 26 BOSTON BAR J. 6, 7 (April 1982). Ironically, both the authors had previously defended the Model Code against similar criticisms that Professor Freedman had made.

[15] *Id.*

[16] The names are, unfortunately, confusingly similar. The best thing to do is to memorize which is which and be done with it.

[17] California has a distinctive set of rules and statutes.

[18] The District of Columbia has adopted a variant of the Model Rules, but the District's version is substantially different in many important respects.

Lawyers (Third) (1998). [19] The Restatement is a mix of improvements, failed opportunities, and bad rules, but it is a major work and cannot be ignored in attempting to understand the rules of lawyers' ethics. [20]

§ 1.04 THE PURPOSES OF CODES OF LAWYERS' ETHICS

Presumably, we write, interpret, and apply rules of lawyers' ethics for one or more purposes. What purposes, then, are we trying to achieve with these rules? Obviously, the answer to that question will make important differences in the rules themselves.

For example, in drafting rules on advertising and solicitation by lawyers, a desire to prevent competition among lawyers will produce a restrictive rule. However, a policy to maximize access to legal services for people who are ignorant of their rights and their need for a lawyer will produce a more liberal rule. Also, a concern that some lawyers might take unfair advantage of unsophisticated clients might require a modification of the latter rule or the inclusion of a separate rule specifically addressing that problem.

Yet another purpose of ethical rules (including those on advertising) might be to improve the "image" of the profession, either by adopting rules that will appear to say the "right" thing or by forbidding conduct considered unseemly. For example, during consideration of the ABA's Model Rules, the managing editor of a news journal for lawyers wrote an opinion piece titled, *Ethics Review Needed to Polish Public Image of Bar*. [21] The same concern with image was expressed by the then-Chairman of the committee that produced the Model Rules. Upon adoption of the Model Rules by the ABA, Meserve announced with satisfaction that "[t]he legal profession has taken a step which should improve its image." [22] As we will see, some of the ABA's difficulties in drafting coherent rules appear to have come from a reluctance to make hard decisions on issues raising problems of image. [23]

---

[19] The ALI is a private organization of lawyers, law professors, and judges that publishes what it calls "Restatements" of various areas of law. Although the Restatement of the Law Governing Lawyers is called the "Third" (because of the date of its adoption), it is the first Restatement of the Law Governing Lawyers.

[20] *See* Monroe Freedman, *Caveat Lector: Conflicts of Interest of ALI Members in Drafting the Restatements*, 26 HOFSTRA L. REV. 641 (1998); Monroe Freedman, *The Life-Saving Exception to Confidentiality: Restating the Law Without the Was, the Will Be, or the Ought to Be*, 29 LOYOLA (L.A.) L. REV. 19 (1996).

[21] Diana Huffman, *Ethics Review Needed to Polish Public Image of Bar*, LEGAL TIMES, Jan. 31, 1983, at 9.

[22] Robert Meserve, as quoted in Kathleen Sylvester, *At the ABA: From Bias to Ethics; Humor in the Court*, NAT. L. J., Aug. 15, 1983, at 5.

[23] Similarly, Professor Ted Schneyer has commented: "To maintain its authority inside as well as outside the bar, the ABA must in a time of professional ferment display its authority. One way to do so is to refurbish its image as lawgiver for the entire profession." Ted Schneyer, *Professionalism as Bar Politics: The Making of the Model Rules of Professional Conduct*, 14 LAW & SOC. INQUIRY 677 (1989). Schneyer's article shows that a concern with institutional image affected the substance of important ethical rules. *See also* William Glaberson, *Lawyers*

§ 1.05　LAWYERS' ETHICS AND CLIENTS' RIGHTS

Some issues of lawyers' ethics require us to go deeper into our purposes and our values than others. In the past thirty years or so there has been an intense debate over whether one can be a good lawyer and a good person at the same time. Put otherwise, can effectively representing a client's lawful interests properly subject a lawyer to criticism on moral grounds?[24]

For example, what should the lawyer do when a client insists upon taking action that is lawful but that, in the lawyer's view, is also immoral? Does the lawyer hire out her conscience when accepting a retainer? Is it justifiable for the lawyer to impose her values on the client? The subject is developed in Chapter 3, but it is useful to introduce it here.

In analyzing the issue of the "good lawyer," commentators have analogized the lawyer's relationship to the client to that of a friend.[25] or even of a spouse.[26] Thus, Professor Charles Fried argues that a lawyer, like a friend, will not (or should not) impose her moral values on the other, while Luban argues the opposite — that a lawyer, like a spouse, will (or should) prevent the other from acting immorally. You might find both of these analogies to be somewhat strained and artificial, and the conclusions that are drawn from them to be less than compelling.

Professor Thomas Shaffer has suggested that we can best understand the issue of the good lawyer by looking to "[t]he distinctive feature of ethics in a profession":[27]

> The distinctive feature of ethics in a profession is that it speaks to the unequal encounter of two moral persons. Legal ethics, which is a subject of study for lawyers, then often becomes the study of what is good — not for me, but for *this other person, over whom I have power*. Legal ethics differs from ethics generally: Ethics is thinking about morals. *Legal ethics is thinking about the morals of someone else*. It is concerned with the goodness of someone else.

Shaffer thus identifies two aspects of the lawyer-client relationship that will affect our view of lawyers' ethical obligations. One is the inequality inherent in the relationship, in which the lawyer frequently has considerable power over the client. The second is a concern with the client's goodness

---

Consider Easing Restriction on Client Secrecy, N.Y. Times, July 31, 2001, at A1, A17 (noting the concern about the public image of lawyers at the 2001 ABA annual meeting at which rules changes were considered).

[24] As Charles Curtis noted a half century ago, "[w]e are not dealing with the morals which govern a man acting for himself, but with the ethics of advocacy. We are talking about the special moral code which governs a man who is acting for another." Charles Curtis, *The Ethics of Advocacy*, 4 Stan. L. Rev. 3, 16 (1951).

[25] Charles Fried, *The Lawyer as Friend: The Moral Foundations of the Lawyer-Client Relation*, 85 Yale L. J. 1060, 1071 (1976).

[26] David Luban, Lawyers and Justice 166–69 (1988); *compare* Curtis, *supra* note 24, at 8 (stating that "[t]he relation between a lawyer and . . . client is one of the intimate relations").

[27] Thomas Shaffer, *Legal Ethics and the Good Client*, 36 Cath. U.L. Rev. 319 (1987) (first emphasis added). *Cf.* Monroe Freedman, *Legal Ethics and the Suffering Client*, 36 Cath. U.L. Rev. 331 (1987). *See also*, Thomas Shaffer, American Legal Ethics (1985).

(or, more accurately, the client's lack of it) and with the extent of the lawyer's responsibility (and perhaps risk) through association with the client as a lesser moral being. As Shaffer accurately observes: "Modern legal ethics assumes that clients corrupt lawyers — that they are, to use an old Catholic notion, occasions of sin, like R-rated movies and bad company."[28]

Although we agree that the concerns expressed by Shaffer are important to lawyers' ethics, our approach to clients and, therefore, to the ethical issues, has a different emphasis. In expressing the distinctive feature of ethics in the legal profession, we would identify the client not as "this other person, over whom I have power," but as "this other person whom I have the power to help." In this view, the central concern of lawyers' ethics is not (as Shaffer says, quoting Plato) how my client "can be made as good as possible." Rather, it is how far we can ethically go — or how far we should be required to go — to achieve for our clients full and equal rights under law.

Put otherwise, Shaffer thinks of lawyers' ethics as being rooted in moral philosophy, while we think of lawyers' ethics as being rooted in the moral values that are expressed in the Bill of Rights. In the words of Justice William Brennan, Jr., "Our Constitution is a charter of human rights, dignity, and self-determination,"[29] and, as explained in Chapter Two, these values have been incorporated into the American adversary system and should inform our rules of lawyers' ethics.

Again, these are differences in emphasis only. Shaffer is not unconcerned about individual human rights nor are we unconcerned about the personal morality of ourselves, our clients, and others. Nevertheless, these differences in emphasis are important when it comes to drafting or interpreting rules of lawyers' ethics.

In varying degrees, the codes of lawyers' ethics reflect the drafters' conceptions of the lawyers' role and of the lawyer-client relationship.[30] To the extent that such a conception is expressed and consistently carried out, a code will at least have coherence. One thing you should watch for, therefore, is the extent to which the rules in each code succeed in carrying out the drafters' expressed conception of the lawyers' role.

The Model Code of Professional Responsibility recognizes that the lawyer's role is grounded in "respect for the dignity of the individual and his capacity through reason for enlightened self-government."[31] Thus,

> The professional responsibility of a lawyer derives from his membership in a profession which has the duty of assisting members of the public to secure and protect available legal rights and benefits. In our government of laws and not of men, each member

---

[28] Shaffer, *supra* note 27, 36 CATH. U.L. REV. at 320.

[29] William J. Brennan, Jr., *What the Constitution Requires*, N.Y. TIMES, Apr. 28, 1996, at D13.

[30] *See, e.g.*, THE AMERICAN LAWYER'S CODE OF CONDUCT, Preamble.

[31] Model Code, Preamble.

of our society is entitled to have his conduct judged and regulated in accordance with the law; to seek any lawful objective through legally permissible means; and to present for adjudication any lawful claim, issue, or defense.[32]

At the same time, the Model Code is affected by a concern with public image. According to the Model Code, ethical conduct is not impelled principally by what the 1908 Canons called the lawyer's "conscience" or the lawyer's "own sense of honor and propriety."[33] Nor does the Model Code view the lawyer's ethical conduct as deriving from what Shaffer calls "character" or "integrity."[34] Rather, for the drafters of the Model Code, "in the last analysis it is the desire for the respect and confidence of the members of his profession and of the society which he serves that should provide to a lawyer the incentive for the highest possible degree of ethical conduct."[35] The Model Code also says that the professional judgment of the lawyer must be exercised "solely for the benefit of his client and free of compromising influences and loyalties."[36] Note, however, how an undue concern for "the respect . . . of the members of . . . society" could be the kind of compromising influence that the Model Code warns against, particularly if the lawyer is representing an unpopular client or cause.

The Model Rules of Professional Conduct reflect a significantly different view of the lawyer's role and of the lawyer's relationship to the client. As expressed by Professor Norman Redlich, who was one of its strongest proponents, the Model Rules "project a different set of values" from those of the Code, and "[t]he fate of the entire project may well hinge on the bar's willingness to accept the altered role model that the Model Rules envision."[37]

Those differences are apparent in the Model Rules' description of the lawyer in the opening sentence of its Preamble. As we have seen, the Model Code begins by stressing the client — "respect for the dignity of the individual and his capacity . . . for enlightened self-government." By contrast, the Model Rules begin: "A lawyer is a representative of clients, an officer of the legal system and a public citizen having special responsibility for the quality of justice." In a sense, of course, the description is simply

---

[32] *Id.*, EC 7-1.

[33] Canons of Professional Ethics 15 and 24.

[34] Shaffer, *supra* note 27, 36 CATH. U.L. REV. at 329–30.

[35] Model Code, Preamble.

[36] EC 5-1.

[37] Norman Redlich, *Disclosure Provisions of the Model Rules of Professional Conduct*, 1980 A.B.F. RES. 981–982. Redlich was referring specifically to the disclosure provisions of the 1980 Discussion Draft of the Model Rules. However, he reprinted this portion of his article subsequent to adoption of the present version of the Model Rules. *See* NORMAN REDLICH, PROFESSIONAL RESPONSIBILITY: A PROBLEM APPROACH (2d ed. 1983). Moreover, as we will see below, the Model Rules also project a different set of values with regard to the client's autonomy. The "altered role model" to which Redlich referred, therefore, is no less significant than his comment suggests.

a truism, but the difference in emphasis is intended to convey the altered role model to which Redlich referred.

§ 1.06   THE LAWYER AS "OFFICER OF THE COURT"

Particularly significant in the Preamble to the Model Rules is the phrase "officer of the legal system," which is similar to "officer of the court." Those who seek to minimize the lawyer's role of service to individual clients commonly characterize the lawyer as an "officer of the court."[38] The implication is that the lawyer's job is primarily to be an agent of the state. The Supreme Court has recognized, however, that the lawyer's traditional function is to serve the lawful interests of individual clients, even against the interests of the state.

For example, Justice Lewis Powell made only perfunctory reference to the lawyer as an "officer of the court" in writing for the Supreme Court:

> [T]he duty of the lawyer, subject to his role as an "officer of the court," is to further the interests of his clients by all lawful means, even when those interests are in conflict with the interests of the United States or of a State. But this representation involves no conflict of interest in the invidious sense. Rather, it casts the lawyer in his honored and traditional role as an authorized but independent agent acting to vindicate the legal rights of a client, whoever it may be.[39]

Eight years later, writing for a majority of eight, Justice Powell sharpened the point: "[A] defense lawyer best serves the public, not by acting on behalf of the State or in concert with it, but rather by advancing 'the undivided interests of his client.' "[40] In short, in a free society the lawyer's function, as an officer of the court, is to serve the undivided interests of individual clients.

In recasting "the officer of the court" as "an officer of the legal system," the drafters of the Model Rules appear to be seeking a substitute for discredited rhetoric. In any event, the intention of some supporters of the Model Rules to reject the client-centered values of the Model Code is clear, and troubling.

---

[38] The question-begging nature of that characterization has been recognized for some time. *See, e.g.*, ABA Opin. 287 (1953); Monroe Freedman, *Professional Responsibility of the Criminal Defense Lawyer: The Three Hardest Questions*, 64 MICH. L. REV. 1469, 1470 (1966).

[39] *In re Griffiths*, 413 U.S. 717, 724, 93 S.Ct. 2851, 2856, n. 14 (1973). *See also* Justice Powell's quotation from *Cammer v. United States*, 350 U.S. 399, 76 S.Ct. 456 (1956), Application of *Griffiths*, 413 U.S. 717, 728–29. *Cf.* Justice Burger's dissent in *Griffiths*, 413 U.S. at 731–32.

[40] *Polk County v. Dodson*, 454 U.S. 312, 318, 102 S.Ct. 445, 450 (1981).

§ 1.07 MORAL VALUES AND ETHICAL CHOICES

As this discussion suggests, you will find it extremely useful in understanding the rules of lawyers' ethics to have an opinion (however tentative) about your role as a lawyer and what your relationship should be to your client. You can then analyze and appraise each rule by asking whether the ethical purpose being advanced by the rule is consistent with your own model of the lawyer's role and of the lawyer-client relationship. That observation takes us to the ultimate reason for understanding the rules of lawyers' ethics — the self-understanding that can come from applying our own moral values to important issues of lawyers' professional responsibilities. An anecdote illustrates the point.

Several years ago, a friend of Freedman's expressed his disappointment that he could never serve on a jury. At that time, the Jury Commission used a questionnaire that asked, among other things, whether the potential juror had moral objections to the death penalty. Anyone answering yes to that question was automatically disqualified from serving. Since Freedman's friend believed, as a matter of religious conviction, that human life is sacred and paramount to all other moral values, he was disqualified each time he submitted the questionnaire.

Freedman suggested to his friend that his conduct was inconsistent with his asserted moral priorities. Human life was not paramount for him — telling the truth to the Jury Commission was. His scruples about answering the questionnaire truthfully made it impossible for him to serve on a jury and, as a juror, to vote against death. On reflection, Freedman's friend decided to lie on the next jury questionnaire.

This decision by Freedman's friend can be, and has been, debated. Our concern here, however, is not whether the decision was right or wrong, but only that you cannot have it both ways. Either telling the truth is more important than saving life, or saving life is more important than telling the truth. Accordingly, when moral values are in conflict, the ways in which we resolve those conflicts show what our true moral priorities are. In that sense, ethics is applied morality, or morality in action. In making a series of ethical decisions, we create a kind of moral profile of ourselves.

You should be conscious, therefore, of how your own decisions on issues of lawyers' ethics establish your moral priorities and thereby define your own moral profile. In understanding lawyers' ethics, you may come to better understand your moral values, and yourself.

APPENDIX A
HOW TO SUCCEED IN LAW SCHOOL

By

Lazar Emanuel[*]

[*] Lazar Emanuel, a graduate of Harvard Law School, has had a distinguished career in law.

APPENDIX A
HOW TO SUCCEED IN LAW SCHOOL

§ 1.01   How to Brief a Case

As you will learn very quickly, all first year classes and most upper year classes are conducted on the case system. This means that you learn by reading cases that have been litigated and decided in the American courts. Each case you read teaches you how to search for the relevant facts and issues, to relate them to each other, and to isolate and learn the principles for which the case stands. By relating one case to another, you develop the concepts and structure which underpin and control each area of the law. In the end, you acquire an overview of each subject which then enables you to analyze and resolve each new problem.

Definition of a "Case Brief"

To help you to get the most out of each case and to integrate it into the pattern formed by it and other cases, it's important to *brief* the case. This means that you reduce the case to a *formula*, which speeds the learning process and helps you to relate it to other cases.

The "formula" can differ from student to student, and no one formula is perfect. The formula described below has worked well for many students. It is based on the case of *Reynolds v. Texas & Pacific Ry.*, 37 La. Ann. 694 (La. 1885).

EXAMPLE: A "Typical" Brief

Title or Caption: List the title of the case, the date, the court and the source in which the text of the opinion may be found.

Reynolds v. Texas & Pacific Ry.
Court of Appeals of Louisiana
1885
37 La. Ann.

Facts: State all the facts that were relevant to the court's decision. These should include a description of the parties, the proceedings that brought the case to this court, and the facts requiring review. Omit any facts that are not needed by the court.

> Plaintiffs are husband and wife. Defendant operates a railroad. Mrs. Reynolds, who weighed 250 pounds, was seated in a brightly-lit waiting room. The train she was waiting for was late. As it

approached the station, the waiting passengers were told to "hurry up." Mrs. Reynolds rushed from the waiting room onto the platform and down a flight of steps, which were unlighted and dark. She misstepped and was thrown from the platform and steps down a slope beyond. She incurred serious injuries.

The trial court, without a jury, found the Defendant negligent and awarded judgment to the Plaintiffs for $2,000. Defendant appealed to this court.

Issue: State the question facing the court. The question should incorporate the most essential facts and state how the relevant rules of law apply to these facts.

Essential facts: Plaintiff was an overweight woman whose excessive weight might have caused her to fall from the platform and down the steps even in broad daylight and regardless of the Defendant's negligence.

Rule of law: A defendant who is negligent is liable to the plaintiff for injuries caused by his negligence.

Issue: On these facts, did Defendant's negligence in failing to light the platform and steps cause the Plaintiff's injuries, or would they have occurred without Defendant's negligence? Even if they would have occurred without Defendant's negligence, was the negligence so essential a contributing cause as to create liability in any event?

Holding: State in simple terms what the court decided. Did the court answer the question before it? How does the answer relate to your general grasp of this subject (in this case, the issue of actual and proximate cause)?

Even though the accident and injuries to the Plaintiff might have been caused without the negligence of the Defendant, its negligence increased the chance of accident and injury and was of a kind that led naturally to the accident. There was an unbroken chain in which Defendant's negligence played an inseparable part. The evidence connects the negligence to the accident. The judgment is affirmed.

Reasoning: Restate the court's reasoning in your own words to help you integrate the decision into a broader outline of the subject and engrave the decision in your memory.

Example:

The court had to consider whether an accident can have concurrent causes: a cause independent of the defendant's negligence and a cause precipitated by the defendant's negligence. Here, the independent cause was the Plaintiff's excessive weight. The cause contributed by the Defendant was its negligence in failing to light the station platform and steps. The facts make it impossible to determine if Plaintiff would have fallen if the lighting had been adequate. It cannot be said that Defendant's negligence was not a cause of the accident. Because this cannot be said, Defendant's negligence was part of a chain of cause and effect that compels liability.

Policy: If the case reflects a social policy, which underlies the rule of law, state it. It will help you to put the case in perspective.

> Tort law is built on the principle that one person is liable to another for injuries caused by his negligence or lack of reasonable care. When a person is negligent, he should be liable for any injuries caused by his negligence, even if his negligence is only one of the causes of the injuries. He should not be relieved of liability unless it can be shown that his negligence did not contribute to the injuries, i.e., that the accident and injuries would clearly have occurred without his negligence.

Comments and Rule: State in your own words what you got out of the case. If you can, phrase it in the form of a rule which will guide you in other cases.

> This case teaches me that there can be concurrent causes of one accident, and that a person whose negligence contributes to the accident will be held liable for injuries caused by his negligence.

Rule: A Plaintiff does not have to show *with absolute certainty* that the accident would not have occurred except for the defendant's negligence. It's enough to show that the accident *probably* would not have occurred except for the negligence.

Tips & Tricks

- Read the case from end to end.
- Make notes as you read.
- Outline the procedural history.
- Write the facts in narrative form and then rewrite to eliminate irrelevancies.
- Before you state the issue, ask yourself how these facts relate to principles and rules you've already studied.
- Conclude with the Rule of the case.

Using the LexisNexis Total Research System to help:

1. Click the **Get a Document** tab.
2. Enter your citation.
   3. Click the **Case Brief** button.
   4. Click **Get**.

You'll get an easy-to-read, accurate and succinct statement of a case that relies on LexisNexis® Case Summaries and LexisNexis® Headnotes.

SUCCESS

§ 1.02 How to Outline in Law School

A good outline of a law school subject is a work of art rarely achieved. That's why students who are capable of writing good outlines are the objects of student envy.

The most important single rule is to write the outline yourself. That's because outlining requires organization and organization requires concentration and commitment, and only you can contribute these ingredients.

It's a good idea to outline in stages as you go through the school year. Your professor will cover the course in a logical sequence of basic subjects. Each subject is reasonably self-contained. In a typical course, the number of basic subjects will range from ten to fifteen. We'll use the course in Contracts to illustrate how a good outline should be constructed.

EXAMPLE: AN OUTLINE FOR CONTRACTS

The first basic subject you'll cover in Contracts is the definition of a Contract. As you proceed in the first days of the course, you will find the following to be a logical and constructive outline for this subject. The outline is hierarchical in structure, progressing from the most important element downward to sub-elements and sub-sub-elements. This may not be the only way to outline but it is the best way. It follows the structure of a good Table of Contents or Index.

Starting Your Outline

    I. What is a Contract

        A. Basic Definition

            1. Must contain at least one promise by one party to act in the future.

            2. May be written or oral

            3. Performance may be imposed by law

        B. Distinguished from Executed Agreements

            1. Examples: barter, sales, gifts

        C. Classifications of Contracts

            1. Formal & informal contracts

            2. Enforceable, void, voidable & unenforceable contracts

            3. Express & implied contracts; quasi-contracts

        D. Sources of Contract Law

            1. Common law: court decisions

            2. The Uniform Commercial Code

            3. The Restatement of Contracts and the Second Restatement of Contracts

Maintaining Your Outline

As you progress through this basic subject, you will want to build on this outline by adding cases and examples. For example, you may want to expand on Item A. above, as follows:

A.   Basic Definition

    1.   Must contain at least one promise by one party to act in the future

        (a)   Example: A pays $1,000 to B, who promises to turn a painting over to A next week

    2.   May be written or oral

        (a)   A contract may be oral, but some contracts must be written

            (i)   Statute of Frauds covers contracts that must be in writing

    3.   Performance may be imposed by law

        (a)   Referred to as quasi-contracts

            (i)   Example: Doctor who provides emergency treatment to heart-attack patient in subway will be permitted to recover in quasi-contract for his services

Refining Your Outline

Other items may be added to your outline as the course progresses. You may want to add such items as:

- a statement of the rule governing a particular element
- a brief statement of an important exception to the rule
- relevant cases and decisions
- your comments on important class discussion
- notes on a statement made by your professor or an insight offered by a fellow student
- a query that will trigger inquiry into an online source

Using the LexisNexis Total Research System to Refine Your Outline

You can use the myriad resources onthe LexisNexis Total Research System to refine the information in your course outline:

- Familiarize yourself with the materials that are relevant to the course you are outlining, including: state and federal cases and statutes; the Uniform Commercial Code; restatements, law reviews, and ALR Annotations. To access these materials, click **Search;** then select the desired source.

- Use Lexis® **Search Advisor** to find cases and other resources from a specific area of law AND to identify the legal issues that are pertinent to specific cases. **Search Advisor** helps you to target your legal issue, identify an appropriate source, and formulate your search request.

- Consult *Shepard's*® Citations Service, available exclusively on LexisNexis, to ensure that your research is timely and accurate AND to identify certain legal concepts or fact patterns within a case's citing references. Use the FOCUS™ feature in *Shepard's* to restrict cases by facts or points of law.

Final Notes

By starting, maintaining and refining an ongoing outline, you will be able to put every case and every rule into perspective and understand how they fit into the general principles that make up the subject. When the final exam comes, you will have a carefully constructed overview that represents your own analysis of the subject. This overview will be your best preparation for the exam and will virtually guarantee a good grade.

Some students will find it hard to build a good outline on an ongoing basis. They won't be able to put the subjects that make up the course into an organized framework until several of the subjects are covered. It's never too late to start an outline. If you begin late in the course, try to integrate your case briefs into the outline. That will help you to reconstruct the course and build an organized overview.

If you find it difficult or impossible to outline, at the very least, write a daily or weekly summary of what you've covered in class and integrate your case briefs into the summary. That's not as good as an ongoing outline, but it does work for some students.

Tips & Tricks

- Start your outline after the first week of classes.
- Build your outline in a hierarchical structure.
- As you build your outline, add cases and rules of law.
- Write and add your own examples — this will ensure that you have understood the issues and will help you to remember them.
- Listen for leads and suggestions from your Professor and highlight them for exam review.
- Don't neglect your outline — review and add to it at least once a week.

Using the LexisNexis Total Research System to help:

Use Lexis® **Search Advisor** to find relevant case and statutory authority for a particular area of law, (e.g., Contracts Law).

- Enter the name of a legal topic to find relevant materials

- Browse the Search Advisor classification system to identify and formulate issues applicable to your case

Once you have selected a legal topic, you can choose to link directly to relevant analytical materials OR to search for related cases. When searching for cases, you may choose to view a list of suggested words or concepts to include in your search request.

When you have an answer set in response to a search request, you can use it to expand your understanding of the legal concept:

- Enter terms or phrases in the Focus™ Terms box and click **Go** to look for those terms or phrases within the cases in your answer set.

Once you find a relevant case, you can use it to expand your understanding of the legal concept:

- Refer to the **LexisNexis® Headnotes** section for an outline of the case's key legal points. Click **More Like This Headnote** to find additional on-point documents.

- Click **More Like This** to find cases that have similar fact patterns to the one you are viewing.

- Click on the ***Shepard's*** Signal indicator or on ***Shepardize*** ® to make sure that your case is still good law and to find additional documents.

§ 1.03 Cite Verification

All American legal writing must ultimately depend on the integrity of citations. A citation is a reference within the author's document to another document that must or should also be read by the reader. The reference may be to a court's decision, to a statute, to a book, to a periodical, or to any other source supporting or explaining the author's position or argument.

Just as all scientific conclusions must be supported by underlying verifiable research before they are accepted as valid, so, also, must all legal arguments be supported by reference to a statute or decided case. Otherwise, the law would be whatever any one lawyer or judge would make it, instead of a coordinated and orderly system based on precedent. Because the law is a system based on precedent, lawyers use citations to show that their arguments rely on legal principles, which have been enunciated and applied in other cases or in existing statutes.

The verification of citations requires careful attention to details. If any one detail is wrong, the reader will be unable to find the case or statute you're pointing to. And the reader may be your professor, your supervising attorney, or a judge deciding a case that's vital to your client.

SUCCESS

Most legal writing conforms to the system of citations defined by a small book entitled *A Uniform System of Citations*, or, more affectionately, the Bluebook. The book is a compilation of contributions by the editors of the Columbia Law Review, the Harvard Law Review, the University of Pennsylvania Law Review and the Yale Law Journal.

Another widely used system of citation is the *ALWD Citation Manual*, prepared by the Association of Legal Writing Directors and Darby Dickerson.

Under the Bluebook and the ALWD system, cases are cited as follows:

1.   the case name; e.g., *Miranda v. Arizona* (the letter "v." stands for the word *versus*, from the Latin verb *vertere*, to turn, face or confront);

2. the place(s) in which the case may be found: e.g., 384 U.S. 436 (volume number first, then abbreviated title of the official reporter, then page number);

3. if needed, a description of the court which decided the case and the date of decision (thus, a case in a federal appellate court might be cited as 456 F.3d 123 (2d Cir. 1998); this would establish that the case was decided in 1998 by United States Court of Appeals for the Second Circuit, comprising the states of New York, Connecticut and Vermont.

A complete citation of the *Miranda* case would read: *Miranda v. Arizona*, 384 U.S. 436 (1966).

Note the following:

1.   the case name is printed in italics

2. the reference to the location of the case is to the official reporter for the United States Supreme Court;

3. the date is in parentheses.

All these components of a reliable citation must be correct. Thus, the case name must be spelled accurately and the parties must be designated properly and in the right order.

The numbers inserted for the volume and page of the reporter in which the case is printed must be correct. In our example, the number 384 refers to the <Liber> of the United States Reports in which the *Miranda* case is located, and the number 436 to the page. Sometimes, we need to quote from or cite to a particular page of a decision. This is referred to as a *pinpoint* cite. In *Miranda*, for example, we might cite to Page 438 of the decision as follows: *Miranda v. Arizona,* 368 U.S. 436, 438 (1966). This would draw the reader's attention immediately to the point of reference, i.e., to p. 438 of the reporter.

Because you're asking the reader to rely on the authority of the case you're citing, you need to make sure that the case stands for the principle you attribute to it. This means that you don't cite a case unless you read it and understand it yourself, and, most important, unless you can vouch person-ally for the content you claim for it. Thus, you can't cite *Miranda* for the proposition that a police officer may not accept a voluntary confession under any circumstances, only that certain procedural and substantive safeguards must be observed before a confession can be considered voluntary.

Also, you don't cite a case without first verifying that it's still good authority. This means that you must personally verify all the following:

1.   that the case has not been reversed on appeal;

     2. that the case has not been affected by some development that needs also to be cited, e.g., remand to a lower court; a decision by a lower court after remand, etc.; or

     3. that the case has not been overruled or distinguished either directly or by implication, e.g., by a later development or decision in another case.

The best road to cite verification is the service called *Shepard's*® Citations Service. The *Shepard's* database contains references drawn from over seven million cases which have been read, analyzed and processed through the years since 1873 by hundreds of editors with special skills in the case verification process. The database contains references also to millions of non-litigation references, including the federal and state constitutions, statutes, regulations, patents, trademarks and copyrights, as well as to such secondary references as law review articles and the various Restate-ments of the Law.

The *Shepard's* service is available in hard-copy, in CD-Rom and on the web. The LexisNexis™ Citation Tools CheckCite and LexLink work with *Shep-ard's* and your word processing program to verify your authority as you prepare your documents.

You start a search in *Shepard's* by inserting the citation for your case. This will lead you directly to the case and will give you the entire history of that case and its relationship to other cases. It will also report any links between that case and a relevant statute or regulation.

By means of its links to on-line search engines, *Shepard's* will also enable you to access, read and download the full text of any case or statute.

The *Miranda* case and its underlying rationale were before the Supreme Court again in April 2000. See if you can find the *Miranda* case in *Shepard's* and look at all the references. It will help to understand the Supreme Court's decision in the case of *Dickerson v. United States*.

Tips & Tricks

- Support all your arguments with citations to authority.

- Be selective about your citations — make sure they're on point. And don't cite every case that supports your argument, only the most significant cases decided in the highest possible court.

- Cite the case or statute first that supports your argument best.

- Check every citation for absolute accuracy — you can't afford to be wrong.

- Don't cite a case or statute unless you've read it yourself and can vouch for the position you're citing it for.

§ 1.04 Law Review

Fifty years ago, law students were appointed to law review solely on the basis of grades. As the first year of classes drew to a close, candidates in the top 5-10% waited expectantly to be told they had been elected.

Today, most law schools have at least a two-track system for law review eligibility: first year grades, first-year writing competition, and/or a combination of grades and a writing competition.

At most law schools, law reviews are both student-run and student-edited. The reviews are usually organized with two basic editorial purposes: the publication of analytical and critical articles by leading legal scholars and commentators, including professors, lawyers, judges and students; and the publication of casenotes written by the student members. At some schools, the law review is published as many as eight times in a school year.

Many of the reviews are regarded as critical sources of vital thought about current problems in the law. Many law review articles frame and influence legal debate and the discussion of issues of public policy and government.

But many observers suggest that the function of student law reviews is not so much to publish scholarly articles as to give student editors an opportunity to become skilled at legal research and at legal editing and writing.

Third-year law review members are often assigned to review and edit the articles of even the most eminent jurists and scholars. The editing process consists most significantly of cite checking. Each case and statute cited by the author, both in the body of the text and in footnotes, is checked for accuracy of citation and for substance. The process is more intense that the process usually followed by a general editor of books, who is concerned normally only with grammar, syntax and style. The law review editor is also concerned with precision of language and argument. She will work closely with the author to suggest revisions that strengthen the reader's comprehension. However damaging to the author's ego, the editorial process is rigorous and demanding. The objective is to publish a piece which may be controversial in tone and content but whose scholarship, accuracy and attention to detail are unassailable.

Each issue of a law review usually contains two or three articles by non-student authors. In addition, each issue contains a number of items written by the students themselves. Most student writing takes the form of casenotes. Three or four student casenotes are published in each issue.

A student casenote is designed to explore a recent development in the law and to stimulate discussion among lawyers about important legal issues.

Occasionally, a note will encourage and influence legal reform or social change.

Case notes may be as long as 20 pages, including footnotes, which tend to be numerous and extensive. In addition to case notes, student editors also review recent cases, recent legislation and books and articles on the law.

Writing for law review is different from most other legal writing. The author is not an advocate asserting or protecting the rights of a client. The article may have a point of view, but it is a more generalized point of view. Often, it will present and discuss both sides of an issue with equal dispassion.

Most critically, writing for law review requires extreme attention to detail. A citation cannot be wrong; misstatements of fact or law are impermissible; accuracy is king. The job of a good law review editor is to check and recheck citations and to write simply and clearly. The objective is to learn and practice "accurate expression of legal data in well-written English."

Among other things, a law review member learns to prepare manuscripts for publication. Some members deal with pre-press production and with the printer; others do proofreading and proof checking.

At some law reviews, all the business functions are handled by the editorial board. Some have a paid business staff which handles circulation, subscriptions, billing, collections and payments, but even on these, the student editors will help to formulate business policies and budgets.

Law school law reviews are proud and important enterprises. The only drawback is that they are limited to so few students.

Tips & Tricks

- Many law firms consider participation in law review a significant measure of a student's enterprise and ability

- In schools which invite members to law review either entirely or partially on the basis of grades, law review is only one first-year target — the real target is pride in your work

- In schools which invite members on the basis of a writing competition — go for it; apart from everything else, it's excellent training in legal research and writing and a chance to work with others.

- Prepare for the writing competition by looking at your school's law review and, especially, at the case notes.

- Pay special attention to your first-year course in legal writing and research; do the exercises; write and rewrite to achieve simplicity and clarity in language.

§ 1.05   Competing in Moot Court

To sharpen their writing skills and their clarity and persuasiveness in oral advocacy, students at most law schools are encouraged to participate in moot court competition.

Moot courts simulate the work of appellate lawyers and judges in the real world.

The steps by a student in moot court competition are the same steps as by a lawyer who is assigned to handle an appeal from a decision in a lower court. After the dispute is defined, the student is assigned to represent either the appellant or the appellee. The student is expected to analyze the issues presented by the dispute, to research the sources that will support his arguments best, to write a brief presenting those arguments, and, then, to appear before a group of judges to state his arguments.

Moot court competition is either intramural or interscholastic. At most schools, all first year students are encouraged to participate in the intramural program. At some schools, first year students advance through a series of competitive rounds. Students who reach the final round then become eligible to represent the school in interscholastic competition.

Representation of a school in interscholastic competition is a serious matter. Every year, teams of students from law schools throughout the country compete in a variety of competitions. Many schools sponsor and hold their own competitions. Competitions also are sponsored by the national organizations such as the American Bar Association and the American Trial Lawyers Association.

Each competition requires the team members to write an appellate brief, usually directed either to the Supreme Court or to a state Court of Appeals, based on a hypothetical set of facts which have been litigated and adjudicated before a lower court. In some competitions, the brief is judged on its own merits and the best brief submitted is awarded a prize.

Following its work on the brief, the team prepares for oral argument before a panel of judges. The judges may be local lawyers or judges, or judges drawn from state and federal appellate courts. Oral argument is combative and intensive, in much the same manner as argument in a vital and crucial litigation. The participants are scored for the quality and clarity of their arguments. An award may be made for the best oral argument separately from the brief, or the brief and oral argument may be combined and judged in one award.

Participation in moot courts instructs the student first of all in the analysis of appellate issues. Remember that the lower courts have already reached a decision that frames the questions you have to deal with in your brief. If you're for the appellant, you want the appellate court to take some action either to change the decision below or to modify it enough to benefit your client. If you're for the appellee, you want the appellate court to adhere to the decision below.

An appellate brief is addressed to a very busy panel of judges with an enormous daily workload. Some commentators have computed that a typical appellate judge spends no more than thirty minutes on any brief. In this short period, the judge has to read the brief, digest its arguments and read all the cases and statutes cited in the brief. What does tell you?

It tells you that you have to get to the issues quickly and to give the court an easy-to-follow roadmap to a decision favorable to your client. The best road is in a straight line through your best arguments, all supported by sound authority. This will enable each judge on the panel to reach the conclusion you want, to explain it to his colleagues, and to write the opinion you're looking for.

Most courts have rules specifying the construction of an appellate brief. The Supreme Court has rules of its own. A good appellate brief has the following structure:

- Title Page
- Table of Contents summarizing the other components
- Table of Authorities. List separately case citations, constitutional and statutory provisions if any, administrative regulations and miscellaneous sources
- Statement of Questions Presented. Unless the appeal concerns only a question of law, link the essential facts to the legal issues. Point the judge in the right direction by framing the question to suggest the answer you want, but don't force the answer on him
- Statement of the Case. Tell the court how the case got here. What kind of an action is it? Who are the parties? What's the dispute about? What relief do the parties want? What did the lower courts decide? Include a Statement of Facts setting forth all the relevant facts in the best light for your client. Remember, you are an advocate. A good brief writer is like a good novelist. He tells the facts to sustain the reader's interest and to mold his responses.
- Summary of Argument. You're out to win. Tell the court why you should win. State your theory of the case, summarize your best arguments, state the rule or principle you're relying on. Your summary should be thorough and succinct enough to enable the court to adopt it as the rule of the case.
- Argument. Divide your argument into point headings, each heading stating in the most persuasive way a principal argument for your position. Use the headings as an outline of your arguments. Follow each heading with a statement of a reason why your client should win.
- Conclusion. This should be very brief and to the exact point. It should state the relief you want and the language "Respectfully Submitted", followed by your name and address as attorney of record.

A good oral argument does not restate the contents of the brief. It draws the court's attention immediately to the principal issues and to your principal arguments. Remember, the judges have read your brief and your opponent's brief, as well as the Record on Appeal. They know the case almost as well as you. They want to get quickly to the questions that have risen in their minds.

Try in advance to develop answers to the questions the court is likely to ask. The judges will inquire most into your weak points. Know what they are and be prepared for tough, incisive questions. Follow these simple rules:

- Don't ignore or evade a question; the judge who asked it really wants a direct and thoughtful answer.

- Never argue with a judge.

- If you don't really understand a question, ask the judge to clarify or repeat it.

- Don't equivocate; if you don't know an answer, say so; if you haven't read a case, say so.

- Fight hard before you concede a point.

- Let the argument go in the direction the judges want, but try to return to the best statement of your position each time the questions drift away.

Tips & Tricks

- Not all law students or lawyers have the skill or temperament to be good appellate lawyers. It's ok if you don't take to oral argument; many of the most successful lawyers have never prepared or argued an appeal.

- Whether you become an appellate lawyer or not, your most valuable tool is the ability to express your thoughts in simple, persuasive language; there's no better way to sharpen this tool than by brief writing.

- Moot court competition will teach you to pick out essential facts and relate them to legal rules and principles.

- The heart of lawyering is skill at persuasion, whether to a jury, to an appellate court, to an arbitrator, or to the other side in a commercial transaction. Moot court competition will hone this skill.

- Moot court competition will teach you to work with others to develop a joint legal argument or position, a skill that will come in handy when you join a law firm or a public agency.

§ 1.06 Participation in a Law School Seminar

Law school seminars, like seminars at every level of education, consist of small groups of advanced students doing original research and exchanging information on a particular subject, under the guidance of a professor specializing in that subject.

At some law schools, the range of seminar subjects is as broad as the mind can conceive. One metropolitan law school offers more than 170 different seminars! At others with more limited resources, the number of seminars can be counted on the fingers of one hand.

Seminars are available to students in the second and third years. Most of them require either the professor's permission, completion of a more basic course in the same subject, or a specialized background such as knowledge of another language. For example, students who wish to enter a seminar in Advanced Trial Practice may be required first to complete a course in basic trial practice; students who wish to qualify for a seminar in Patents may first be required to take a general course in Intellectual Property.

Whatever the core subject, the seminar is likely to require an original research project and the submission of one or several papers during the course of the semester. At one school, the students in one seminar are assigned weekly reading material and are expected to submit a short discussion and summary of the material each week. At the end of the semester, they are required to submit a long paper "of sufficient scope" to justify course credit. For another seminar at the same school, the students are required to submit two long papers and also to make an oral presentation.

One seminar at a leading law school focuses on Advanced Legal Research Techniques. After studying and working with electronic sources for cases and statutes, the students cover statutory and legislative materials, case law, regulations and regulatory decisions, court rules, ethics materials and many secondary sources. They also review transactional documents such as contracts, wills, deeds and other legal forms.

Seminars are generally conducted in groups of 15-25 students. Some are even smaller. This permits broad inter-student discussion and exchange and maximum contact between student and professor. In the larger law schools with lecture-hall classes of 150 students, the seminar is often one of the few means for direct faculty-student contact.

The seminar format gives each student the opportunity to develop her own research and verbal skills and to gain confidence and knowledge in an area of law that may ultimately become her life's work.

Let's suppose you have a special interest in Ethics and Professional Responsibility and you enroll and are accepted in a seminar entitled *Professional Responsibility: The Law of Lawyering.* Your professor is Samantha Straightarrow, who has written the major casebook on the subject and is frequently quoted (and identified as an expert) in newspapers such as the New York Times.

At your first session, Professor Straightarrow tells you that you are expected to submit a term-end paper of 40 pages on the issues created by the following set of facts:

Lawyer A was admitted to the bar two years ago. He is employed as an associate in a large metropolitan law firm. His supervising attorney, Lawyer X, is the head of the firm's mergers and acquisitions section. X has been involved for many weeks in negotiations for the sale of the Bosworth Corporation, a leading manufacturer of widgets. Lawyer A has been present at several meetings between X and various Bosworth officers and directors, as well as Bosworth's accountants. Lawyer A has reason to suspect that Bosworth's president and one of the firm's accountants are withholding information which would cause the buyer either to walk away from the sale or to demand a reduction in price. Lawyer A also suspects that X knows all about their scheme and has agreed to go along with it. What are Lawyer A's obligations? To himself? To the law firm? To Bosworth's directors? To Lawyer X? Construct your answers first under the American Bar Association Model Rules of Professional Conduct and then under the Code of Lawyer Ethics of our State.

This assignment is designed by your professor to tax all your resources and energies for the balance of the term. She will expect you to find and read a great deal of material, including:

- the relevant rules under the ABA Model Rules
- the relevant rules under the Code of Lawyer Ethics of the State
- lawyer disciplinary proceedings involving the issues raised by these facts
- state court cases deciding any of the issues raised by these facts
- cases of the federal courts deciding any of the issues raised by these facts
- Ethics Opinions of the American Bar Association on these issues
- State and local bar Ethics Opinions on these issues
- the reports of Committees or Panels appointed by the State Bar or by the ABA to consider these issues
- provisions of the Restatement of the Law Governing Lawyers
- the rules of the state courts and of the federal courts applicable to these issues
- relevant federal or state penal statutes or other statutes governing the conduct of lawyers

In short, you are expected to do broad research into a very narrow area and to submit an erudite and illuminating paper that offers original insight into a complex legal problem.

But that's not all. You're also expected to participate in class discussion and to offer your ideas on a variety of topics included within your subject. And, in the best of seminars, you're expected to draw upon your professor's knowledge and experience to develop your own skills in a specialized segment of the law.

The ultimate purpose is to make you a better lawyer, to increase the demand for your services, and to enable you to earn your way in the most satisfying of all professions.

Tips & Tricks

- Give some thought in your first year to the areas of law that interest you most.

- Apply early to enroll in the seminar that fits your interests best; many seminars are offered only once every two years and many require prerequisites you have to fulfill.

- Get your professor's advice on the project to research and write on.

- Participate actively in class discussion.

- Talk to your professor as often as possible.

§ 1.07 The Law School Clinic

Most law schools now offer clinics in a variety of areas of the law. Each clinic concentrates on a particular kind of client or a particular set of practical legal problems.

The number of clinics varies from school to school, but the purpose of all clinics is to give the law student "hands-on" experience in the law as it relates to real clients and real problems.

Law school clinics are generally organized under the umbrella of a nonprofit corporation formed by the law school. As one example, the school may form a Community Legal Assistance Corporation. The Corporation applies for and is issued a Student Practice Order. This Order enables participating law schools to practice in clinics without the charge that they are engaged in the unauthorized practice of law. Each clinic is under the supervision of a faculty member.

Most clinics offer their services to the poor and the indigent. In this way, they make competent legal services available to clients who would ordinarily find them beyond their reach. In most schools, especially those in large urban communities, clinics tend to concentrate on those areas of practice that touch the largest number of people. Among these are housing disputes, the custody and care of children, and minor criminal proceedings.

Students are organized into teams. This makes for intra-group discussion and the exchange of ideas. The team approach also enables the faculty advisor to develop a solution to a legal problem by drawing from the skills of each student on the team.

EXAMPLE: A "TYPICAL" CLINIC SCENARIO

Suppose you are a member of a two-student team in a clinic devoted to the defense of persons charged with the commission of misdemeanors. The

SUCCESS

charges are brought in a county court in a large metropolitan area. The clinic will have a name such as the Criminal Justice Clinic. Usually, it will be housed in a building on the law school campus.

In order to qualify for this clinic, you will have taken courses in Trial Practice, Evidence and Criminal Procedure. During the year, you will attend several seminars, write several papers and memoranda, and participate in discussion and preparation of several courtroom appearances.

Today, your team is instructed to appear in court and accept an assignment from the judge in Part II. The calendar is called at 9:30 AM. The first two defendants are charged with petty larceny, a misdemeanor in your state. Each appears with his own attorney and pleads not guilty to the charges. Both matters are put over for trial at a later date.

The third defendant is a Hispanic woman who is charged with loitering for the purpose of engaging in prostitution. This is a Class B misdemeanor in your state. The judge asks if she has a lawyer. With the help of an interpreter, she answers that she does not. She establishes to the judge's satisfaction that she is unable to afford the services of a lawyer.

You and your supervisor are asked to step before the bench. In the presence of an interpreter, the defendant is told that her defense is about to be assigned to a law school clinic, which will represent her throughout the proceedings. If he is satisfied that the client consents after being fully informed, the judge will assign the case to your clinic. He will then adjourn the case for several weeks to permit you to plead to the charge and to prepare for trial, if necessary.

Outside the courtroom, you instruct the client to appear at your office at a specified date and time. You ask her to bring with her a list of character witnesses, proof of her immigrant status, proof of her employment, and any other facts she considers relevant to her defense. Before the meeting and in constant consultation with your supervisor, you prepare by reading the complaint, checking the applicable provision of the Penal Code, visiting the scene of the arrest, reading the police report, and discussing the basis for a possible defense.

At your meeting with the client, you develop the following facts: The defendant is a legal immigrant who has been in the country for four months. She lives with her aunt and uncle and six cousins. She has recently found employment with a woman who offers housecleaning services.

She has never been charged with any crime and is a loyal churchgoer who would never offer herself in prostitution. When she was arrested by a plain clothes policeman, she was not loitering for any purpose but was instead asking for directions to a local school that conducts evening classes in English. She had stopped a number of passersby, but only because no one seemed to know where the school was and she had become confused.

Satisfied that your client is telling the truth, you prepare for the arraignment and the trial.

In your preparation, you look for and interview possible witnesses, including eyewitnesses and character witnesses. Finally, you reduce your recommendations to a memorandum which you review with your supervisor.

On the return day, you appear before the court and enter a plea of not guilty. Thereafter, you pursue the other steps necessary in trial preparation and the conduct of the trial itself.

All these steps are done under the guidance of your supervisor.

Tips & Tricks

- If participation in a clinic is compulsory at your school, pick a clinic you can participate in with enthusiasm.

- If clinics are voluntary, join one. You'll remember it as the best thing you did in law school.

- After you join a clinic, become an active team member. Pull your own weight. Don't let the others do it all.

- Think of yourself as a lawyer with responsibility to the client or to the cause. Develop the attitudes that distinguish dedicated lawyers.

- Take advantage of the opportunities to appear in court, to argue before the judge, to write a cogent memo . . . in short, develop the skills of advocacy.

LexisNexis Total Research System HINTS:

- Understand the entire process of legal research, from finding relevant cases and other sources to ensuring that your research is timely and accurate. Log on at *http://www.lexisnexis.com/lawschool/research/* for all of your legal research needs.

- Familiarize yourself with the comprehensive state materials available on the LexisNexis Total Research System including: cases; statutes; bill tracking; full-text of bills; administrative codes and registers; regulation tracking; state Constitutions; and, state court rules. Under **States Legal -US**, click your state or click "View more sources."

- Use Lexis® **Search Advisor** to find cases and other resources from a specific area of law, (e.g., Family Law) AND to identify the legal issues that are pertinent to specific cases.

- Consult *Shepard's®* Citations Service, available exclusively on LexisNexis, to ensure that your research is timely and accurate AND to identify certain legal concepts or fact patterns within a case's citing references.

APPENDIX B
AMERICAN LEGAL SYSTEMS:
A RESOURCE AND REFERENCE GUIDE

By

Toni M. Fine

*Lecturer in Law & Director of Graduate and International
Programs
Yeshiva University
Benjamin N. Cardozo School of Law*

APPENDIX B
BASIC CONCEPTS OF AMERICAN JURISPRUDENCE

§ A. Summary of Basic American Legal Principles

What follows are some of the fundamental principles that comprise the American legal system. Each of these is discussed in greater detail in this and other chapters of this book. They are summarized below in order to give the reader an overview of some of the basics of American common law.

1. Impact of Precedent—The Principle of *Stare Decisis*

The defining principle of common law[1] is the requirement that courts follow decisions of higher level courts within the same jurisdiction. It is from this legacy of *stare decisis* that a somewhat predictable, consistent body of law has emerged. See Chapters I.F. and II.G.

2. Court Hierarchy

Court level or hierarchy defines to a great degree the extent to which a decision by one court will have a binding effect on another court. The federal court system, for instance, is based on a three-tiered structure, in which the United States District Courts are the trial-level courts; the United States Court of Appeals is the first level court of appeal; and the United States Supreme Court is the final arbiter of the law. See Chapters I.F., I.G., I.H., II.G.1.

3. Jurisdiction

The term "jurisdiction" has two important meanings in American law. One meaning of "jurisdiction" refers to the formal power of a court to exercise judicial authority over a particular matter. Although the term most often is used in connection with the jurisdiction of a court over particular matters, one may also speak of matters being within or beyond the jurisdiction of any other governmental entity. See Chapters I.C.2., I.F., and I.H.1., 2., and 3.

Second, the federal court system is based on a system of "jurisdictions," the geographic distribution of courts of particular levels. For instance, while there is only one Supreme Court, the court of appeals is divided into 13 circuits, and there are 94 district courts. See Chapter I.H.3. In addition,

---

[1] See Chapter I.B. for a discussion of the term "common law."

each state court system comprises its own "jurisdiction." As indicated above, the jurisdiction in which a case arose will determine which courts' decisions will be binding precedents. See Chapter I.F.

4. Mandatory/Binding versus Persuasive Authority

Some of the various sources of law that will be examined are considered to be "mandatory" or "binding," while other sources are considered to be merely "persuasive." See Chapter I.G. Indeed, a court may completely disregard precedent that is not binding (*i.e.,* not even consider it to be persuasive). The issue of whether authority is mandatory or persuasive relates directly to the application of *stare decisis* principles. See Chapter I.F.3.

5. Primary versus Secondary Authority

The various sources of law may also be broken down into primary and secondary sources of law. Primary sources of law may be mandatory on a particular court, or they may be merely persuasive. Whether they are binding or persuasive will depend on various factors.

Secondary authority is not itself law, and is *never* mandatory authority. A court may, however, look towards secondary sources of law for guidance as to how to resolve a particular issue. See Chapters I.G., II.B. Secondary authority is also useful as a case finding tool and for general information about a particular issue. See Chapters I.E., 1b. and 2.

6. Dual Court Systems

The American legal system is based on a system of federalism, or decentralization. While the national or "federal" government itself possesses significant powers, the individual states retain powers not specifically enumerated as exclusively federal. Most states have court systems which mirror that of the federal court system. See Chapter I.H.

7. Interrelationship Among Various Sources of Law

One of the more complex notions of American jurisprudence is the extent to which the various sources of law, from both the state and federal systems, interrelate with one another. There is a complex set of rules that defines the relative priority among various sources of law and between the state and federal systems. See Chapters I.H. and I.

§ B.   What Is Common Law?

The term "common law" evokes confusion and uncertainty—which is no surprise given its duality of meaning. The term "common law" may refer to any of the following:

1. Common Law as Differentiated from Civil Law

The American system is a "common law" system, which relies heavily on court precedent in formal adjudications. In our common law system, even when a statute is at issue, judicial determinations in earlier court cases are extremely critical to the court's resolution of the matter before it. See Chapter I.I.3.

Civil law systems[2] rely less on court precedent and more on codes, which explicitly provide rules of decision for many specific disputes. When a judge needs to go beyond the letter of a code in disposing of a dispute, the judge's resolution will not become binding or perhaps even relevant in subsequent determinations involving other parties.

2. Case Law

Common law may refer to "judge-made" law, otherwise known as case law. Cases are legal determinations based on a set of particular facts involving parties with a genuine interest in the controversy.

a. Case Law May Be of Several General Types:

(1) *Pure decisional case law*—Court called upon to decide cases on the basis of prior court decisions (precedent) and/or policy and a sense of inherent fairness. In cases of pure decisional law, there is no applicable statute or constitutional provision that applies. This type of decisional law is what is referred to as "judicially-created doctrine." Historically, the term "case law" referred to certain areas of law (*e.g.*, torts, property) that began as judge-made, or pure decisional law.

(2) *Case law based on constitutional provisions*—Court called upon to consider whether a particular statute or governmental action is consistent with the United States Constitution or a particular state constitution. Court interpretation may rely upon prior decisional law interpreting same or some other constitutional provision.

(3) *Case law based on statutory provisions*—Court called upon to interpret a statute. Court interpretation may rely upon prior decisional law interpreting the same or similar statute.

b. Subsequent Case History (see Chapter II.B.5):

(1) Subsequent Case History defined—What a higher level court has done with respect to a lower-level court decision on appeal.

(2) Importance of Subsequent Case History—If a higher level court has taken action on a lower level case, it is the opinion and

---

[2] Civil law systems are found in many European, Eastern, and Latin American countries, as well as in Louisiana.

holding of the *higher* level court that will constitute the precedent in the case. A higher level court opinion will in effect abrogate the lower level court opinion in the same case.

c. Subsequent Case Treatment (see Chapter II.B.5):

(1)   Subsequent Case Treatment defined—What other cases have said about the initial case. Has it been followed? Reversed? Distinguished? Applied in a specific way?

(2)   Importance of Subsequent Case Treatment—Will indicate how the same and other courts interpret the initial case.

§ C.   The American Judicial System: A System Based on Advocacy and the Presence of Actual Controversy

The American legal system is adversarial and is based on the premise that a real, live dispute involving parties with a genuine interest in its outcome will allow for the most vigorous legal debate of the issues, and that courts should not have the power to issue decisions unless they are in response to a genuine controversy. Hence, federal courts are prohibited from issuing "advisory" opinions, or opinions that do not involve a live case or controversy.[3]

1.   Threshold Issues Designed to Preclude Advisory Opinions

Given the prohibition against advisory opinions by the federal courts, there are certain threshold prerequisites which must be satisfied before a federal court will hear a case. Issues surrounding the applicability of these prerequisites may also arise in state courts and on petitions for review of agency orders. See Chapter VI.C.1.

The principal prerequisites to court review are the following:

Standing—The parties must have an actual, cognizable, usually pecuniary or proprietary, interest in the litigation.

Finality—In the case of appeals or agency review, the action by the trial court or administrative body must be final and have a real impact on the parties.

Exhaustion—The parties must have exhausted any possible avenues for relief available in the trial court or administrative body.

Ripeness—The dispute must present a current controversy which has immediate rather than anticipated or hypothetical effects on the parties.

---

[3] These principles are based on Article III of the U.S. Constitution, which limits federal court jurisdiction to "cases and controversies."

Unlike the federal courts, some state *do* allow for the presentation of cases that are not based on live controversies, and hence do not share the federal court bias against advisory opinions.

Mootness—The dispute must not have been resolved. Nor must the circumstances have changed in any way that renders the dispute no longer subject to controversy.

No Political Questions—Courts will not involve themselves in nonjusticiable disputes that are between the other two branches of the federal government and are of a political nature.

While these prerequisites are well-established, the courts tend to apply them in a pragmatic way and allow exceptions to these requirements when warranted by the facts.

2. Courts Generally Confine Themselves to the Dispute Presented for Resolution

As a jurisdictional matter, courts are supposed to restrict their holdings to the narrowest terms possible in resolving a dispute.

This limitation relates to the principle of *dictum,* under which portions of the opinion not required for the resolution of the precise issues before the court on the facts presented by the parties are of diminished precedential value. See Chapter II.C.

3. Tendency to Avoid Constitutional Issues When Possible

Federal courts also tend to avoid deciding constitutional issues when they are able to decide a case on a procedural, statutory, or some other ground.

§ D. Institutional Roles in the American Legal System

1. Attorney

Depending upon the circumstances and the needs of the client, the lawyer may be a counselor, a negotiator, and/or a litigator. In each of these roles, the lawyer will need to engage in factual investigation.

With respect to each of these roles, the lawyer will do the following:

Counselor: Attorney will help advise the client how to order the client's affairs, how or whether to proceed with a proposed course of action, or how to proceed with respect to pending or potential litigation or settlement. Often, this is when the lawyer will prepare (or ask that someone prepare) an interoffice memorandum of law (see Chapter X.), which will examine the client's legal position and help the lawyer counsel the client.

Negotiator: Lawyer will work with opposing counsel to try to get a favorable resolution for the client with respect to a pending dispute. The parties may already be in litigation when they negotiate, or the parties, through their attorneys, may be negotiating a resolution to a dispute not yet in court. The art of negotiation involves many techniques individual to particular attorneys and the circumstances. The client always retains the right to accept or reject a settlement negotiated or offered by the opposing party.

Litigator: In litigating, the attorney will help pick a jury and participate in pre-trial motions. At trial, the attorney will present evidence through testimony of witnesses, documents and perhaps demonstrative evidence (*e.g.,* charts, diagrams). The lawyer will also present an opening statement and closing argument, and will make and respond to evidentiary objections lodged by the opposing party. The lawyer may also make motions, sometimes supported by a memorandum in support thereof (see Chapter XI) before the court, and propose to the court a set of jury instructions. See Chapter V.B.

Fact Investigator: All of the lawyer's roles require the investigation of relevant facts, including locating and interviewing witnesses.

A lawyer is to be a zealous advocate of his/her client. In this respect, the lawyer must advocate on the client's behalf and avoid conflicts of interest. The lawyer is also an officer of the court and is required to deal fairly and honestly with the court and with its other officers, including the lawyer's opponents.

There are specific ethical rules applicable to these issues, but in most circumstances, when the client's interests and those of the lawyer as officer of the court conflict or otherwise interfere with each other, the lawyer is generally expected to favor his or her role as advocate of the client.[4]

2. Judge

The judge is the final arbiter of the law. The judge is charged with the duty to state, as a positive matter, what the law is.

At trial, the judge takes a passive, "umpire" role in connection with the presentation of evidence by counsel. The judge must also make evidentiary rulings, and charge the jury as to the law to be applied. In addition, the judge is to maintain order in the courtroom.

Occasionally, when the parties agree, the judge may also act as trier of fact. This is known as a "bench trial." See Chapter V.B.

Judges in federal courts are appointed by the President with the "advice and consent" of the Senate. Many state court judges are elected by popular vote.

---

[4] Most states have adopted some variant of either the American Bar Association (ABA) Model Rules of Professional Conduct or the ABA Model Code of Professional Responsibility. The federal bar as well as many professional bar associations have also adopted standards based on these rules. There is also a special code of conduct applicable to government attorneys.

In addition, Rule 11 of the Federal Rules of Civil Procedure requires that a lawyer have a reasonable basis for believing the allegations set forth in all writings submitted to the court. See Chapter V.B.

3. Jury

The jury, a group of local citizens, is the fact-finder in most trials. The jury will receive instructions from the judge as to the law, and its members will assess the facts as they perceive them in light of the law as instructed, to return a verdict. See Chapter V.B.

§ E. Sources of Law

1. Overview of Primary and Secondary Authority

There are many sources which comprise "the law" in the United States. At least two major divisions between sources of law may be identified. First, there are primary and secondary sources of law, which are identified and discussed immediately below and in Chapter I.E.2., respectively.

Second, there are both federal and state sources of law. State sources of primary authority are addressed together with the primary sources of federal law, below. Some secondary authorities are state-specific, or have sets that relate specifically to state law. See Chapter I.E.2.

a.   Primary Sources of Law Primary authority as a body constitutes "the law," the set of enforceable legal rules and principles. The following are the most significant sources of primary authority:[5]

(1) Constitutions

Constitutions are government charters. They provide the fundamental rights and obligations of citizens within the charter, and establish and ordain government systems.

U.S. Constitution: The document that establishes the federal government of the United States. No state or federal law can contravene any provision of the U.S. Constitution.

The U.S. Constitution establishes three branches of federal government:

- (a)   Legislative—2 houses (Congress = Senate + House of Representatives) with power to make laws.
- (b)   Executive—President and others to carry out laws.
- (c)   Judiciary—Supreme Court; Congress given authority to establish other federal courts.

State constitutions: Each state also has its own constitution.

While a state constitution may confer rights greater than those conferred by the U.S. Constitution, it may not purport to limit or take away rights conferred by the U.S. Constitution or by federal statutes.

---

[5] Treaties—international agreements—are also a form of primary authority. In some cases, treaties are self-executing. In other cases, they must be given effect by implementing legislation.

(2) Statutes

Federal: Laws passed by a majority vote of each house of Congress and then signed by the President. A presidential veto may be overriden, and in limited other situations, a bill can become law without presidential approval. See Chapters III.C. and D.

State: Each state may pass legislation according to rules applicable in that state.

No state law may contravene any provision of federal statutory or constitutional law.

State action may be preempted in certain areas when federal law so requires.

(3) Rules, Regulations, and Orders

Federal: Federal agencies issue rules and regulations, and adjudicate, pursuant to statutory authority. See Chapters IV.A. and B.

States: States also have administrative agencies, which act pursuant to state legislative authority.

No action by any state agency may contravene any federal law nor may it deal with any matter preempted by federal law.

(4) Executive Orders and Proclamations

U.S. Presidential issuances. See Chapter IV.E. Presidential orders cannot legislate or reverse an act of Congress.

State governors may also issue orders and proclamations.

(5) Case Law/Common Law

Judge-made law/legal doctrine.

Case law is issued by federal and state courts.

b. Secondary Sources of Law Secondary sources of law are not themselves law, but comment upon, analyze, discuss, interpret, and/or criticize primary authority. See Chapter I.E.2.

Examples of secondary authority are the following:

Treatises

Restatements

Law Reviews

American Law Reports (ALR)

Hornbooks

Legal Encyclopedias

State law may be discussed in any of the foregoing secondary authorities. Some states have their own legal encyclopedias.

c. Nature of Primary Versus Secondary Authority As Precedent Primary authority may be mandatory *or* persuasive. Secondary authority may be persuasive, but is *never* mandatory. See Chapters I.A., F. and G.

2. Secondary Sources of Law

Secondary sources are not law, but they comment upon, summarize, restate, criticize, or advocate changes to the law. *

Among the purposes they serve are as case-finding tools (they cite to cases[6]), and as background information on an area of law.

Because secondary authorities are not themselves law, they are *never* binding authority. Depending upon the authority, they may be more or less persuasive, as indicated below.

Common sources of secondary authority are treatises, hornbooks, restatements, legal encyclopedias, law reviews, American Law Reports, Uniform and Model Acts, commercial looseleaf services, and litigation manuals.

a. Treatises

General Description/Overview	Specific treatment of multitude of issues in a particular area of law.
Special Features	Multi-volume; detailed; updated frequently.
Usefulness	Provides detailed information about a particular area of law.
Credibility As Authority	Certain writers considered to be most well-known authorities in a particular area. Some carry significant prestige with courts.

---

* Some secondary sources, such as case digests (see Chapter II.B.1), Shepard's Citators (see Chapter II.B.2.) and annotated versions of the United States Code (see Chapter III.B.) are case finding tools and do not share the functions of the secondary sources described herein. Unlike the secondary authorities discussed here, case finding tools may not be cited or quoted.

6 The citations provided in secondary authorities are often *not* consistent with the *Bluebook*. See Chapter IX.

b. Hornbooks

General Description/Overview	Very general, background information.
Special Features	Not comprehensive; very concise and clear.
Usefulness	Useful if you have no familiarity at all with a topic.
Credibility As Authority	Generally do not carry much weight.

c. Legal Encyclopedias

General Description/Overview	Am. Jur. (American Jurisprudence) and C.J.S. (Corpus Jurus Secundum). Organized topically by legal issue, subject. Gives overview and guides user to primary authority and other resources.
Special Features	Am. Jur. has some state versions in addition to the national version.

Usefulness	Case-finding tool—Leads to cases in many jurisdictions. Background; good place to begin when you know little or nothing about the subject.
Credibility As Authority	Very little authoritative value—do not cite except for most basic, well-accepted propositions (even then, only if necessary).

d. Restatements

General Description/Overview	State and analyze common law on national basis; show trends, make recommendations.
Special Features	Joint effort by scholars, judges, practitioners; panels of noted specialists in area. State general principles and give comments thereto.
Usefulness	Deal with various substantive topics, focusing on overview of state approaches. Appendix volumes contain case digests and citations.
Credibility As Authority	Excellent analyses, given considerable respect by courts, often adopted as law of state. Respectable to cite as secondary authority.

e. Law Reviews

General Description/Overview	Scholarly writings on discrete, fairly specific areas of law.
Special Features	Journals are usually student edited and operated. Journals are general or specific (by theme/area of law).
Usefulness	General scholarly interest.
Credibility as Authority	Not usually used or cited by practitioners. Nor will a court often consider a law review article to have persuasive value.

f. American Law Reports (A.L.R)

General Description/ Overview	Two components: • Cases—Limited number of cases "reported" [Note: never use the ALR "citation"]; • Annotations—Discussion of reported case and related cases; detailed discussions along lines of narrow topic.
Special Features	Sets: A.L.R. FED; A.L.R. 1st; A.L.R. 2nd; etc. Federal cases are reprinted and annotated in A.L.R. 1st and A.L.R. 2nd through1969. Since 1969, (select) federal cases are reprinted and annotated in A.L.R. FED.
Usefulness	Topics in A.L.R. are discrete—many important topics are not addressed at all.
Credibility	Very little authoritative value—do not quote from or cite.

g. Additional Secondary Authorities: Looseleaf Services, Practice Guides, and Form Books

Commercial Looseleaf Services	Specialized and administrative fields.
	Organized by area of law—often by agency or other responsible government entity.
	Common commercial publishers are CCH and BNA.
	Often publish daily issuances of federal administrative agencies.
Practice Guides	Most common for litigation practice and procedure.
	Useful practice guides include those that detail various federal rules and portions of Title 28 (see Chapter I.H.3.a. note 12).
Form Books	Organized by area of law and jurisdiction.
	Judicious use of form books can save time/money; should be accompanied by practitioner evaluation for each potential use and modification as may be necessary.

§ F. The Use of Precedent—The Principle of *Stare Decisis*

The use of court precedent—earlier court decisions in factually analogous cases—is one of the defining elements of the common law system. In short, the use of court precedent, known as the principle of *stare decisis,* requires that a court follow the rules of law established by the same or higher level courts in the same jurisdiction (see Chapter II.G.). Indeed, given the laudatory purposes served by the principle of *stare decisis* and its fundamental significance to our system of common law, many courts who are not required to follow precedent established in an earlier case will nevertheless apply the principle of *stare decisis.*

1. *Stare Decisis* Means "Let It [The Prior Decision] Stand"

Principle by which courts follow precedent (prior decisions in factually similar/analogous situations).

2. Rationale

    a.   Judicial economy

    b.   Fairness to parties

    c.   Predictability

    d.   Check on arbitrary behavior

3. Applies Only if Precedent is "Binding" or "Mandatory"

The principle of *stare decisis* does not apply to authority that is merely "persuasive."

4. Application of *Stare Decisis* Depends upon Two Main Factors

The determination whether the principle of *stare decisis* applies is based mainly on two factors: Jurisdiction and court level (hierarchy):

    a.   *Jurisdiction*—The geographic region from which the case in question arose:

        (1) State court? If so, which state?

        (2) Federal court? If so, which district or circuit?[7]

    b.   *Court Hierarchy*—The level of court from which the case arose:

        (1) Trial level, appellate level, or court of last resort?

Jurisdiction and court level are critical to the application of *stare decisis* because the doctrine applies only with respect to cases decided within the same *jurisdiction* by a *higher level court*.

In addition, courts from the same jurisdiction are to consider and generally will follow precedent established at the same court level.[*]

Courts need not but may consider precedent established by courts in other jurisdictions.

5. Additional Factors to be Considered in Applying *Stare Decisis*

    a.   Similarity of legal issue(s)

    b.   Similarity of facts

    c.   More recent precedent has greater persuasive value

    d.   Whether precedent emerged from a court that the court at hand tends to follow or that is recognized as a leader in that subject area

    e.   Whether precedent was well-reasoned

---

[7] If the precedent was issued by the United States Supreme Court, that precedent will be treated as binding upon all courts, with one possible exception: If the Supreme Court precedent nvolved a matter of state law, it will not be binding upon the highest court of the relevant State. See Chapter II.G.

[*] In the case of federal circuit courts, a panel is required to follow decisions rendered by another panel within the same circuit. See Chapter II.G.3.b.

6. Importance to the Principle of *Stare Decisis* of Analogizing and Distinguishing Precedent

The application of *stare decisis* thus requires—in addition to a consideration of the jurisdiction and level of court of precedent—a consideration of the similarity between the issues of law and facts presented in the earlier case and those in the instant case. See Chapter II.D.

a. *Analogizing:* If the court finds that the issues of law and fact are similar as a legal matter, then the court will likely analogize to the earlier case and apply the precedent to the later case.

b. *Distinguishing:* If the court finds that the issues of law and/or fact are dissimilar from a legal perspective, then the court will probably not apply the precedent.

7. Deviations from the Principle of *Stare Decisis*

Despite the principle of *stare decisis,* courts will at times deviate (or appear to deviate) from earlier precedent.

The following points bear mentioning:

a. Courts rarely explicitly overrule earlier applicable authority. Rather, they are more likely to distinguish facts or otherwise find that the earlier precedent does not apply on the merits.

b. When courts recognize that earlier precedent in that jurisdiction should be overruled, they will rely on considerations such as the trend of other jurisdictions, newly developing policies, and the arcane nature of the earlier precedent.

c. A court can (but rarely does) overrule its own precedent, but a court may not overrule precedent established by a higher level court in that jurisdiction. Lower courts may indicate in their opinions their preference to rule in a manner contrary to precedent established by a higher level court, but only that higher level court is empowered to overrule earlier precedent.

§ G. Binding/Mandatory versus Persuasive Authority

Of the many sources of American law, some are considered to be "mandatory" or "binding," and others "persuasive."

While some sources of law are mandatory in some contexts, they may be merely persuasive in other contexts. For instance, a case that is binding on one court may not be binding on a court in another jurisdiction.

In addition, if authority is considered to be "persuasive," it does not mean that a subsequent court will consider it to be persuasive—only that the court *may* consider it in evaluating a case before it.

Mandatory/Binding Authority Defined	Authority a court must/is bound to follow.
Examples of Mandatory/Binding Authority	Applicable constitutions and statutes. Cases: General Rule— *Holding* (*i.e.,* not dictum); From a *higher level court;* In the *same jurisdiction;* In a *factually similar* case; Applying the *same law* (federal; particular state). See Chapter I.F.
Persuasive Authority Defined	Authority a court may, but is not required to, follow.
Examples of Persuasive Authority	Cases that are not binding (see above). Secondary sources. See Chapter I.E.2.

Factors Court May Use in Determining Whether to Consider and Apply Persuasive Authority	Jurisdiction Court hierarchy Factual similarities Policy Intervening authority Attractiveness of reasoning Date of prior authority Split among courts
Importance of Question Whether Authority is Mandatory or Persuasive	Relates to application of *stare decisis.* See Chapter I.F.

§ H.　Federal and State Systems

1.　Dual Federal and State Systems

The American legal system is based around a system of federalism, which basically refers to shared powers among the state and federal governments. The federal government is a government of limited powers, which are prescribed in the U.S. Constitution. The states retain all powers not expressly left exclusively to the federal government.

The federal government and most state governments have court systems based on three tiers. Cases proceed from the lowest level court to two separate levels of appeal. A few states have only a trial level court and one level of appeal.

(a) **U.S. Government System Based on a System of Federalism**

1. Shared powers between federal and state governments

2. Federal Constitution delegates to federal government specific powers; remaining powers are reserved for the states

(b) **Federalism Results in Dual Court Systems**

1. Federal court system

2. State court systems

(c) **Consistent With Limited Power of Federal Government, Federal Courts Have Jurisdiction to Hear Cases Involving:**

1. Federal constitutional issues

2. Federal statutory issues

3. Diversity cases—disputes between citizens of different states or of a citizen of a state against a citizen of a foreign country, if they meet a certain "jurisdictional amount" (currently $50,000, exclusive of costs)

4. Cases in which U.S. is a party

5. Other cases as specified by law—*e.g.*, admiralty, antitrust, maritime

6. Removal jurisdiction—if plaintiff could have brought case in federal court but brought case in state court, defendant can "remove" case to federal court, unless case is in defendant's home state

(d) **State Courts May Review the Following Types of Cases**

1. Any case, including those over which federal courts have jurisdiction

2. Exceptions to state court jurisdiction: State court jurisdiction may be precluded by federal statute either expressly (*e.g.*, admiralty, patent, copyright) or implicitly (*e.g.*, antitrust damages and injunctions)

(e) **Typical Federal and State Court Structure**

1. Three-tier structure is most typical

2. Three-tier structure:

    (a) Lower court—fact-finding

    (b) Intermediate court—appeals from lower court

    (c) High court—appeals from intermediate court

(f) **Federal Court Structure**

1. District Courts—Trial-Level Courts

      (a)   Factual finding and development

      (b)   Each state has one or more "districts" depending upon the size of the state

      (c)   Several "districts" are combined to form one "circuit"

      (d)   94 districts form 12 circuits

  2.   Court Of Appeals—Intermediate Level Court

      (a)   Appeals from trial-level (district) courts

      (b)   Original jurisdiction over orders of many federal agencies

      (c)   13 circuit courts—one for each number 1-11; D.C. Circuit; Federal Circuit for certain specialized matters

      (d)   Except for Federal Circuit, circuits are geographically-based

  3.   U.S. Supreme Court

      (a)   Supreme court of the land

      (b)   Original jurisdiction in very rare cases, *e.g.*, when there is a controversy between two states

      (c)   Generally hears appeals from U.S. Court of Appeals

      (d)   Hears some appeals from highest state courts

See Chapter I.H.3.

(g) State Court Structure

  1.   Most state court systems mirror that of the federal court system, *i.e.*, they generally are three-tiered, with two levels of appeal

  2.   Some states have only two-tiered court systems, with only one level of appeal

See Chapter I.H.4.

2. Illustration of the Dual American Court System

FEDERAL COURTS	STATE COURTS
Court Levels	
U.S. Supreme Court	Court of last resort
U.S. Court of Appeals [circuit courts]	Intermediate courts
U.S. District Courts	Trial courts
Court Jurisdiction	
Federal Question	Anything not expressly or implicitly reserved exclusively for federal courts

Diversity
U.S. a party
Others as specified
by law

Parallel Systems
A case will normally go through one system or another;
there is some overlap in unusual cases.

3.   The Federal Courts: An Overview

The federal court system is a three-tiered system with one court of last resort (the U.S. Supreme Court, see chart immediately below), one intermediate court of appeals (the U.S. Court of Appeals, divided into 13 circuits, see Chapter I.H.3.b.), and a level of trial courts (the U.S. District Courts, of which there are 94, see Chapter I.H.3.c.). Several district courts are combined to form one circuit court.

a. United States Supreme Court

Formal Court Name	United States Supreme Court.[8]
Type Of Court	Court of last resort. Original jurisdiction in limited cases (*e.g.*, conflicts between states).
Basic Court Structure	One Supreme Court. Nine Justices. All justices hear and decide each case (unless recused/disqualified).[9]
Reporters	United States Reports—U.S. [official]. Supreme Court Reporter—S. Ct. [West]. Lawyers' Edition—L. Ed. [Lawyers' Cooperative]. United States Law Week/Supreme Court Bulletin—newest Court decisions.
Digests[10]	United States Supreme Court Digest [West]. Federal Practice Digest [currently in 4th series] [West]. Modern Federal Practice Digest [older cases] [West]. Federal Digest [older cases] [West].

---

[8] Also referred to as the "Supreme Court" or the "Court" if it is clear from the context that the reference is to the United States Supreme Court.

[9] Federal judges at all levels may be recused or disqualified for conflicts of interest (real or perceived) and other reasons. Grounds for disqualification are found at 28 U.S.C. § 455.

[10] Reporters publish cases, while digests are a case finding tool. See Chapter II.A. and B.1.

Applicable Statutes And Rules	Rules of the United States Supreme Court.[11] Title 28 of the United States Code.[12]
Access To Court	Right of appeal: Limited classes of cases, generally involving state court declaration of unconstitutionality of federal law, federal court declaration of unconstitutionality of state laws, high state court upholding state law against claim of unconstitutionality. Original Jurisdiction: Involving ambassadors, controversies between states, etc. Petition for a *writ of certiorari:* Review completely discretionary with Supreme Court. Certification: Request by Court of Appeals that Supreme Court give instructions on a question of law. The Supreme Court may give binding instructions, or may hear the entire matter in controversy. Writ of Habeas Corpus: Limited right of redress for prisoners.[13]

b.   United States Court of Appeals

Formal Court Name	United States Court of Appeals; United States Court of Appeals for the __ Circuit.[14]
Type Of Court	Intermediate court of appeals. Initial court review for some cases, especially appeals from agency action.

---

[11] All federal courts have their own rules of practice and procedure which should be consulted by the practitioner.

[12] Title 28 of the United States Code provides important information to the practitioner regarding many issues of federal court law, including issues of jurisdiction, venue and other areas of federal court review. Title 28 should be consulted whenever an action is taken or planned to be taken in any federal court.

[13] A petition for a *writ of habeas corpus* should normally be filed in the first instance in a United States District Court. The Supreme Court will entertain an original request for the *writ* only under exceptional circumstances, including showing that adequate relief can not be had in any other way.

Basic Court Structure	Court of Appeals divided into 13 circuits: 1-11 (geographic), District of Columbia Circuit, Federal Circuit.[15] Each circuit (except Federal Circuit) comprised of one or more districts.
	Each circuit has varying number of judges, from six to twenty-eight, depending upon the size of the circuit and the volume of cases.
	Most cases heard and decided by 3-judge panel, selected at random.[16]
	Entire court may hear case *"en banc."* See Chapter V.B.
Reporter	Federal Reporter—F./F.2d./F.3d [West]
Digests	Federal Practice Digest [currently in 4th series] [West].
	Modern Federal Practice Digest [older cases] [West].
	Federal Digest [older cases] [West].
Applicable Statutes and Rules	Federal Rules of Appellate Procedure—applicable to all circuits.
	Local court rules adopted by and applicable within each circuit. See Fed. R. App. Proc. 47.[17]
	Local operating rules adopted by and applicable within each circuit.
	Title 28 of the United States Code.
Access to Court	Direct appeal from determinations of district courts.
	Direct review of final action of some federal agencies.

---

[14] Also referred to as the "Court of Appeals for the __ Circuit" the "__ Circuit" the "court of appeals" or the "circuit court," if the reference is clear fromt he context. The term "circuit" comes from the old practice of circuit court judges to travel around the circuit to hear cases. Now, most appellate judges are assigned to a court in a single geographic location.

[15] Unlike the other circuit courts in which venue is based on geographic considerations, the Federal Circuit has jurisdiction over specialized matters, including intellectual property, international trade, government contracts, and other miscellaneous matters. The location and composition of each of the twelve geographic circuits may be found in a diagram in the front of each volume of the Federal Reporter and the Federal Supplement. See also 28 U.S.C. § 41.

[16] On occasion, a panel may not be selected at random if there is a particular reason to call a panel comprised of specific members. For instance, if a panel has already heard the same case and ordered a remand, the same panel may be assigned to hear that case on a renewed appeal or petition for review.

c. United States District Courts

Formal Court Name	United States District Court [for the District of __].[18]
Type of Court	Trial court—deals with issues of fact, including motions relating to evidentiary and other matters.
Basic Court Structure	94 District Courts—one to four districts for each state.[19] Each District has a varying number of judges, from 1-28. Cases heard by a single judge.[20] Cases may be, but are rarely, heard *en banc*.
Reporters	Federal Supplement—F. Supp. [West]. Federal Rules Decisions (selected district court cases on procedural issues)—FRD [West].
Digests	Federal Practice Digest [currently in 4th series] [West]. Modern Federal Practice Digest [older cases] [West]. Federal Digest [older cases] [West].
Applicable Statutes and Rules	Federal Rules of Civil Procedure. Federal Rules of Evidence. Local court rules adopted by and applicable within each district. See Fed. R. Civ. Proc. 83.[21] Title 28 of the United States Code.
Access to Court	Initial level of court review.
Other "Courts" at Level Similar to District Courts	U.S. Tax Court. U.S. Bankruptcy Court. Judicial Panel on Multidistrict Litigation.

4. The State Courts: An Overview

a. State Court Structure For the most part, state court systems are analogous to the federal court system in that they have three-tiered structures: a trial court, an intermediate court of appeal, and a court of last resort (a supreme court). A few states have only one appellate-level court.

At the trial court level, there may be divisions or departments for specialized matters such as family issues, probate, and juvenile matters.

Many states also have inferior courts, which are not courts of record but are very informal and handle lesser forms of recovery, such as small claims court.

States are often separated into districts or other geographic divisions for purposes of court allocation. These districts operate much like—but are completely distinct from—federal districts.

b. State Reporter Systems Each state has either and/or an official or a West case reporter which report intermediate appellate and high court cases. *

Most states' appellate and high court opinions are also published in West regional reporters, which combine the published cases of several states into West "regions." [Note: the combination of states together in a West regional digest has no bearing on the relative precedential value of the cases from the states that happen to be combined by a commercial entity (West) into a single regional reporter. These regions and the states that form them have nothing to do with jurisdiction or anything else other than the convenience of the publisher.]

The most efficient way to learn which reporters contain the opinions of a particular state court is to consult Table T.1 of the Bluebook. See Chapter IX.

---

[17] See 28 U.S.C. § 2071.

[18] If the district is the only one in a particular state, the name of the district will be the abbreviation of that state's name [D. Ariz.]. If a state has more than one district, the district will have a geographical designation accompanying the abbreviation of the name of the state [S.D. N.Y.]. Also referred to as "district court" if the reference is clear from the context.

[19] See 28 U.S.C. §§ 81-131 for the location of and distribution of districts among the states.

[20] Even though cases are heard by a single judge, reference to "the court" is preferred to reference to "the judge."

[21] See also 28 U.S.C. § 2071.

* Most trial court decisions are not published because such decisions often take the form of jury verdicts which, have no precedential value in subsequent litigation.

c. **State Court Digests** Each state has its own digest.

Some state digests are published by West; other states have digests that are published by another private company or by the state itself.

Some states have a West digest *and* a digest published by some other entity.

Many published state cases are also digested in one of the West regional digests.

d. **State Court Rules of Practice and Procedure** Each state also has its own rules of practice and procedure applicable to each court. Most states will have annotated versions of their rules of practice and procedure, or practice guides describing the application of such rules.

§ I. Interrelationship Among Sources of Law

1. Interrelationship Among Federal Government Institutions

a. **Three Branches of Government** The American federal government is comprised of three branches of government—the legislative branch, the executive branch, and the judicial branch. Each arm of the federal government has unique functions and responsibilities.

b. **Federal System of Checks and Balances** The federal government was designed with a system of "checks and balances," in which each branch in some way acts as a restraint on the other branches. For the practitioner's purposes, the judicial oversight function over the legislative branch is most significant.[22]

c. **Authority of Federal Courts** Federal courts have the authority to review acts of Congress for their constitutionality. When an act of Congress establishes and/or authorizes an agency to take action, court review may include the question of whether that delegation of authority is constitutional.

Federal courts also have the authority to review actions of administrative agencies. Inquiries a court may make of agency action include whether the agency has acted in a manner consistent with the authority granted by Congress to the agency; whether the agency's actions are consistent with

---

[22] Other examples of checks and balances built into the federal system include congressional oversight of the executive and executive oversight over Congress. For instance, the Senate has the authority to try the President and other executives who are impeached (brought up on charges) by the House, and to approve certain presidential nominations. The President, for his part, has the authority to veto legislation passed by Congress. See Chapter III.D.

other statues;[23] and whether the agency's actions are consistent with prior court and agency decisions.[24]

d. Congressional Authority To "Overrule" Court Precedent Prospectively

While the Supreme Court is largely considered to have the "last word" on the legality of acts of Congress and actions of federal agencies, Congress has authority to "overrule" or modify *prospectively* through legislation even Supreme Court precedent. But Congress cannot "overrule" a constitutional decision.

For instance, if a court has held that an agency acted beyond its statutory authority, Congress can amend the relevant legislation to more explicitly authorize the agency to take the action in question. However, if the Supreme Court holds that legislation to be unconstitutional, only a constitutional amendment can override that decision.[26]

2. The Judicial Review Function: The Interrelationship Between Congress and the Federal Courts

ACTS OF U.S. CONGRESS		FEDERAL COURT REVIEW FUNCTION
Passes laws	♦	Is law constitutional?
Creates and authorizes agencies	♦	Is delegation to agency to act constitutional?
ADMINISTRATIVE AGENCIES		
Issue rules and regulations	♦	Is action consistent with Constitution?
Resolve disputes via adjudications	♦	Is action consistent with congressional delegation and other laws?[25]
	♦	Is action consistent with case law?

AMER LEGAL SYS

---

[23] Under the U.S. Constitution, Congress is charged with law-making authority. To the extent Congress is seen to have delegated excessive law-making authority to an agency (or, for that matter, any other entity), a court will invalidate such delegation. Invalidation of an act of Congress on this ground is rare, but remains a potential source of judicial inquiry of which to be aware.

[24] While agencies are not bound by strict principles of *stare decisis,* they are generally required to explain departures from earlier decisions. As for rulemaking, agencies are required to explain the need for changes to existing rules.

[26] A constitutional amendment requires a proposal by two-thirds of both houses of Congress, or two-thirds of the state legislatures, and ratification by three-quarters of the state legislatures.

[25] Agency authority is generally derived from specific statutory authority to that agency. Agency actions are also governed by the Administrative Procedure Act, a more generic statutory scheme applicable to federal agencies generally.

CONGRESS
[Prospective
Only][27]
Codify case law
Modify/amend case
law
Reject/"overrule"
case law
(unless based on
constitutional
infirmity)

3. Relative Priority of Sources of Law: Hierarchy of Authority

In any given legal situation, many sources of law may be applicable. For instance, a case may present a federal constitutional issue, but may also implicate issues of statutory law (state or federal). There is a complex reaction to the issue of which law has "supremacy" over others.

First, there is the issue of federal supremacy over state law. A complex area of jurisprudence, this principle basically stands for the proposition that when there is conflict between a federal law and a state law, federal law supersedes the state law. In addition, there are certain fields over which federal law preempts the possibility of any state law.

In addition, even within the federal system or a state system, there are rules of supremacy governing the relative priority of sources of law applicable *within that jurisdiction*. As indicated below, the U.S. Constitution takes priority over federal statutes and regulations, which in turn take priority over federal case law. The U.S. Constitution, of course, also takes priority over state statutes, regulations, and case law.

It is critical that case law be examined *whenever* interpreting a statutory or constitutional provision. As an example, consider the sources of federal law: Although the U.S. Constitution and then federal statutes take priority (under the principles of constitutional supremacy and legislative supremacy, respectively) in interpreting the Constitution or a statute, case law will be critical; under the principle of *stare decisis*, the way in which the same or similar constitutional and statutory provisions have been interpreted in the past will have an enormous impact on the way in which a constitutional or statutory provision will be interpreted.

a. Federal Law

(1)   U.S. Constitution

(2)   Federal Statutes

---

[27] These actions of Congress, in turn, would likewise be subject to judicial review.

(3)   Federal Rules and Regulations

(4)   Federal Cases—Cases must be consulted in interpreting Constitution, statutes, and agency issuances

b.   State Law

There are several principles of law that must be considered when dealing with an issue of state law. Although a comprehensive examination of these rather complex rules is beyond the scope of this work, they are as follows:

(1)   *Federal Supremacy:*

Federal law prevails over conflicting state law. State law may not be inconsistent with federal law. Nor may there be state laws covering areas that have been preempted, or fully covered, by a federal statutory scheme.

(2)   Erie * *Rule:*

Federal courts will apply state "substantive" law (*e.g.,* torts, contracts) and federal "procedural" law when state law creates the cause of action.

(3)   *Choice of Law Issues:*

A federal court deciding which state's law to apply to a state claim will use the choice of law rules of the state in which the federal court sits.

Apart from these issues, the following hierarchy of authority would apply to state sources of law:

(1)   State Constitution

(2)   State Statutes

(3)   State Rules and Regulations

(4)   State Cases—Must be consulted in interpreting state Constitution, statutes, and agency issuances

A Note On Citations To Authority: When citing to federal or state law, citations should include all relevant sources, in the order of their respective hierarchy. See Chapter IX.C.

---

* *Erie R. Co. v. Tompkins,* 304 U.S. 64 (1938).